Some Notes

for

the Guidance of Parents

by

Daniel A. Lord, S. J.

Catholic Authors Press
www.CatholicAuthors.com

First published 1944
Reprinted 2007 Catholic Authors Press

ISBN: 978-0-973198-3-0

Catholic Authors Press

www.CatholicAuthors.org

With Ecclesiastical Approval

CHAPTERS

SOME NOTES

for

The Guidance of Parents

INTRODUCTION

This is a book for parents by one who doesn't happen to be a parent. Yet I, the guide who hopes to take parents and the teachers of parents through these pages, am called a father. Perhaps because of the priesthood that is mine and the title of father that was given me, I have seen your children more objectively than you have. And an objective vision is sometimes the one which sees truth most clearly.

At any rate I can plead, as I start to write, that I have a deep love of your children and a sincere admiration for you who are their fathers and mothers. For a good many years now my work has been almost entirely among those sons and daughters of your homes. I have talked with them, and they have talked with me. Fine boys and girls and strong pure young men and women have shown me without ostentation the virtues that came to them from their splendid parents. Weak youngsters and adolescents who faced life embarrassed, ashamed, and almost trembling have without words on their part made me know the irreparable loss that has been theirs because their parents were careless and uninterested and their homes were schools of future failure.

I have talked to these young people at crucial times in their lives: as they entered school, as they sought to decide their vocations, as they planned to enter marriage, as they faced their first brutal temptation, as they puzzled over some problem that left them weary and sick and frightened. I have met them in English classes and in religion and philosophy seminars. I have noted with approval the good manners of some and been annoyed and regretful over the brashness and ill-breeding of others.

Yet whatever the situation in which I met them, one thing I always sensed: the impact that had been made upon their lives—for good or evil—by their parents.

PARENTS, DIFFERENT KINDS

Of deliberately evil parents I have met almost none, thank God! I have however seen the effects of careless and selfish parents more times than it is pleasant to remember. But mostly parents as I have found them fall into two classes, the good and the unprepared. The good might be good out of a natural genius for parenthood or a real love of their children or a deliberately developed insight into the problems and needs of their youngsters. They might be trained to successful parenthood by their reading and study and perhaps by their being in the right sort of class. Or their ability to handle their children might be an instinctive thing that came right out of their own youthful experience and their prayerful desire to give their children not merely what was easiest and sweetest but what was strong and of lifelong value. But they were good, this pleasant majority, and their goodness showed in the fabric of their children's character.

The unprepared were usually good too. They wanted to be successful parents, as any decent person wants to be a success at the job he undertakes. But they didn't know quite what to do. They felt at a loss in the presence of their own children. When their children were young, they thought all that were needed were love and a good home and two tender arms and a warm shoulder and food and more love. When the children grew older, they hesitated between the stern duty of giving commands and the dear pleasure of wooing their children's affection by unmeasured love. When adolescence brought its cloudy problems, they hadn't even the words in which to answer the asked or unspoken question. They were embarrassed that their children must learn "the facts of life" from themselves, embarrassed because they were their children's forebears. They found it hard to speak of personal matters to a growing boy and a growing girl whose questioning eyes keep asking, "Was that true of you, dad? . . . Are you speaking from experience, mother?"

No Substitutes

So the unprepared, like all those who take up a job for which they have not been fitted and trained, seek to pass off their responsibility to others. Yet no others will do. That is all there is to it. Not the most inspiring teacher nor the most skillful guide of youth has any right to attempt to supplant parents or substitute for them. Only the hesitance of parents facing the problem of guiding and directing their own children has been the excuse for their calling upon outsiders to do for them the job which God and nature made inescapably theirs.

These Notes of Mine

With the good parents and the unprepared parents in mind I drew up the original notes for this book.

It was not however my good luck to be able to assemble a large group of parents and talk directly to them. I prepared the talks then, not directly for parents, but for those priests and religious teachers who do have the opportunity to meet parents and help them prepare for the task of parenthood. I gave the talks first at the Summer School of Catholic Action during the summer of 1941 in St. Louis, Pittsburgh, Boston, New York, and Chicago.

Those notes I was asked to put into fuller form. Hence this book.

For Parents or Teachers

So as you see, I have written it primarily for parents. But it is written for the use of either parents themselves, in so far as it will help them, or those whose responsibility and opportunity it is to help parents prepare for the most important natural vocation in the world.

I shall be very happy if mothers and fathers and future mothers and fathers read the book and find it useful. But I shall be quite as delighted if it is used by priests, religious teachers, the directors of groups of parents, and the guides of future parents in the talks they give and the classes in parenthood they conduct for those who are the fathers and mothers of our children.

How Used

I conceive of the book's being read straight through by anyone, parent or guide of parents, who wants a little help with the guidance of young people. But I also see it used as a textbook or a discussion-club guide for those who want to study quietly and more at length. Perhaps young parents will form a club, use the book as a sort of simple text, and then call in to talk to them experts in the fields indicated.

Priests may wish to assemble young parents in their parishes and give them talks on their duties and opportunities. The constantly growing parent-teacher associations established now in so many sections of the country may find suggested topics indicated for them. Sometimes the parish Confraternity of Christian Doctrine or discussion club may think it wise to carry a group through the entirely practical problems of men and women who want to give their children competent guidance and wholesome instruction. There is many an alumni association in which the fathers would be glad of help in their mysterious job of helping to guide their own children. Alumnae associations that find their programs a little vague and not too appealing may draw larger crowds to meetings if the young mothers know that the subject to be discussed and threshed out among them will be that of the handling of the children God gives them.

But whether the book is privately read, used merely as a point of departure, or employed as a text, I hasten to assure the reader that in it I have as much as possible avoided theory and stuck to what I have learned from experience.

I am not a specialist in child psychology. I do not set myself up as an expert on child training. I am merely a Catholic priest who has the unusual opportunity to meet thousands of modern boys and girls, young men and women, to keep up constant correspondence with hundreds of them at a time, to talk to them on easy and friendly terms, and to listen to them under the most favorable circumstances. They have been my teachers.

What they have taught me of their likes and needs, of their problems and difficulties, of their desire for parental guidance, and of the approach that they feel parents should use toward them, I have embodied in this book. This book is really a symposium back of which stand thousands of young people who talk through me as I write.

EXPERIENCE

To the whole question of the training of young people by their parents I bring my own happy experience as child, boy, and youth. For I can speak as one whose mother gave him the full devotion of maternal love and wise if instinctive direction. As the years go on, I come to know that my father, who in all his life never spoke one word of advice or counsel to me, was yet tremendously powerful in that he set me the example of what a father should be and gave me powerful lessons by his own living and conduct.

So when I speak of a happy home, I can think of my own. The gratitude I feel toward my parents is something that must profoundly affect my whole attitude toward the parents of the young people I have known, know at the present moment, hope to know in the future.

So with the consciousness that it is merely the resultant of pleasant experiences, I offer you this book.

To You Who Do the Work

If you are a mother or a father, engaged or about to engage in the God-given assignment of training the sons and daughters of God, I sincerely hope you will find this book practical, sympathetic, and alertly concerned with your rights and privileges quite as much as with your duties and obligations.

If you are a priest, I sincerely hope the book will help you even a little to train your young people to Christian parenthood and to carry young parents over the shoals and rapids of their job. Can't parenthood and its duties and privileges be preached from the pulpit? Certainly it can be carried with great effect into discussion clubs and other like groups where the laity are constantly asking that "religion be made practical and applied to life."

Religious teachers should find the subject of parent training almost exciting in its possibilities. Alumni and alumnae will return to the school that offers adult education along these lines. I see no reason why into the senior class of high school and into the forums of collegians should not be introduced a subject which vitally concerns the overwhelming majority of the students. For of the young people in school today eighty per cent will most likely become parents. Shall we send them out trained and prepared for that all-important assignment and career? Or shall we let them drift into it, flounder about in timid and uncertain fashion?

The Great Profession

As one who believes in the tremendous importance of the profession of parenthood and who has loved and worried over the children of today, I offer this little book to parents and future parents and the guides of parents. May it help them a little to become or to help form the splendid mothers and fathers of the future.

With the world clamoring for a thousand remote and impossible solutions of its problems, we are convinced, I think, that nine tenths of the difficulties today would be solved if out of fine, pure, well-disciplined, and loving homes came strong, adequately trained, honest, and decent children prepared for life by parents who understood their job and loved it.

The esoteric solutions of world problems can in large measure be shoved aside when the homes of the nation take on the pattern of the holy house of Nazareth, where Mary set the example for all mothers of all ages, and Joseph— though only a foster father—gave mankind the perfect example of a father's training of his boy. Out of that home came the perfect Son, who was Jesus Christ.

In His image all the sons and daughters of men and women, who are the sons and daughters of God Himself, are to be fashioned. If this small book helps even a little in so glorious a work, I shall be humbly grateful.

Feast of Our Lady's Maternity, 1941

The Guidance of Parents

I

THE IRREPLACEABLE PARENT

Parents are the world's most influential professional people.

That, like much of what we shall have to write at the beginning, is commonplace, almost axiomatic.

Yet parents are the one group of professional people who are almost never trained for their work in life.

It seems strange that people bearing the enormous responsibility that rests upon parents should be tossed into their job with almost no preparation. For the magnitude and significance of their profession is too clear to need more than a passing gesture of recognition.

Parents produce the new life of the race. Parents support and nurture that life until such time as it is capable of becoming self-sustaining. Parents prepare the background against which will be lived the most impressionable years given to a human being. By nature and by the will of God as well as by the force of circumstances parents are the original teachers of everyone except the chance orphan or the waif who becomes immediately dependent upon charity, organized or disorganized.

SOURCE OF ALL

From parents, the preordained teachers, the child gets all the fundamentals of living. The gift of language is a parental gift. His first human habits are formed in imitation of his parents' actions. If there is religion in his life, it rises in the first instance from the religious conduct of his father and his mother. Good manners or bad, a sense of morality or a primitive criminal code, the first glimmers of culture come to the child either from the direct teaching of his parents or from the conduct which the infant observes and notes for future reference.

All this is plain platitude—or it should be.

The facts of the case are however by no means in line with the platitudes. For parents themselves and those who are interested in parents are constantly bemoaning what can be called the complete parental collapse.

PARENTAL COLLAPSE?

There are, thank heaven, splendid parents, strong, competent fathers and mothers who love their children both wisely and well—an important combination of adverbs in that particular case. Yet in thousands of cases young parents look at their newborn baby with a bewildered air of "What in the world do I do with him now?" Then as the child grows into adolescence, the parents come close to stifling over the necessity for explaining to the youngster the simplest facts about himself. Somewhat later the full-grown mothers and fathers, who dominate a thriving business or dominate a social world, find themselves embarrassed and afraid when they are faced down by their own offspring.

AMERICAN FATHERS

As for the American father, he seems to be about the most generous of his kind in the world—and almost the most incompetent. If he provides the money for a happy home and adequate education, he thinks he has done his full duty. Indeed in this he has been encouraged by the women of our race. For American women have fostered the conviction that the children belong to the mother alone. We have no admitted matriarchate in theory; we have it everywhere in practice. Mothers in America want to run the children and ask of their spouse no more than an occasional contribution of trouble shooting. American fathers, long accustomed to accede to the wishes of their wives, bow themselves out of any matters of discipline or guidance, content to be the walking checkbooks and the occasionally evoked bogeyman.

That is not (let us be honest) entirely the fault of American women. American fathers are either so desperately busy or have so systematically built up the legend of their intense preoccupation with the job of holding up our high standard of living that they have had little time for the profession of fatherhood. They are great doctors or fine businessmen or excellent members of their labor union. They have turned the job of the training of their children over to their wives with almost a sigh of relief. Strong men are always afraid of babies anyhow. Any smart child can browbeat a grown man. And American fathers have known what it means to be cowed into submission by a coalition of their wives and children.

Beyond all that however the American male is simply never given even the most fundamental lesson in how to be a father. I doubt if in half a dozen Catholic colleges or high schools in our land (and half a dozen is a very generous hazard) there is during the year even one chapel talk on the subject of parenthood. As for a class where the future father might learn a little child psychology or even his own rights and duties as a father, where does it exist?

I have run my finger down long lists of suggested subjects for men's discussion clubs; I have read over the topics handled in college and high-school forums; I have never yet hit upon anything that sounded like "The Duties of a Father," "How You Can Someday Instruct Your Young Son," "The Place of the Father in the Home," "The Example of the Father As the Inspiration to Purity."

Young men stumble into marriage, usually with some preliminary information and guidance. They almost abruptly find themselves fathers, only to realize that they are utterly unprepared for the job. Often enough they remain, unless nature's kindly instinct or their own developing wisdom enters in, unprepared for the rest of their parental days.

FATHER AND MOTHER TOGETHER

Yet a father is one half of that important professional firm in which the mother is only the other half, even if you insist she is the more important half. For the training of the son the father is all-important. Only the father can give the boy that perfect male example which is the basis of the boy's soundest education. From the father the son gets his first glimpse of the masculine virtues and the basic training in courage, gentleness, truthtelling, purity, the spirit of work.

In the life of every man there are what we recognize as the male ideals. No woman can present or inculcate them adequately. It is the father who establishes the male attitude toward religion. Quite clearly in the case of those Catholic nations in which the men do not go to church, the boys give up their attendance at Mass and the frequenting of the sacraments the minute they slip away from the strings of their mothers' aprons. The noble attitude a boy will take toward women is about an equal blend of his love of his mother and the respect he has read in his father's conduct with women.

Even the daughter is profoundly affected by her father. His attitude toward women may become an important ideal in the shaping of her character. She finds strength in his ideals of women's virtues.

The Father's Authority

Ultimately, we must never forget, the authority of the family rests with the father and not with the mother. The father is the head of the family; and though under American customs he shares that authority generously with the mother, he cannot nonetheless completely relinquish his right to govern. As a matter of fact I don't believe that the normal woman likes her husband to relinquish that right. I have never known a woman who in her heart of hearts did not want her husband to be her intellectual, physical, and even —where possible—her religious and social superior. Women are far more comfortable when they are looking up to a man than when they are looking down on him.

American Mothers

Mothers in our country have had the task of the training of children laid quietly and finally in their laps. And at the same time they have found problems entirely in their own realm as mothers. There is the developed contempt for motherhood that is so frankly and widely expressed. Almost any other career is regarded as superior to that of motherhood. The woman who produces a novel looks down her nose at the mother who has only three lovely children to show as her achievements. A woman who makes a success of a dress shop is regarded as a remarkable woman; a mother who beautifully dresses two little daughters on a carefully worked-out budget is a nobody who can be treated with amusement. It is praiseworthy for a woman to be an interior decorator and furnish the homes of other women; it is nothing meriting attention for a woman to make her own home a thing of joy and loveliness.

CONTEMPT FOR MOTHERHOOD

Each year when one or other of the magazines or national polls selects the country's ten most outstanding women, you may be perfectly sure that two professions will be ignored: No one will pick a nun or a mother. If a married woman who has children happens to be on the list, it will not be because of her achievements in motherhood but rather for the truck she drives, the surgical operations she performs, her radio broadcasts, or her part in a movement that is working to eliminate children and make motherhood, not a career, but an accident.

Indeed the young married woman these days begins almost on the day of her marriage to be bombarded with advertisements telling her how stupid she is to have children at all. Any woman who has to her eternal credit four children is regarded by her contemporaries—always the pagans, often the Catholics—as clearly a stupid ninny who hasn't sense enough, wit enough, or courage enough to protect herself against the aggression of children.

Motherhood is distinctly a minor profession. Even the woman who breeds terriers or Persian cats is encouraged to regard with condescension the woman who gives birth to what once we all considered the children of God and the springtime of our race.

RIVAL JOBS

Even the good mother these days, the one who regards her profession with respect and affection, is likely to be harassed to the point of inefficiency. Once on a time motherhood was easily a woman's whole career, her full-time job. Now she may have to earn a living, not through any desire or greed on her part, but simply to keep the family together.

Or she is forced by the current of modern living into varied time-consuming activities. She must belong to clubs. She has to take part in charity work. She is asked to serve on committees or even to renew her youthful love of the amateur stage. She must be hostess to her husband's business associates, or she must travel with him when he goes on those tours which blend vacation with the making of "important contacts."

She is a busy woman, this American mother of the present era. Even the enslavement of electricity to her service has, far from making life simpler for her, opened the possibility of more and more varied demands upon her time and energies.

Untrained

Again, as in the case of the father, she may feel toward her job of motherhood that fear and apprehension and desire for flight that is common to all unprepared people. If anyone were to ask me to go out onto the flying field and take a bomber up, I should beg to be excused. Quite obviously I am totally unprepared for the job. Indeed a perfect nightmare would consist in my finding myself in the air at the controls of a plane, which I know myself utterly unable to handle. We do with joy the job we feel prepared to do and adequate to handle. We are miserably ill at ease in any situation for which we know ourselves to be unfitted.

That is always true of untrained people, whatever the situation into which they are catapulted. So why be surprised that modern mothers shy away from the job of motherhood and are abjectly conscious of their lack of ability to handle it?

Girls in college will get splendid biology courses that make no slightest reference to the life of children. They will be trained to be excellent librarians or secretaries or teachers or laboratory technicians, and they will take up those jobs with relish. Then they transfer to marriage and motherhood, their real job, with the alarming realization that no one has given them any preparatory help for the doing of this all-important job even passably well.

It seems to me that our schools have a real responsibility there. Priests and religious teachers and those in charge of youth must not blame young people if they fumble at parenthood. Untrained people are necessarily inadequate people. How many young people get any real preparation or training to be adequate fathers or mothers?

Love Is Too Easy

Modern mores have done much to develop a destructive sort of maternal selfishness. I am not thinking of the unnatural woman, too common today, who renounces motherhood entirely in the hope that she will preserve her figure or remain a girl, when she should be a grown woman giving new life to the world. I am thinking instead of the mother who looks to her child merely for the love she can find there and for the gratification of her own desire for affection. She will not correct the child because she is afraid that then it will not want to run to her arms. She will spoil it and pamper its vanity and make a doll and plaything of it—as if she herself were a child—not rear a strong young character, but drain from the baby or the little boy or girl adulation and easy affection for herself.

It is so easy to be easy with children. It is so hard to be strong enough in love to discipline the little ones we love.

Competition From Schools

Now there is another factor that has made for parents' distrust of themselves: the unfair competition presented by the schools.

Seldom these days does it happen that a group of public-school teachers meet in solemn convention without there being speeches or resolutions that demand that more rights be taken away from the parents and given to the schools. In high educational councils parents are regarded as positive menaces to the progress and development of their children. The school, backed by the unlimited taxes of the state and in large part controlled by what someone has unkindly but truly referred to as "old maids of both sexes," demands an almost exclusive suzerainty over the youngsters. Homes are regarded as places from which the school must rescue the children; parents are those incompetents who should be obliged to yield up their boys and girls to the real experts, who know what to do with them.

So the magnificently equipped school competes with the poor or plain little home. Parents are told to deliver up their children to be taught not merely the elements of formal education but all those things that the school was never remotely intended to handle: how to play, care of the health, good manners, even the most personal matters of private living.

Children are pulled away from home in the early hours under the dawn and returned at the end of so long and strenuous a day that they come to look at their parents only through drowsy eyes and to use their homes as mere hotels where they park for the night.

You'd think that all homes were like some of the backwoods hovels from which children have to be snatched as quickly as possible before they become incurably infected with disease and ignorance and bad language and vermin.

All of this is clearly enough wrong and against the plan of nature and the designs of God. If some educators had their say, parents would bear the children only to deliver them over to the state educational systems, where experts would encase them in human-sized test tubes until they had sufficiently developed to resist the love and example and training which parents might otherwise have tried to inflict upon them.

And even Catholic parents have been infected by this unnatural heresy.

Parents Walk Out

The attitude has of course a twofold effect upon parents. The constant repetition of the charge that they are unfit to train their children breeds inevitable doubt in their own minds. "Maybe," they think, "we aren't fit to handle the development of our children." And as they are already aware of their lack of training, their unpreparedness for their job, they are easy to convince when the salesman for school supremacy is glib and persuasive.

Or if they are lazy or selfish or indifferent or bad parents, this popular attitude is the pleasantest excuse they can find. Gladly enough they turn their children over to the schools. They can wash their hands of all responsibility. They merely send their children on to the experts and let the experts do their proficient job.

THREE PERIODS?

So it has happened that even good Catholic parents have often divided the lives of their children into these periods:

1. There is the period of birth and earliest infancy. During that period parents must of necessity feed and clothe and warm and nurture their babies. They may feel incompetent, but there has as yet been developed no extensive schools in which to park infants. There will one day be those schools, never fear. But for the present both parents and infants have to wait.

2. There is the period of babyhood. This is a somewhat static period. The parents wish there were some haunt of the expert to which they could send their babies. Since there usually is no such place, parents and children wait expectantly for the arrival of the happy third period.

3. This is the instant when the child is old enough to get into some sort of school—first grade, kindergarten, pre-kindergarten, and (most recent) classes for youngsters who are learning to walk. The happy parent sees his or her child off to school, the child toddling a bit and alarmed at this sudden expulsion from the nest.

The parents breathe a sigh of real relief. They've done their full duty, haven't they? At very considerable expense to themselves and the sacrifice of a lot of luxuries they could otherwise have enjoyed, they have sent their child to an expensive school. Fine! Now let the school handle the child. The parents have no further responsibility.

So the father turns to his business, his golf, and his friends. The mother has an empty house for eight hours of the day, while the school trains her child to that full maturity which the professional educators guarantee so glibly.

Parental Alibi

Today schools become finer and finer, more complete in their control of the child, longer in the hours they take the child from home, and more of an alibi for delinquent parents. Even the Catholic parents (and I am not sure of the correctness of that word "even") are inclined to put the whole burden of the education of their children on the school. Already they think that because religion and morality are included in the Catholic curriculum they need not worry about their own duty of teaching their children to know and love God and to honor the right and hate the evil. Let the priests and brothers and sisters in the magnificent parochial and private schools take up that duty.

And all the while the experimental facts are completely against this shifting of parental responsibility to anyone else, even to the most expert educator. The school cannot remotely take the place of the home. Teachers cannot except most inadequately take the place of the parents.

Schools Are Only Substitutes

Any intelligent child, no matter how young he is, feels the institutional character of even the best and the most modern school. The intensely personal relationship of parents and children in the intimate environs of the home cannot even be imitated in school surroundings. Children recognize that and in the vast majority of cases, like Shakespeare's immemorial schoolboy, still drag reluctantly to school.

At best schools are unnatural. There is something formal in the most informal, something regimented in the most systematically homelike. Perhaps the child instinctively knows that schools exist merely to supplement homes or because homes have failed their natural purpose. For certainly in the majority of cases the child resists school with a competence that is one of his most significant achievements. What he would have drunk in naturally at home he regards as a chore in a classroom. Education that he was meant to absorb through his pores from the delightful association with his parents and his brothers and sisters now serves to stiffen his spine resistingly.

Schools were not in nature's plan. Children seem to know that. Hence it takes long years to teach children in school what they should be able to learn in a matter of months in a natural home environment.

Schools Are Too Late

Besides if parents have waited for the school to start the education of their children, they have waited much too long. School comes too, too late. Even with the incubating process common nowadays, where the fledglings are tucked away in educational brooders, the school still comes too, too late for its training really to affect the child. Children are established for life before they are five years old. After that they merely build on the foundation already laid. In fact some more modern psychologists are convinced that all essential foundations are laid in the child before he is two years old. And I don't know any schools that take children quite that early.

Homes First in Everything

Any parent who thinks that he can shove off onto schools the training of his children doesn't know either his children or the schools. Homes are the places where children learn easily, instinctively, without resistance, and under nature's own perfect conditions. Schools furnish merely the supplement to what the home has already given.

Hence it is that we who have taught in schools are grimly aware that the difference between the varied types of students before us is largely a matter of the training and preparation each received before he ever set foot in a classroom. The child from the good home is alert, interested, keen, on his toes, well mannered, possessed of quick and right instincts. The child from the sloppy, inadequate home is dull, uninterested, uncooperative, bad mannered; he fails to catch on, fails even to try to catch on.

The Difference in Children

The difference between this child and that one is often largely a matter of what he saw in and heard from his parents. His religious response, his sense of honesty, his ability to play with other children and be unselfish toward them, his attitude toward books, his appreciation of the beautiful, his sense of what is right and what is wrong, his quick apprehending of the charming and noble, his ready reaction to music that is good, his approval of heroism and his rejection of evil and cheapness—how happy the teacher who finds that all these things have already been established in the child's mind by the parents, who alone can deeply and strong-rootedly establish them!

We have to remind parents with all the insistence in our power that schools, even the most expensive or the most expert, cannot supply for fine heredity or wholesome environment. School does not give first impressions or second or third or ten thousandth. It can only correct, if possible, the false impressions made by parents, or it can continue the child's progress in the happy grooves established by a noble father and a gracious mother.

We teachers work on the material that is sent us by the parents. That material is already so formed and shaped and set and established and concreted that our modifications can often be only amazingly slight. No wonder then that we pray for good homes and parents who take seriously the inescapable duties of their profession. From fine parents come, except in rare and almost abnormal cases, fine children. From slovenly, slipshod, careless, badly trained, neglectful, or definitely selfish and evil parents come . . . Ask any educator in his moments of honesty to finish that sentence. He can build with fine material. He works hopelessly with material already spoiled by the master builders who are the parents.

Educate the Parents

All of which points of course to the wonderful field for the Catholic educator who will regard his task perhaps less as the education of the children and more as the education of parents and future parents to their own glorious possibilities. Through the sermons on parental duty and opportunity, through the introduction of parental problems in discussion clubs, through the presentation of Catholic attitudes on fatherhood and motherhood to alumni and alumnae and to the students in our senior high schools and colleges the Catholic priest and religious and lay leader can move far toward the restoration of nature's right order and God's plan for the shaping of the child's character. This work must not be done entirely by outsiders and aliens. It belongs under the direction and example and inspiration of the father and the mother, whom the child loves.

Four Classes of Parents

The relationship of the parent to the adult child and his problems lies outside the range of this book—unless perhaps he happens to be a grandparent who wants to help make his grandchildren successful men and women or to throw in the way of his own children guides to successful parenthood.

Among the other parents with whom we are concerned there are four main classes:

1. The parents whose children are beyond grammar school and are either in high school or in college or are still below voting age and are living at home and working.

2. The parents whose children are of grammar-school age.

3. The parents whose children are not yet eligible for grammar school and hence are about six years old or under.

4. Finally the future parents, the boys and girls, the young men and women who in the normal course of events will be the fathers and mothers of the future.

Though in this preliminary survey I want to discuss each of the four classes separately, still much that is said of the first group will apply to the others. There are however factors which are individual to each class. Hence the division.

Parents of Older Children

When we come to the first group, the parents of children who have passed beyond grammar school, we have to start with a note closely approximating pessimism. If the parent and the child have not before that time established a satisfactory relationship, they probably never will establish it. It is too, too late to start training the youngster after he has received his eighth-grade diploma and has come to regard himself as a pretty big boy or she as a pretty smart girl.

Parents who wait until this period of the child's life to form a comradeship, to start to talk to him or to her, to begin to give advice and try to shape conduct, are going to meet a lot of unpleasant obstacles. Chiefly their children will regard them with startled amazement. What in the world has come over their parents?

These children will run a mile from any attempt their parents may make to establish camaraderie. If the parents try to give them intimate, personal information, they will blush, grow painfully confused, and on the slightest pretext or opportunity take to cover. I sincerely doubt that parents can take adolescent children and then for the first time make pals of them or sit them down for serious conversation and interchange of confidences or information. That should have been done years before. The boy or the girl beyond grammar school is too self-conscious or too self-assured, too timid or too brash to be otherwise than startled, resentful, suspicious, or indignant at the intrusion if suddenly after years of silence and parental neglect he sees his mother and father abruptly bearing down upon him with proffers of friendship or the unwanted and unwonted gifts of good advice.

Yet discouraging as the prospect is, parents who have neglected to establish that relationship should be made aware of their failures and shown that with real tact and a deep study of their children they can still do more for them than can anyone else in the world. A slow, tender, patient siege of an adolescent's heart will bring ultimate surrender. For children, whatever their age and however they have been weaned away from their parents, can, if the parents really want to gain an entrance into their lives, be won over with kindness, interest, justice, and sympathy.

Reunited Families

What I should like to see is groups of parents meeting in one another's homes to talk, perhaps under the guidance of a priest or a physician or a psychologist, about what they can do for their children and how they can do it. I know one priest, Father Raphael McCarthy of St. Louis University, who organized such informal parent clubs. He was simply besieged by mothers and fathers who desired membership in those clubs.

Anything that helps to bring parents and children together is right and should be encouraged. There are the father-daughter and the father-son evenings that have been initiated by parishes, schools, and clubs. Paralleling them are the mother-son and the mother-daughter events. In these the two generations meet, not on terms of the ordered and the ordering, but on terms of happy equality and comradeship. There is only one thing wrong with these meetings: There should be a thousand times as many of them as are now provided.

Part in Social Life

You see, one of the barriers between parents and children who until the children's adolescence have not discovered each other or built up confidence and comradeship is that the children are likely to regard their parents as absurdly old. Anyone under twenty years of age, cynicized Somerset Maugham, is sure to regard anyone over forty as slightly ridiculous. So if parents and children have never played together, the youngsters probably look upon their oldsters as ancients tottering rapidly toward the cemetery. Naturally it is difficult to establish an easy relationship with a person who, to our way of looking at it, is separated from us by a long bridge of painful years.

Hence as the first approach of a parent to his adolescent child we offer the suggestion of almost any form of social life.

Suppose the parish undertakes to supply that. Suppose the high school or the college sees that parents and children have a chance to meet on pleasant terms, to play together, dance together, take part together in games and sports.

PARENTS AS CHAPERONES

No other chaperone can possibly be so satisfactory for, let's say, the parish young people's party or the school dance as mothers and fathers. If the older people are present when their offspring are at play, an electric current of sympathy and friendliness is established between parents and children. The trouble with so many families is that the children have never seen the parents enjoying themselves, while all the parents know of their children's good times are the weary sighs that echo across next morning's breakfast table.

Now by a chaperone I do not mean a policeman in evening dress. Quite aside from the horror of being asked to fill a job like that, chaperones who stand along the wall and supervise a party are likely to be as unwelcome as a bad cough and as ineffective as the potted palms. An effective chaperone, male or female, is really part of the party. He or she in having a place in the fun. The chaperones dance as their children dance. They drop from their shoulders that supposed cloak of the years in order to prove to their children that one doesn't need to be sixteen or eighteen in order to dance without a crutch. They laugh as easily as the youngest. They are good fun, and they relish good fun.

I think there is nothing more doleful than a platoon of chaperones, smiling fixed and painful smiles, lined up along a wall while dancers glance at them over their shoulders in youthful pity and distaste. If the parents at these young people's parties don't want to dance with the youngsters, if the thought of attempting a fox trot of the twenties while their small fry are jitterbugging makes them nervous, then they can play bridge on the balcony of the ballroom. Or they can rally round the punch bowl. Or they can amuse themselves in other adult fashion while their children are risking life and limb in obedience to a vibrating tom-tom.

Parents should be invited to their children's parties. Once there, a little resumption of the youth they have relinquished not so long ago, a little appreciative participation in the gaiety on the floor, a little sharing of the evening's social events will make their children realize that mother and dad are not quite ready to be stuffed for the Smithsonian but are really charming and alive people when the band begins to swing.

Parents As Sponsors

Parents should fight for the right to sponsor their children's entertainments, not accept a place on the program in such a way as if thereby they were inscribing their names on a mortuary tablet. They are the logical and appreciative audience at all the school events: the school play, which they should applaud even if their dramatic sensibilities have been trained on Broadway; the athletic events, which are vastly dear to the youngsters' hearts and which absorb their deep interest and awake their real enthusiasm; the elocution contest, the school glee-club concert, the music recital; open house at school, when the pupils count the number of other pupils who have managed to induce their parents to attend.

Boys and Girls Together

After adolescence is reached, young people will not voluntarily make the approaches to their parents. From that point on they must be stalked in the haunts where they most often congregate and where they think real fun is to be had and for which real people head to enjoy themselves.

Happy the parish that brings together the old and the young in social events! Smart the school that regards the parents as natural chaperones and inevitable audience—if not actual participants—at all its social events. And wise, oh very wise the parents who collaborate with the school and the parish that make parent participation possible and persuade elders to attempt it if they have thus far been uncooperative.

I know one school which has an annual field day for its pupils and their parents. The event starts in the afternoon with the arrival of the mothers; it gains real impetus and momentum with the arrival of the fathers, who come straight from their offices or places of business. All the races are run by teams made up of parents and children.　If there is a relay, it is a child, a mother, and a father against another child, mother, and father.　If it is a three-legged race, a mother and a daughter are tied together.　If it is the human wheelbarrow, a father propels his long-legged offspring down the cheering field.

So much more could be done to bring parents and children together.　Wise educators and leaders will plan and execute the strategy to accomplish this "more."　Indignant parents will demand this "more," which is really their simple rights.

Parents' Rights and Duties

Perhaps at this point we should insert a section to remind parents that they have rights and that they have duties.　Such a section would be solid with chestnuts and platitudes.　Maybe chestnuts and platitudes are exactly what are needed to buck up the modern parent and reinstate him in the position from which he has been rudely shouldered.

God's Model Society

The family is meant to be God's model society.

Even the great, inclusive civil state is only an amplified family, with the same basic powers of the family extended and increased to meet the wider needs of the state.　We are quite right when we talk of the "family of nations."　Family is the correct word.　We are not far astray when the sentiments we hold for our country come very close to those we feel for our family.

Within this natural, God-ordained society which is the family there is that authority which is essential for right government, unity, and proper social functioning.　That authority rests first with the father, who is the head of the family.　It is shared by the mother, who is the cocreator of the children and mistress of the home.　Together the father and the mother make the council of state for the family; and no matter how democratic the country's mode of thought may become, the parents hold that authority over their children, with their consequent obligation to use it wisely, justly, and well.

A bad parent will be punished by God . . . and probably, if he is caught, by the state. Every so often the newspapers play up the case of some utterly unnatural parent who chains a child to a bed or locks him permanently in a dark closet or starves and beats him for the cruel satisfaction he himself derives thereby. Parents who are like that, unnatural and inhuman and lower than the mother cat or the casual rooster, will one day face an angry Father in heaven, whose judgment of them will be terrifically severe.

That is the negative side of parental conduct.

PARENTAL AUTHORITY

That Father in heaven will ask much more than whether the earthly father and mother refrained from getting their exercise by beating their children, or whether they treated those children as cowed slaves and kept them from light and air and decent food and the recreation necessary for normal development.

How, God will demand, did they use their authority constructively? Were their commands firm and just and reasonable? Did they recognize and exercise their unavoidable obligation to form their children into mature and self-controlled adults? Did they, when the children could be corrected and deterred from evil in no other way, punish them, even when to punish them was hard on parental affection? Did they set the personal example which made abstract orders clear and attractive to their children?

The bad parent will undoubtedly be punished by God, as all bad people are punished. The eternal joy eventually allotted to parents will be measured on the simple terms of how well they exercised their duties toward their children.

Children may fail, may become criminal failures despite the best efforts of parents. But if the parents have through neglect or too much love or sheer laziness failed to give their children the things that make for full character development and a sane and successful maturity, God will regard them as the real delinquents. Parents are professional people of the highest order. God and their fellow men judge professional people, not on the basis of what crimes they may not have committed, but by the standard of how well they have carried out the duties of their profession.

No parent can escape the obligations of his God-given authority.

No parent can hide behind the teacher, the school, the priest, the parish, the club and say, "I asked them to handle my child for me." Parents' duties toward their children cannot be tossed into the lap of anyone else.

With this brief reminder of their authority and their duty we can turn to some of the pleasanter aspects of parenthood.

Children Must Be Wanted

For the adolescent boy and girl, the student of high-school age or just beyond, the wise and competent parents make home the normal center of their entire life. Children are quick to feel whether or not they are welcome. We grownups find their noise disturbing and their heavy clatter annoying. We are inclined to allow ourselves at their expense the luxury of nerves.

Boys and girls spot that attitude at once. If the returning boy flushed and excited from the victory of his team over the traditional rival is greeted with the loud command to pipe down and cut the shouting, he crawls up to his room with the feeling that he is unwanted by a pair of utterly unsympathetic parents. When the girl rushes in with a bevy of her schoolmates and finds mother regarding them as an unwelcome squad of storm troopers, the girl takes her friends elsewhere and thinks of her home as the place to which she goes only when she can't find another place where she will be welcome.

Even though parents may not have established a close and comradely relationship with their young children, they can woo them with this air of loving to have them around the house and of being delighted when they bring their friends home.

Natural Love of Fun

The desire of young people for recreation is a perfectly normal and wholesome one. Fathers and mothers rise high in the children's estimation when they seem to recognize this and make possible a decent amount of wholesome fun. Children sometimes get the idea that their parents have lost the power to enjoy anything more strenuous than the shuffling of a deck of cards. They take it for granted that any youthful voice raised above a stage whisper is going to set all the parental nerves atingling. Parents who want to win the approval and esteem of their children will be extremely wise to smile cooperatively on their children's good, healthy animal capers and afford elbow room for their strenuous games and dances and laughter, which are part of expanding humanity.

If parents feel themselves outside the circle of their children's confidences, if they have isolated themselves or allowed themselves to be insulated, they had better start winning back their children, not with wise council and solemn man-to-man and woman-to-woman sessions, but with a game of catch or badminton in the back yard, with an invitation to have their children teach them the current dance, with a picnic for which they provide the food and during which they take part in even the most strenuous games, and with a party thrown by the whole family for the whole family and the family's young friends.

Any child who suddenly realizes that his parents are still very much alive and not at all the ancients they seemed to be, people who like youngsters and are quite capable of sharing their games, laughing at their jokes, and taking part in their recreations, has found a new respect and the beginnings of that friendly confidence and comradeship which should be the goal of all families.

Cultural Tastes

From the parents normally come the children's cultural bents. The youngsters get their first taste in books from those books which their parents hand them. Even after they enter high school, they are not beyond an interest in what their parents may be reading. If parents actually set this cultural example and threw in the way of their children the fine books of the world, books read by themselves and made accessible to the youngsters, we should not be afflicted by the avalanche of uncomic comics and ghastly unhumorous "funnies" that are now giving children a lasting attack of mental indigestion.

During these adolescent years parents are really shaping or at least giving a final polish to their children's cultural tastes. These tastes may be manifested in the musical records they collect and play, in the use they make of a camera, in the interest they take in decorating their rooms, in a thousand youthful hobbies or enthusiasms.

Whatever the form, the children's tastes spring directly from the tastes of the parents. And if instead the children are allowed to squander their time in daydreaming or in paging through the movie magazines, if they get their exercise in petty rows among themselves, the parents had better make a sincere examination of their own consciences and follow it with a feeling of deep sorrow and a firm purpose of amendment.

All this we'll talk over in much more detail somewhat later.

Parental Rights

Whatever the age of the children, parents must remember, be conscious of, and if necessary enforce their parental rights.

Just because we are a democracy, we have thought we should repeal all or most parental authority. On the contrary—if we understood democracy at all, we should be grimly aware that there is no decent democracy without obedience to law and that we cannot hope to secure our rights under law unless we first have a respect for authority.

Yet for authority American parents have had a way of substituting wheedling, bribes, recriminations, prayerful entreaty, and occasional bursts of exasperated oratory. None of these has any real connection with parental authority, which must be exercised wisely and well if the children are not to grow into obnoxious little anarchists. What the American home has tended to produce is, not a race of democrats, but a race of anarchists. And God help the country that is entrusted to the tough mercilessness of citizens who think they are democrats when what they really are is hoodlums with no slightest respect for even those laws that they themselves make.

No Escape From Authority

Parents cannot escape the authority which God has given to them. If they have any real love for their children, they had better not try to escape it. I am perfectly willing to admit that it seems easier to woo a child's love than to exercise necessary restraint. It is much simpler to shrug the parental shoulders with a fatalistic "I simply can't do a thing with Junior" or "Sissy never pays the slightest attention to a thing I say" than to lay down clear orders and watch them through to fulfillment. But the parent who puts aside his authority is simply putting aside his obligations to God, the country we call a democracy, and his own children.

"Honor thy father and thy mother," runs God's commandment. Primarily that seems to speak to the children. They must obey their parents or be guilty of sin. In a much more vital way however that commandment affects the parents. They must with justice and love bring right order into their children's lives or there can be neither obedience nor honor on the part of the youngsters.

So even the democratic American father and mother are obliged to give those orders and exercise that authority which are essential to a well-governed household. Within the family father and mother must assign the division of work and of responsibility. They set the hours for meals. They establish the relationship of the children to the care of their rooms and of their clothes. They appoint the time for rising and retiring. Indeed they are harming no one but the children when in slack and lazy fashion they let themselves be coaxed or bullied into running a house that lacks dignity and order and the reasonable time schedule essential to civilized living.

As long as the children live in their parents' house, the parents have to exercise a reasonable authority over them. Even when the children become in whole or in part financially independent, that authority remains. For whether it is an apartment or the quarter-deck of a ship, a dinner table or (forgive the somewhat dubious juxtaposition) a battlefield, someone must give the orders if chaos is not to reign and inevitable devastation not to ensue.

WISDOM AND JUSTICE

Hence in simple justice to themselves and to their children parents accept the authority God gave them and use it wisely and with loving justice. They know that it is their obligation to regulate the comings and the goings of their children. For it matters a great deal to the whole future of children when and where and with whom they go out and when and in what condition they return.

It is the parents' plain duty to regulate the spending of money, though they are wise if they teach their children early how to appreciate the value of money and how to use it generously yet not wastefully.

Parents have the final word on who shall come as guests to the house. Here they will be smart to show a great interest and leniency. They will be keen enough to know that if their children bring their friends home it is because those children are proud both of their friends and of their home. It is only the friend the parents are not allowed to meet that needs to worry them.

Father and mother have a certain jurisdiction over correspondence, though again with restraint. If letters come from an unknown source, parents have the right to ask to see them. If letters between their young son and some girl or between their daughter and some boy become far too numerous and suspiciously important to the child, they have the right to exercise a curb upon the momentary fervor.

Assigned Jobs

In the well-ordered house the parents have given an assigned job to each of the children. They simply take it for granted that the children will show a willingness to carry out those jobs.

Meals should naturally enough be furnished by the parents. So should comfortable beds, warmth in the house, and pleasant recreation. But as members of an important natural society, the children soon begin to earn these things. They do so by their execution of the small assignments through which they contribute to the happiness and smooth running of the entire household.

Recreation At Home

If parental authority seems to entail unpleasant orders and a certain amount of discipline, it also affords wide opportunity for fun. In fact parents should know that they have a real obligation to make life happy for their children. This is not a task they can pass over to the professional entertainer on stage or screen or athletic field or—least of all—night club or tavern.

Family recreation is one of the things that must be arranged for by the parents. I love to see parents and children going to the movies together. When children have seemed a little reluctant to go with just "a family party," I've seen smart parents invite some of the neighbors' children—to the great delight of their own youngsters and to the real enjoyment of all.

Reading aloud is not out of possibility in these days. Parents should see to it that the radio doesn't become a source of family rows; it can become a means of learning family cooperation. If the boy wants to hear "Gang Busters," he gets his chance, provided he doesn't insist on Tommy Dorsey when mother wants to listen to the broadcast from the Metropolitan. Sister is encouraged to tune in on her favorite tenor, but she is expected to be willing to step aside while dad listens to the commentator who makes him feel that all is not lost in the world.

As part of the recreational program which they must develop, parents of high-school children should encourage home games, especially when young friends come in and take part. The dart board has moved from the English tavern into the family living room, with pleasant effects in family unity. Tournaments around the ping-pong table are grand sources of competition and fun. Since badminton is much less expensive than tennis, the back yard has again come into happy use.

I know families where family bingo has kept the youngsters and the oldsters intensely engrossed and has gathered the kids of the neighborhood in alert participation. If the stakes are small, a penny or a nickel a card, the gambling instinct may be exhausted and yet gratified under wholesome family conditions.

I can see the mother herself teaching her young son to dance, or watching him being taught, or even playing the piano for the lesson, or changing the records while his older sister takes over the job of teaching. The boy will be grateful if when he goes out to his party he is able to do something more than hold up the ballroom wall.

I can see the dinner table as a center of sociability. If the parents make it so, the children will respond. If it is the center of a gay rehearsal of all the events of the day, an interchange of pleasant banter, the children will not rush madly from meals or spend their time with one ear alert to the phone and the other ear cocked in anticipation of a car's honking at the front door.

PRACTICE, NOT THEORY

All this, needless to say, is a matter of doing, not discussing. Parents are most effective when they simply take their authority for granted and discuss it not at all. They need not theorize to their children about "the value of home recreation" and "games as the unifying influence in the household" if they are making possible that recreation and are providing and taking part in those games.

Religion

Almost too patent is the part that parents of high-school boys and girls play in the religious training of their children. If they go with their sons and daughters to Mass and in their company approach the communion rail, a profound impression is made upon youthful religious spirit. Family prayers may be difficult in the easy flow of an American family. But grace before meals is one prayer that can become a sort of family liturgy. Families even in this present age of restlessness have established during the month of October the family rosary.

When it is announced that the parish will hold special devotions, the response should be that of a united family. There will be a special novena; fine; the whole family will attend. The missionaries come to give a parish mission. Without discussion all take part. The parish inaugurates a new society; the members of the family who are of the correct age for it are there to cooperate.

In all this the parents are the natural leaders. And just because their children are passing through the preoccupied and harried age of adolescence, parents are in no way excused from their God-entrusted authority.

Comradeship

In their use of authority parents who are wise realize that what they are really aiming at is the establishment of trust and comradeship. They give orders to secure cooperation and a pleasant home atmosphere. They are quick to let their children know that they use their authority only because they look to their children's happiness and the continuance of real happiness in the home, a fine, healthy spirit of fun, and the development of those strong characters which alone make possible the difficult form of government known as democracy.

Parents of Grammar School Children

The second group we can consider is made up of the parents of children in grammar school.

I like to see these parents forming into parent-teacher associations. These organizations always seem to me a little like parents' unions or parents' protective associations. Parents should, since they cannot have the exclusive privilege of teaching their children, be very close to the teachers who supplement their work. Never for a moment should their job be relinquished. So through a parent-teacher group the mother and the father join with the teacher to form a co-operative enterprise.

Almost all that I have said about the parents whose children are of high-school age could be repeated for this group. There is this important difference though: Since the children in grammar school are younger than those in high school, the chances of influencing them are much higher. The general principle always is this: The younger the child, the greater the possibilities for adult influence. So when parents decide during their youngsters' grammar-school days to take up in all seriousness the questions of influence, authority, recreation, culture, and religion, their chances for success are enormously better than if they waited even only a few years.

INVITING EXPERT HELP

Parent-teacher groups make wonderful clearinghouses and schools of adult education for parents. So do alumni and alumnae associations where the presence of young parents is recognized and the programs arranged to include their needs. For that matter parish discussion groups might well drop theoretical questions in favor of the problems of parenthood. I should much like to see Sodalities of parents, particularly young parents, meeting to ask Mary their mother to help them with the guidance of their children and to discuss among themselves or with experts just what they can do most effectively to bring their children to successful maturity.

Parents have a right to look to the experts for help. In fact around this most important of natural professions should swing the other professions. Doctors should of their own accord or at the invitation of these parents' unions be brought in to discuss the care of children's health, their food, exercise, adolescent developments, needs. Priests are often natural experts on morality and on the way of instilling a quick sense of right and wrong into the youthful soul. I can see sisters teaching mothers a great deal that they themselves learn from their patient observing of the girls: what young girls really think and how they really feel and what makes or mars their psychological development.

A trained nurse could give mothers a great many invaluable pointers on the care of their daughters' developing bodies.

PSYCHOLOGICAL PROBLEMS

Catholic psychologists (but unless they are Catholic, their attitudes are not likely to be beyond suspicion) can give information that will solve many parental perplexities. What causes boys to be sullen? How do sexual temptations arise? How is self-abuse corrected? What about the worries caused children by temptations to impure thought? How can the boy's loyalty to his gang be turned from evil and to good? What about his abruptly developing interest in girls? How far should parents intrude upon or be interested in the boy's possibly quite harmless secrets? Why do boys like to keep these secrets, even in such harmless matters as their back-lot clubs, their hobbies, their collections? Why are they noisy, and how far should their general gaucherie be curbed?

In the case of daughters a Catholic psychologist can explain the value as well as the obvious peril of vanity. How is cliquishness among them turned to leadership? to wider charity? toward a real social horizon? If they show a lack of truthfulness, is it because they are afraid or filled with a sense of physical or mental social weakness? How can wheedling and pouting be cured? What is the difference between the affectionateness of a girl and the dawning passion of a boy?

It would be wonderful if parents really got the straight of all this from experts. Though I firmly believe that for many a tired woman an afternoon of bridge is an excellent way to relax with her friends . . . still if the friends are mothers like herself, couldn't they together with other mothers' bridge clubs combine occasionally and bring in someone to speak to them about their problems of child guidance?

Though I think that fathers have a right to their occasional evening of poker or the mild boxing show put on for their release from the awful grinding of modern life, still their jobs as fathers would be perhaps more readily and effectively accepted if at intervals some persons experienced in the ways of young people explained for them problems that all fathers meet with in their children.

Several years ago I was called into an all-male club which on normal occasions met to eat good food and drink good beer and heckle some political speaker or some globe-trotter or writer. They asked me to talk to them about their own children. I did—for an hour and a half—following which they asked me questions until after midnight.

Sex Problems

During the days that children are in grammar school, a lot of change is likely to take place in them. Their sexual development begins, and with it all the problems of adolescence. If the child has been properly trained from childhood, these problems are in all likelihood already prepared for and armed against. It is during his grammar-school days however that parents begin to suspect that their boy is practicing self-abuse. Perhaps they note in him a morbid growth of curiosity about women.

The girl returns announcing blithely (or worse still concealing) the fact that they played kissing games at the evening's party. Brothers and sisters begin to manifest sex temptations toward each other. The parents stumble on immodest pictures or cards that the youngsters have found and hidden away in what they thought was a safe place.

I shall handle some of these problems in another chapter. Just now all I mean to do is indicate that parents during this period of the children's development have a set of unique problems which they must care for adequately. If they do not care for them, some stranger will have to scrape these children free from the wreckage in years to come.

Interest Awakens

Take for example that suddenly awakened interest of grammar-school children in the other sex.

Up to this point the boy regards girls as silly little nuisances who by their mere presence tend to clutter up the important projects of the male of the species. They pursued them with contemptuous looks and unfriendly snowballs and classify them all as snitches and tattletales and cowards afraid of such interesting things as snakes and toads and angry dogs. During that same brief period of hostility the girls want nothing to do with the dirty, noisy, destructive breed known as boys. They hide their dolls from the boys as pioneer mothers might have hidden their babies from the Indians. The mere sight of an approaching boy causes them to break up their games while they look at his advent as an insult, a disturbance, and an annoyance past enduring.

That attitude lasts through the early years of grammar school—until the coming of the great change. Then boys begin to wash behind the ears, unreminded and on their own initiative. Girls begin to smile coyly at the boys of their acquaintance. Clumsy male feet are voluntarily disciplined to dancing measures, and grave concern is felt by fluttering feminine hearts over whether the important he will or will not notice that the dress is new and the mouth adorned (or inadvertantly distorted) with a lipstick filched from mother's dresser.

The parents at this period of amazing transition may take the heretical attitude of laughing at their offspring. That unkind laugh simply cuts them off from the possibility of their ever sharing the confidences or new enthusiasms of their children.

No Laughter; No Importance

"Willie's got a girl!" may be chanted at the boy by his male associates, and the boy will forgive them. His new love cannot be used as an occasion for banter by parents or family without their gaining Willie's hatred or deep-red fury.

After all this first interest of boys in girls can be a very wholesome thing, something that can turn an unkempt barbarian into a pleasantly clean and polished gentleman—not however if his parents treat his new attitude as something right out of Tarkington at his funniest.

The sensitive girl who feels a first heartthrob over the seventh grader who carries her books home from school and saves his money all week in order to treat her to a chocolate marshmallow sundae regards her new concern as far, far too sacred for the blasphemy of mirth.

Parents who laugh at their children's first timid forays into romance are giving the bonds between themselves and their children a terrible wrench and a perilous stretch.

On the other hand nothing could be more ridiculous than for the parents to take these salad love affairs as things important and serious.

I remember sitting in indignant anger one evening while in his presence the doting mother and father talked about the calf loves of their eighth-grade boy. You'd think he was a Don Juan, of whom they were both proud and fearful.

"Oh Henry is certainly a terror with the girls," cooed his mother. And addressing the smirking Henry, she added, "Aren't you, Henry?"

Whereupon Henry from the conceited heights of his already inflated male vanity smirked back in agreement.

Choosing Companions

If the mother and father have been taking wise, protective care of their children up to this point, they may rest secure in the goodness of their girls and boys and the trustworthiness of their companions—rest secure, that is, as long as they continue to keep a watchful vigilance without making scenes or suspecting evil in each shy and rather pathetic new interest. Parents know there are bad boys whom their little girls may meet and bad girls who may stretch their juvenile webs about their boys. But most parents can swiftly detect the difference between a sweet young affection and a dangerous association which is not making the child better but—so that the effects are visible on the very surface of his life—plainly worse.

When children's interest in the other sex dawns, parents alertly watch for possible dangers. They do not let themselves be thrown into panic or dither by the simple development of nature through which millions of rightly guided children move unharmed.

Nor is there the slightest reason for parents' regarding each new affection as if it were prelude to marriage. Their boy will fall in and out of love a dozen times or more before the right girl captures his love for life. The girl has reached a point where, being deeply interested in the attentions paid her by the boys in her class, she may like the most ungainly hulk who plays puppy at her heels, though in years to come she will probably marry his elder brother, who is even now a junior in medical school.

So wise parents regard this whole transitional period as interesting, apparently natural, something they may laugh about in private, but not a problem to worry them into excessive brooding over or hedging round their children nor a sign that their dear little ones are planning an elopement to take place come Michaelmas.

SPORTS

During this period the interest of boys in sports reaches a generally high level. By the time they get into high school, boys have by the force of bitter experience been divided into those who are good at games and those who never play without muffing an important throw or breaking a finger. So there is strong probability that by the time youngsters come to high school they are already classified as players or spectators, the latter confining their sport to much energetic rooting and a little amateurish fun about which they do not do much bragging, the former working might and main to make a place first on the class team and then on the school team.

During grammar school however nature, acting as guardian for God, gives every boy the healthy conviction that he can knock the ball over the fence and, given a few more pounds and a little more experience in open-field running, that he will be all-American halfback on the Notre Dame team.

That is as it should be. Games are not played for the games' sake of course but simply to lure the unsuspecting child into the exercise so vitally important for his full development. He thinks he enjoys throwing a ball around, and he does; what nature is arranging is that he will use that arm, bend and twist and run, and develop muscles that could hardly be discovered otherwise. He thinks he is madly bent on pushing the Little Tiger Cats on to victory. He does take the long end of the score, proudly leading his baseball team to a close victory of thirty-six to thirty-one over the rivals, the Iroquois Invincibles — practically a pitchers' battle in the sand-lot league.

Yet who will ever remember that famous victory? Long years later he will realize that in the heat of the game he was free from the heat of young passion and that, having worked off his excessive animal energies as he circled the base for the thirty-sixth and winning run, he returned home too tired to be troubled by temptation. There on the vacant lot he was learning much about cooperation and sportsmanship that was to help him be a better democrat.

Nature was luring him into precisely the exercise of body and soul and social instincts that carried him safely into developed manhood.

Hence any interests of parents in the long-winded and usually pretty incoherent sports reporting of their sons is all to the good. Hence the willingness of wise fathers to invest in moderate supplies of athletic equipment, even though they know after one glance at their boys' playing that the Yankees won't have a scout following him around from his first year in high school.

Hence too the wisdom of the mother who encourages her boy to tell her all about his victories: that one-hand catch of that long fly in the sixth; and that new kid who arrived on the lot, carrying a "swell new catcher's mitt, and boy, can he use it!" If he finds her attentive in this, he may have important things to tell her later on: his victories over self or the new companion toward whom he feels a strange attraction and who creates in him a still stranger revulsion that puzzles and disturbs him.

The interest of parents in the sports program of their gangling youngsters all through grammar school is a wonderful breeder of confidence and a prelude to lifelong comradeship.

DRESS

Then there is the girl's quite rightful interest in dress. Nobody really admires a dowdy. No one regards slovenly clothes as a sign of intelligence or of high virtue. So when of a sudden the girl begins to be concerned about her clothes, to spend time putting on her hat at precisely the right angle, and to ask mother to teach her how to sew, she is offering her mother a powerful lever of control.

If the girl is good, pleasant around the house, and attentive in class, her mother sees to it that she is rewarded with more or better clothes. A real nexus is established between daughter's personal conduct and her blessed reward in adornment. If on the other hand she neglects her home duties and is annoying or negligent at school, there is no worse punishment than mother's "Sorry, but you can't have that new hat you wanted," or "I had planned on getting you that bright new sweater, but I couldn't give it to you when you have been so remiss in what you know I expect of my daughter."

During grammar-school days, when youthful hands are ready for expert development and the mastering of skills, that love of girls for dress makes possible real training. The girl can be shown that if she learns to make her clothes she will have more clothes than if she has to buy them all ready-made. Material is not as a rule so expensive, she learns, as bought, ready-made dresses. So the youngster may develop a real skill in dressmaking. Her vanity may be transmuted into a care for her clothes. She learns the importance of putting her clothes away carefully, of hanging them in bags or drapes, of keeping them clean.

Her vanity may also help her understand a budget: "There is just so much money to be spent on your clothes, dear; let's work out a way of getting the most value for that money." Thriftily, with her eye on which item will make her most charming and personable, the girl decides between a new hat and a new pair of shoes.

PARTY FLIGHTS

It is during the grammar-school days that the parents supervise the first flights from home. Those are perilous occasions, the parents think, for the children; they are worrisome days, the parents know, for themselves.

Yet these first flights can be safely supervised by the parents without their own visible intrusion or undue heaviness of hand.

All their life thus far should have been marked by a training in good manners. The final advice in consequence resummarizes lessons which, while they are old to the child, are now going to be put into practice.

The parents restress . . .

The proper manner toward the hostess: greeting her on their arrival; thanking her on their departure.

The simple fact that noise is not fun and that noisy children aren't invited a second time.

A respect for the property of others: no handling of things which at home they would not be permitted to paw; no breaking up of furniture or bric-a-brac in the interest of hilarity.

The value to oneself of being kind to the less attractive, not joining the line that forms to the left of the obviously charming.

If the parents of grammar-school children have really been doing their duty, without too great a show of supervision they have been long selecting the companions toward whom their children will gravitate. These playmates should normally be the children of the parents' own friends.

Hence very simply, if the parents have chosen the right friends for themselves, they have stored up for their children a fine endowment of associates for all the years. When they selected a Catholic school for their children, they assured their meeting other wholesome Catholic boys and girls from much the same type of wholesome Catholic homes and with exactly the same standards of conduct as those of their own youngsters.

During their grammar-school days children have a natural respect for the opinions and judgments of their parents. Hence when at that time the father and mother approve of a companion and of his home, their verdict is accepted largely without question. On the other hand when the parents spot a youngster who is obviously bad-mannered and badly trained and a poor example to others, or if they know that the home to which he invites the children is not a place where they would want their children to visit, their tactful handling of the situation will not be resented by the children at that age.

In fact if parents wish to have a say in matters of this kind later on, they had better exercise this subtle selection from the very beginning of the child's social life. Later on supervision will be furiously resented, unless it has been the practice of a lifetime.

Social Life at Home

The first flights from home will of course be successful largely in proportion to the success of the social life that has already been provided at home. Children will be invited by those children whom they themselves have entertained. Parents can stimulate a series of wholesome and approvable invitations by first giving parties for their children in their own houses.

Hence the vital importance of plenty of social life at home under the eyes and sponsorship of the parents.

If all this has been taken care of during the grammar-school days, half the social problems of later life have been anticipated and forestalled.

Parents of Preschool Children

Yet it is to the parents of children not as yet in school that I turn as to far and away the most important group.

Psychologists may differ on a great many things. On one platitudinous detail, essential and significant, they are unanimous: As the twig is bent, the tree is inclined; as the child is trained from birth to the age of five, he will probably in the main continue to the day of his death.

For a long time, as I noted, we have been expertly told that no one learns anything really new after the age of five. Now we are hearing that the fatal dead line has been pushed back further still: At the recent gathering of psychologists I referred to, it was maintained that all basic habits and character bents are developed before the baby has arrived at the ripe maturity of his second birthday.

You can choose whichever date you prefer as the ultimate boundary. Either one would make the responsibilities of the parents to their very young children almost frightening.

Well Trained, Early Trained

Certainly this would make all honest, sincere parents take their early responsibilities pretty seriously. They would not be likely to turn their children over for long hours a day to some little girl or some practically unknown woman hired for a few dollars a week. They would know that during those impressionable years the child's whole future is made or ruined. Education does not begin with school; almost in a way it ends when the child leaves home for school. The best the teacher can do is supplement and build on the virtues and strengths and character elements long since given to the child by the mother and the father.

No wonder teachers welcome a well-trained child from the hands of responsible and skillful parents. And no wonder they regard with something like despair the unkempt, untrained, weedy youngster, no matter how exquisitely he is dressed, who by careless, indifferent, weak, or bad parents has been pampered or neglected or abused or misshaped into a little caricature that can never be corrected or redrawn to the pattern of a fully developed human being.

Simply stated, everything important for the child's future begins during that period before ever he sets foot in a classroom. During this period the confidence between parents and children is established, and education is brought to its most important developments.

WINNING EARLY CONFIDENCE

I shall repeat in various forms the all-important fact that if fathers and mothers want the confidence and comradeship and trust of their children they must develop this in infancy and during the years that immediately follow infancy. There is something indescribably pathetic about an adolescent's mother and father who decide all of a sudden that they have not the child's trust and confidence (or confidences) and that right here and now, say at about the child's fifteenth or sixteenth birthday, they must go about getting that trust and confidence. They are exactly fifteen or sixteen years too late. That intimacy must be established when the child is utterly lacking in self-consciousness and when he looks up to his parents as to his whole world.

If when he is five years of age there is not a close bond of trust and fellowship between parents and child, only with miracles of labor and grace will that bond be established later.

Hence once more: The wise parent encourages his child to ask questions, and he answers those questions with all honesty. Even though the prattling youngster asks the same question over and over again to the point of complete boredom, even though he seems to pay no attention to the answer given and five minutes later makes the same query once more, the parent must talk, listen, and answer. The important thing gained through this is, not that the information is given to the child, but that the child slowly realizes that his parent is willing to answer.

At this period of the child's life the questions may be as trivial as "What makes a cow moo?" A question like that may leave the parent stumped for an answer and make him feel very silly when he replies, "Because it's a mother cow and very lonesome for her little boy." The child probably will pay no attention to the answer anyhow. But the child will have the unforgettable memory of his mother's or his father's being interested enough to answer even his silly chatter.

There is nothing else like that attentiveness for the cementing of lifelong trust. It guarantees an instinctive giving of confidences later on.

During that early period of life all true comradeship between parents and children is established. Then too law comes to life in the firm, loving discipline administered by the parents. The first and all-essential sex instruction is given at a time when no harm can possibly be done and wonderful foundations can be laid for ideals and right conduct.

Yes; we may as well face the fact that all education is really over at the age of six. After that the things that have been learned are developed; fuller knowledge is built upon the foundations already established; tastes earlier acquired are improved, clarified, made less instinctive and more reasonable. But all basic training has already started.

Everything Starts Before Six

During those first six years or less good manners come into the child's life. His religious reflexes are established and his bent toward God and goodness fixed. During those years he learns how to deal with others. He masters those queer appendages that are his hands, and he learns to manipulate (a wrong word but still vivid) his feet. He acquires basic skills in speech and movement and the handling of external objects. He gets a taste for music and perhaps for beauty in pictures. He hears the first of the great stories and learns to love good literature before he has even been told that there is such a thing as literature and that some of it is good.

At the age of six he is in other words the mental, social, religious being that he will be in later years. Some violent change or shock or some accident for good or for evil may shake him away from this first formation. But that is most unusual, and there is no use in planning or counting on the unusual. For the normal child in normal society these years are the really formative ones. During these years no teacher can possibly supplant his parents, nor can any other environment adequately take the place of his home.

The parents of young children should meditate long and carefully on their high responsibilities. Let the rest of mankind work with brick or steel or clay or ink or paints or bread or "herbs and simples" or the letters of the alphabet. They work, these fathers and mothers of young children, with the immortal stuff of God's sons and daughters, the citizens of the civilized states, the men and women who, themselves successes, will make others deeply happy.

Parents and priests both work in human souls.

FUTURE PARENTS

The final group of parents of whom we are thinking are the future parents.

These are the boys and girls in senior high school or the young men and women in the parishes and the colleges today.

The insistence placed on other careers, the focusing of the spotlight on medicine and social service and law and government and literature and art and the entertainment world, has made many a young man and woman forget that parenthood is first in importance among all natural jobs. There can not possibly be any decent civilization without success in that profession.

So I look for the day when there will be in sermons and in lectures much less talk of marriage and much more talk of parenthood.

If their parents are the right sort, it will not be necessary to give these young people much instruction in how to be a successful and efficient father or mother. The children have seen the art practiced before their eyes. That is the best possible way to learn how any profession is carried out.

Talks on Parenthood

Yet as the parents of our young people are not always too successful, what about classes in parenthood for students in high school and in college? It seems to me that before graduation—on the supposition that many of the graduates will not go on to college—high-school seniors should be given a series of good instructions on homemaking, the authority and responsibilities of parents, the training of children, and the relation of both the father and the mother to the full development of the child.

I hasten to insist that there is no least touch of sex education in all this. It is merely a discussion of what to plan for the children when they are on their way and what to do for and with them after they have arrived. Indeed while talks on marriage necessarily bring in the matter of sex, talks on parenthood can be remarkably free from that whole question, except in its most wholesome and reassuring aspects.

I certainly think that college students should be prepared for life by frank and effective discussions of child psychology, child problems, and the training of children by the parents.

For those who do not have these opportunities in school, the thousands of discussion clubs throughout the country can well handle this question that is so vital to the vast majority of young men and women. If experts can be introduced into the school discussion groups, these same experts can and should be brought into the young people's clubs of the parish and into the Sodality meetings, where are gathered the future mothers and fathers of the race.

I should like to see priests talk much more on parenthood.

Sermons on marriage always suggest themselves to the young priest. They seem to be attractive and hence are likely to attract a crowd. As a matter of cold fact unless they are extremely well done, they give the people little that is new and often serve to excite a degree of amusement and perhaps a bit of morbid curiosity. I should say that from my experience I have seen where too many talks and sermons have been given on marriage . . . while almost none is given on what is the great objective of marriage, the care and education of children.

People will always rush into marriage. Once in it, they often find themselves completely baffled by the mystery of the children who bless that marriage. Parenthood is the real problem. Parenthood is the vocation for which young people should be prepared.

II

THE JOY AND GLORY OF PARENTAL RESPONSIBILITY

Though we outlined four groups of parents as subject for our interest, we shall find ourselves thinking more and more in terms of the young mother and father, the parents with the child under six years of age. These are the really important parents. If they do their work well, everything will be almost simple for them as the years advance and their children grow older.

I don't think we need to do more than make a swift gesture toward those responsibilities which any decent parent, even the most casual or ignorant, recognizes as resting upon him. Clearly parents are supposed to provide food—and good food—or the child starves. They are supposed to put a leakproof roof over the head of the child and an adequate bed or cradle under its helpless body. They are supposed to wrap the youngster in sufficient and clean clothing. They are expected to give the child normal love and care and disciplining.

Now that we have put all those obvious points in one paragraph, we can leave them for the rest of the book.

AXIOMS FOR PARENTS

Instead let us lay down a few axioms, without which we can hardly hope to develop our treatment.

Axiom One: The home is the laboratory of living.

Axiom Two: The home is the school of life.

Axiom Three: The home is the university for the development of the full man.

Axiom Four: The parents are the rulers of the home.

Axiom Five: The parents are the faculty of the school and of the university.

Axiom Six: The entire day within a home is a developing program of youthful education.

Axiom Seven: The student, the child, begins to learn at birth.

Like all other axioms these demand only a presentation. We need not delay to discuss or prove them. Anyone with any knowledge of civilized living admits them without further argument.

But like all other axioms ... it is one thing to admit them intellectually, and another to act upon them and make them dominate one's conduct.

Consequences of the Axioms

Hence we come back to those all-important truths that flow immediately from the axioms: that the responsibility of parents for the education of their children cannot possibly be shifted to anyone else; that the school can never supplant the home; that the education of children is a job that requires all the ingenuity and resourcefulness and devotion of parents; that there is never a moment so early in a child's life that the parents can say of it, "This moment is not important and can be slighted."

From Infancy

Education begins with earliest infancy. No more serious mistake could be made than the assumption by parents that "Our child isn't old enough as yet to understand." Probably his mind is not yet manifesting itself. He may actually seem a charming little vegetable, eating and sleeping and soaking up sunshine, whose every gesture is instinctive and whose intelligence is as yet hidden deep down in his soul.

Even so his education has begun.

The lasting quality of early impressions is one of the things we all know from experience. We remember vividly the things that happened to us long before the age of reason: the time that, hardly able to walk, we rode the tricycle down the cellar stairs; the time we stuck out our tongue at our mother and came in intimate contact with the reverse side of a hairbrush; the times our father sat us on his knee and built up for us an idyllic childhood by telling us of the days when he was a boy; our visits to church with mother; the trips to the market when we were just barely toddling.

Yet the impressions that mattered most to us are not necessarily the impressions that we can consciously recall now. They may be impressions that left their mark upon our character though we are to this day unaware of the time or the circumstances under which they were made—or for that matter of the very fact that they ever were made.

Apparently that soft, impressionable brain of the child is like a wax gramophone record as yet unmarked but waiting for the first sensitive contact on its surface. When later on the human being plays a melody or performs some other action, he may be reproducing subconsciously the impressions left on his waxlike brain long before the dawn of consciousness.

Youthful Impressions

That is why psychologists try—rightly or wrongly—to force a mental patient to recall things from his earliest youth. Though long since forgotten, these things may still be the motivating influences for action that he finds hard to explain and feelings and ideas for which he can consciously discover no origin.

That youthful impressionable brain constantly registers what goes on around it. The impressions are stored up for later use. Sometimes with advancing maturity the impressions are recalled, mulled over, puzzled about, or understood. Often they become, without our meditating or planning or even clearly understanding, the standards of our future conduct. For good or evil they modify the future development of the human being.

Hence for two different reasons parental characteristics may turn up in the children. It is possible that these are passed on in the life germs transmitted by the mother and the father to their offspring. Characteristics may lie hidden in the chromosomes, waiting for manifestation in later life: the way the father crooks his little finger; the way the mother laughs or smiles; the parents' liking for music or lack of interest in art; a pleasant manner or a churlish disposition.

Beyond these inherited factors however the child, a natural mimic, copies what he sees in and hears from the parents who lean over his crib. Their actions, their smiles, the sound of their voices, the tricks of their speech, their instinctive gestures—these are the first impressions left on the youthful brain. They create the first grooves.

If these qualities appear later in the child, if the mother says, "Why that's just like his daddy," or the father thinks, happily, "Everyday she grows more like her mother," the little imitator who is the child .may merely be reproducing what he or she has seen and registered and retained as part of his or her basic equipment.

THE CHILD RECORDS

Even a few seconds at the crib of a baby reveal the intense activity of his eyes and ears. Long before he begins to speak, these are at work. His eyes and ears are simply soaking up everything that goes on around him. They are the direct channels leading to the baby's soft, expectant brain. They are the phonograph needles leaving behind a trail of vital impressions to be played back when the child has grown old enough to use the record he is making.

Of course all the early learning done by a child is instinctive. If a child never hears people speak, he will never speak. He may make arbitrary signs that signify the ideas in his mind, but he will never express them in words until he has heard over and over again the sound of words uttered within reach of his receptive ear.

What is true of the development of his speech is true of so many other human faculties, the listing of which would be catalogic.

The child watches and observes. What he sees his parents do, he tries to do. What he hears them say, he tries to repeat. When they clap their hands together, so does he. He learns to echo their laughter with his imitative crow. His eyes follow their gestures. His ears drink in their inflections, the timbre and character of their speech.

So it is that the baby becomes a little copy, a record of his environment, and for the first few months an inarticulate copy of those people who are closest to him.

Even the most careless, thoughtless parent in the world is in consequence of all this incessantly teaching the child. His teaching may be all to the bad; the teaching itself goes on without interruption.

First Recorded Words

But where the parents are good, they are pouring their own goodness into the child—everything from the charm of their speech and the grace of their movements to the ideals of love and God that lie in their souls.

Only because it is so important a fact do I even mention that the first spoken words of the child come straight from the lips of his parents. That is why most children say mamma and daddy first. Blessed egotists that they are, the parents have trained the child—in fact they have besought him—to say the words they wanted to hear. Under the constant parental bombardment of "Say mamma! Say daddy!" the child at last picks up the sounds and gives them back, to the unending joy of the dear ventriloquists who have put the words right into his mouth.

That is why occasionally we read in history of saintly mothers and fathers who, loving Christ and Mary more than they loved themselves, heard their children, future saints, say as their first words, not mamma and daddy, but Jesus, Mary, and Joseph. That too was the reflex of the parents themselves, the holy echo of the names they loved best.

First Thoughts

So too the first thoughts put into the child's mind come from the parents. The parents point, call attention to, or are merely present and filled with these ideas. The child in that endless mimicry of infancy picks up these gestures, cries, ideas. First habits are born, not of reasoned planning or conscious mental operations, but of the frank copying of the habits of mother and father.

Parents Like Minor Gods

In Kenneth Grahame's lovely book "The Golden Age" the youngsters consistently think of the older members of the family as the Olympians. They tower above their youthful lives like blissful gods leaning down from Mount Olympus. Like the ancient gods of Greece they are often unreasonable, whimsical, uncertain, and hard to understand. Always they are godlike in size and proportions, godlike in thinking and planning, godlike in the shadow they cast over the lives of the earth dwellers who are their sons and daughters.

That, in poetic fashion, is the way in which all children think about their parents. Perhaps for that very reason God chose as His favorite title for Himself, Our Father. For to the dawning intelligence of a child his parents, his strong father and tender mother, brood over his cradle as God broods over the world. They take God's place in the little world of infancy. Not only have they created the child; they are God's providence manifested toward him, feeding him and caring for him and actually, like God Himself, holding him in the crook of their arms.

It easily happens then that during those early years the growing child regards almost any attitude or custom or speech of his parents as inevitably right. They are his little gods; they are his supermen. In very truth they stand by the order of God in His place. Their majesty and might and power seem all-enveloping.

PARENTS IN PLACE OF GOD

That admiration for parents is simply part of God's economy of childhood. I remember so clearly my own attitude toward my father. Our family had been marked by doctors and lawyers, a minister or two, professional men of various kinds. My father was not a professional man; he was merely a man of business, which made him seem very different from someone who had a title and a standing of dignity. Yet when I was asked by some visiting guests what I intended to be when I grew up, I shocked the visitors and alarmed my family by announcing, in a very childish soprano, "I am going to be nothing, like my daddy."

Parents stand in the place of God. The child takes it for granted that in their "perfections" they are right, entirely imitable, patterns according to which young characters are to be formed.

Hence in no time at all the child's unconscious imitation is abetted by conscious imitation. He tries, this small god of his little world, to be like his parents. Half consciously, half instinctively he picks up his parents' tag phrases, their tricks of language, the codes of conduct they express casually in his presence, their moral attitude and religious principles. He even tries to imitate his parents when they raise their eyes in appreciation of a picture, or to copy the intentness with which they listen to music.

IMITATION STARTS EDUCATION

On these instinctive and half-conscious factors will be established the education of the growing child. If the parents realize the unexcelled opportunities that are theirs and really try to capitalize on their children's youthful admiration, they can do wonders toward the developing of their children's ability. If their training is sketchy and their language, conduct, codes, habits far from worthy of imitation, even a long lifetime of later education and training may not undo the neglect of those first five years.

A little reminiscing on our own parts makes us realize how very soft and impressionable were our minds before the dawn of reason. I always feel quite safe in challenging an audience of adults to repeat nursery rhymes. If they really learned them in the nursery, they remember them today.

We can without difficulty rattle off the stories of "Cinderella" and "Jack and the Bean Stalk" and "Sindbad the Sailor" because we were told these stories when we were offering to our parents a blank mind all ready to be impressed with first contacts. We can remember stories that our dad told us. We can even recall the name of his favorite dog. We can remember what our mother wore on a certain occasion and how beautiful she looked.

Against that just try to recall that clever little verse you read the other day with the determination, "Now I'm going to remember that and tell it to my friends." Repeat that

joke that made you laugh so heartily at dinner yesterday.
What was the plot of that magazine story you read in your
favorite weekly a few days ago? What did your friend say
was the name of his prize Boston terrier? Or was it a Boston
terrier? Perhaps it was a fox terrier—or maybe an Airedale.
What did your wife wear the last time you went out together
—unless you happen to remember, not the outfit, but the bill
that came as an unhappy accessory to the dress.

First Memories

In "High Tor," Maxwell Anderson presented a situation
that the audience recognized and found amusing. His two
villains are captured in the crane and hang perilously over
the cliff. It's a time for praying, no doubt of that; but the
two old scamps can't recall either a prayer or a method of
praying. Then one of them rakes up out of the past a child's
prayer. He can pray, and he does:

"Now I lay me down to sleep," he begins—certainly no
prayer for a man hanging in danger of his life over a steep
embankment.

The only prayer he can recall is one that was rutted in
his brain when he was a baby, when childhood prayers became
part of his ineradicable experiences.

In summary of all this we simply have to remember that
long before the child's first conscious effort to speak or
the parents' first conscious effort to teach him, the human
learning process has been going on. Even the most casual and
thoughtless parents have been teaching their child things
they never dreamed they were teaching him. He has been
instinctively observing them. He has been making permanent
records of speech and conduct. He has been storing up experiences that will last him forever. Already his character and
cast of thought, his speech and his ideals have been shaped
into lines that will continue throughout a lifetime.

Life's First Lesson, Love

The great commandments of Christ the Savior concern
themselves with the very first lesson that parents give their
children: love.

For without the shadow of a doubt good parents can give their children, from the babies' infancy, lessons in the purity and self-sacrifice and beauty of the love of man for God and of man and woman for each other.

Over the baby's crib and under the restless, hardly focusing eyes of the baby the parents manifest their deep, pure, mutual love. Instinctively, without knowing what is happening, the baby watches the father put his arm around his wife's waist and kiss her tenderly. Sometimes the parents laugh as the baby in seeming response crows. Perhaps that is a real and not a seeming response. Perhaps the infant is made happy by the radiations of love which come from his parents to warm him and light his life.

Certainly the parents can give the child from the start of his life a demonstration of love in its purest human form. His first impression may be that of the kiss his father bestows upon his wife when he kneels at her side in the sick-room and she draws back the coverlet to show him the new-born child. As the weeks progress, the child unconsciously records the passing history of his parents' love. He sees enacted before his eyes the drama of their affection. He notes the change in their voices as they speak to each other. He records on his soft brain the pet names they use for each other. He is made happy by the joy they feel in each other's company.

As important to a child as the sunlight streaming through the open window or the pure milk from his mother's breast is the atmosphere of love that is created by his mother and his father in their unselfish, deep love, a love which envelopes him.

Marred By Dislikes

On the other hand the infant may be exposed to the stormy, lightning-charged, black atmosphere of parental dislike. Over his crib the parents may quarrel, and he is frightened by that as he is by the crash of thunder outside his window, more frightened because this danger seems terrifyingly close to him. He may record their sharp speech, their dislike expressed in hot, burning, searing words. He may keep embedded in the soft fiber of his brain the memory of their cruelty as they strike at each other. His emotional nature may be twisted and warped before he has any glimmer of consciousness—simply by the atmosphere of recrimination and hatred that is generated by parents who have grown to dislike each other.

God help the poor youngster whose infancy is blurred and shocked and distorted by a mother and a father who hate each other openly and in bitter words or secretly but in waves of emotion that vibrate around the bed of their helpless little baby.

Their Love for Him

Flowing from this love for each other is the love his parents feel for him. This too is constantly touching his emotions. This too is leaving upon his mind and heart a record that will sound sweetly when consciously or unconsciously he plays it in later years.

Union Through the Child

The love of the parents for their child should of course result in an increased unity. How terrible when parents struggle for the love of even a baby! when they fight each other to take first place in his affection! when the mother nullifies the commands of the father or the father cuts the ground from under the orders of the mother in the case of older children! when each tries to outdo the other in love and leniency so that he or she will be the one loved more— because he or she is the gentle, affectionate, easygoing parent, while the other is the stern and law-enforcing one!

How terrible when the child actually divides the parents! when the father in the hearing of the child—even though the child be an infant—taunts the wife with her neglecting him for the sake of the baby and loving the baby more than she loves him! or the mother early develops a jealousy of the father's devotion to the child and lets that jealousy radiate above the child's awakening perceptions!

Few things could more powerfully affect for good the infancy of a child than the warmth and truth of paternal and maternal affection cooperating to care for him. Such a baby is literally bathed in affection. And such affection may serve to orientate his whole emotional life in the most wholesome fashion.

LOVE WITH JUSTICE

On the other hand even in infancy the child can become aware that, much as they love him, his parents cannot by their love be swayed from the strict justice that is his due. He cannot stretch out his arms, squeeze forth a few easy tears, and immediately melt their determination to punish him when punishment is called for.

It is amazing how quickly infants realize that they can put it over on their parents and with what facility they proceed to do so. Love their children they surely must. But they must love them enough to punish them when punishment is necessary to curb an already bad disposition or the habit of whining or a vicious temper displayed in the cradle. Bad dispositions, whining, and rotten tempers do not develop in children after they are conscious of the meaning of sin; these develop when the baby is still feebly kicking, still gripping his inept hand.

Then and there love must be strong enough to do the thing which in the long run is for the child's happiness. Without any conscious process of thinking or recognizing, the child knows strong love from weak love, justice from an inordinate desire on the part of the parents to be loved and thought tenderly loving.

THE CHILD AS A BOND

All around the infant God and nature meant that there should be displayed a real family unity. The child was intended to bind the mother and the father closer together. As the fruit of their love, he was to give their love fullness of meaning. So if such family unity does result, the child is very lucky indeed. In his soft brain and upon his flexible emotions is recorded an ideal of home life and family harmony that will profoundly affect the home he himself later comes to establish. That ideal may be the very basis on which, arrived at maturity, he will build his own fine paternity, on which she will establish the virtues of a fine mother. Perhaps the quality of the home he will build is established before he has said for the first time the word mamma or daddy.

Lucky indeed is the child whose growing life is surrounded by an atmosphere of love, the frank love of the mother and the father, their united love for him.

He watches and approves and long remembers his parents' kissing one another on the father's returning from the day's work or on his leaving to be gone even for only a few hours. I have never forgotten the fact that my father invariably kissed my mother even if he meant to be gone only from the room for a little longer than usual and that she greeted him on his home-coming each evening with outstretched arms and an affectionate kiss.

Gracious Memories

The happy symbolism of birthdays becomes a part of his emotional background. The gifts that are given within the family are signs of the welcome felt for the child who added his presence to the family or an indication of the children's gratitude to their father and mother.

As sounds begin to gather in his mind and become coherent words and intelligible sentences, he grows to approve of the gentle tones that mark the voices of his parents as they speak to each other. When his father calls his mother dearest, the child may already be aware that this is an adjective in the superlative, reserved for his father's superlative woman. The poetic word darling, as yet not understood by the child, is still on the lips of his mother clear indication of the affection she feels for his dad.

He comes to know their frank enjoyment of each other's company. He makes an effort to fit himself into their joy.

Love is the first lesson that should be taught to every child. He should find it in the love of his brothers and sisters for each other and for him. He should see it in the attitude his parents take toward their friends, the real pleasure with which they welcome them. Charity in the true sense of love must begin at home. If it does, it is the warm cushion that protects the new little human being against the harsh shocks of the world that has just received him.

The Impressions of Home

Love, we always like to remember, is essentially productive. This is why the love of a mother and a father results in that wonderful production which is a home.

To all of us the home of our childhood remains the most important house in the world. With the years we come to magnify it. We spread out its proportions and invest its rooms with an ample spaciousness they did not really possess.

Priests who have spent quite a time in the seminary, or religious who for a period of years have been living in a religious house, or for that matter a man and a woman who have been long absent from the home of their childhood are amazed upon their return to find how really small the house is. In their absence they dreamed of the living room as being big enough to contain all their young friends at the same time, plus possibly a couple of swing bands and a small army of secondary acquaintances. They thought of the dining room as being little short of a banquet hall; King Arthur's knights wouldn't be too crowded around that ample table.

Then still under the spell of the magnifying power of childish memory they return and find the house quite tiny and the rooms they had remembered as stretching out into space really cramped and almost oppressively narrow.

Such is the simple influence of a sense of importance upon a memory of size. That first house of our childhood was enormously significant; therefore it must have been vast in proportions and capacious in its power to welcome our friends.

The first observations of an infant—after those he makes on his parents—may well be directed toward the room in which he is cradled and then toward the house that surrounds that room. He soon develops a perception of the attitude his parents take toward their home: the song that his mother sings as she goes about her work; the gaiety that seems to fill her soul when she carries him down to the kitchen or moves him about with her as she dusts and vacuums the house.

He notes in a permanent record the interest his father takes in the house. He gets the impression of dad's cutting the lawn while he himself sits in the sun in his perambulator. He hears the discussion of the new draperies for the windows or the new rug for the floor. He drinks in the charm of furnishings, which, as anyone knows, need not be expensive to be delightful. The home improves as the earnings of the family increase; after all since it is the setting against which they live their lives, his parents want it to measure up to their advancing income.

VISITORS

The visitors who come to the house certainly make an impression upon him.

I have thought that some brilliant cartoonist might well do two contrasting pictures, both dealing with childhood.

Both pictures would show a cluster of little children behind the staircase railing on the second floor of the house. They are looking down, wide-eyed with interest, their faces thrust out between the spaces in the balustrade, their young brains drinking up the party that is in progress on the lower floor.

The first picture would show a gay, happy, decent, utterly wholesome yet thoroughly enjoyable party. The adults would be having a wonderfully good time. There would be excellent food and drinks either nonintoxicating or if intoxicating handled with the mastery of civilized men and women over a friend who might prove an enemy. The games would be gay. The conversation would be brisk. The laughter would be clean, sincere, and from the heart.

The artist would not have much difficulty in painting upon the faces of the young observers their total approval of the scene and their delight in the gaiety that fills the house.

The second picture would show a very different type of party. There would be drunks, both male and female. The men would be amorous and the women easy. The games would destroy all sense of dignity. The laughter would be raucous and of that unmistakable timbre that follows the vulgar, obscene jest.

This time the childish faces above might be hard to paint. For they would be frozen in horror, rigid in a paralyzed fascination, revolted yet acutely curious, shocked yet drawn to drink it all in with unblinking stares.

I wonder if even the sounds of the party that float up to the infant in the crib, sounds blending subconsciously with his dream phantasms, might not leave a lasting impression. Certainly there must be a jolt and a shock when a pair of giddy parents drag up to the nursery their giggling, tipsy guests, who into the face of the baby wheeze their foul-smelling breath as they lift him with uncertain hands and drool over him in a fashion that inevitably frightens him and excites an instinctive repugnance.

Is it possible to emphasize too strongly the importance of the first impressions left upon infancy by parents and home? I frankly doubt it. Yet otherwise smart people will imagine that education begins when the youngster packs his first school books in a brand new strap and wanders off to a classroom. Almost I am tempted to repeat that his basic education ends, rather than begins, at that moment.

PARENTS PROFESSORS OF SPEECH

Once on a time it was my destiny to teach English. I had a year with the boys in high school. I had three years of teaching English in college. I met boys who wrote extraordinarily well and boys who made a simple sentence go through contortions that were ruinous to the sentence and a source of real pain to the listeners. I have met college freshmen who had a quick appreciation of literature that made my teaching merely the happy job of handing out books to be read; and I have met freshmen in the same class who regarded Charles Lamb's delicate essays as the most unintelligible moonshine and the poetry of Francis Thompson as the ravings of a dope fiend or—as they themselves would express it—the windjamming of a dope.

I allow much for innate genius and the fairy godmother who presides over the christening of those destined for the creating of literature. Yet I knew that with the vast majority of students the difference between the young man who found English easy and delightful and the one who beat a sentence to death with his fountain pen and faced the classics with sweat on his brow was almost entirely a matter of the type of language and the kind of books each had received from his parents.

Parents are the English professors par excellence. For years the children's speech is entirely a matter of parental construction. Their sense of words, their mastery of sentence form, their use of slang as substitute for speech or as the spice and flavoring of speech, their breadth of vocabulary—whether it will consist of one hundred and fifty hackneyed and threadbare words or swing out into a comprehensive and exact list that presents each object and each occasion by the use of the correct term—all this is so absolutely within the control of parents that teachers in later years labor in vain to overcome in their students the defects of speech imparted in youth.

On the other hand correct speech presented as an early gift by the parents will survive the battering of companions and the pressure of bad luck and bad association with the gutter language of the world.

Some years back I visited one of our better Catholic grammar schools—established however in a section of the city where the families have to battle for their living. The parents of the children were in the main first-generation immigrants or the descendents of families who had been lucky if they had been able to send their sons and daughters through grammar school. The speech these youngsters heard at home was flavored with foreign idioms. It was less a use of English than a struggle with it.

The teacher, a magnificent nun who not only knew pedagogy but who loved the sound of correct speech, was struggling with the crippled language of the youngsters. She was doing a splendid job.

On this occasion of my visit the grammar lesson was being dramatized. Across the room a young lady called to a young man (both children were rounding their tenth year), "Who is that speaking?" Whereupon the boy replied, in almost prim accuracy, "It is I."

They worked on the elegant solicism — you know, the correct use of the phrases you and I and you and me. I heard several children say, with absolute correctness, "He gave the apples to you and me," where the elegant misgrammarian would have insisted on the polite "He gave the apples to you and I."

They clipped their speech until they had said "give me" and "won't you?" instead of "gimme" and "woncha," and they tossed pronouns around into the baskets of the correct cases.

"Magnificent," I applauded. And the sister and the youngsters beamed at my approval.

Somewhat later I wandered out into the yard, where recess was in progress. There were my exact grammarians of a few minutes ago, now at play.

"Yeah; gimme dat ball. Ya hoid me de foist time. You and me is gonna mix it right here if ya don't come tru."

"Who d'ya tink youse is trowing to anyhow? I ain't had no crack at dat ball for de last week. Gimme!"

And on their side of the yard the girls were mutilating the English language in the same inhuman fashion.

The labors of an enterprising and devoted teacher simply went to pieces on the rocks of home training and the speech their parents used.

Speech Ruined From Youth

For a brief time I had in my class as a young Jesuit one of the most brilliant young men novices I have ever met. His vocation eventually led him elsewhere; his impression upon us all was profound—in two senses. He read Latin as if it were the language of the family dinner table. Greek he tossed off with a careless proficiency that made one think of the young De Quincey. He would have done admirably on an

"Information Please" program — if the radio had been invented in those days. But when he sat down to eat or when he launched forth into a conversation in English, any man of sensibilities simply shuddered in shocked and involuntary pain.

For his treatment of food was symphonic. He whistled his soup and masticated fortissimo and handled his knife, fork, and plate in the manner of a drummer beating out fresh rhythms for a tavern orchestra. Slightly exaggerated, I confess, but only slightly.

Then when he began to talk ordinary conversation, all his book learning fled back to the books, unhonored and unsung. I have heard him in class give a recitation in faultless English; so he undoubtedly could use it as the shapers of our language meant it to be used. Then he would come into the recreation room and talk something like this:

"Dat's de funniest guy I ever seen. Wot's de matter wid de gink? Ain't he got no sense of de way a feller oughta act? Dose kind of guys gets me down! an' I tink we'd be doin' de bloke a favor, if we'd put him wise dat dat ain't no way to bang aroun'."

It was excruciating, the complete triumph of environment and parent training—or lack of it—over the years he had spent collecting A+es throughout high school and college.

At the time I thought, and I have since become convinced, that to anyone who has been brought up on really bad grammar correct grammar sounds thin, emasculated, definitely sissy. Any man who has cried, "He ain't got no chance to grab dat," finds it positively effeminate to say, "He hasn't a chance to get that." If he is accustomed to a double negative like "I ain't never done it," a single negative like "I haven't done it" or "I've never done it" sounds like bare poverty of language.

TABLE MANNERS

Bad table manners and bad speech may be corrected with years of practice. But the man who makes the corrections after a childhood spent speaking and behaving at table incorrectly will always do the right thing self-consciously and with a stiffness that will make his actions and his speech seem formal, stilted, and just a little put on.

THE TRAINED VOICE

So the ordinary conversation that parents use around the house is the greatest training in speech that a child will ever get. The infant is alert to sounds. They register on him, I must repeat, in soft, permanent grooves. If the parents' grammar is correct and their choice of words pleasant and accurate, the child's speech from the beginning moves toward delightful English. If the parents are victims of bad grammar, bad grammar will mark their child's speech and cause him in later years to slip disastrously, like the heroine of Shaw's "Pygmalion."

Clean speech is picked up by children from their parents. But so is the casual vulgarity which the father (or, heaven help us, the mother) thinks the child is too young to register or understand. The father who curses around the house in the presence of his children is likely to have children who curse arrogantly before the children of the neighbors—unless it happens that they are shocked into a distaste for evil language that may be part of their instinctive distaste for the father who introduced that language to them.

Observant parents will notice that their inflections and modulations of voice are picked up and repeated by the children. Charming speech in a mother will be copied by a daughter, exactly as she will copy, while she is still a youngster, her mother's style in clothes. When on the other hand parents are noisy, crude, harsh, loud-mouthed, what can they expect but noisy, crude, harsh, loud-mouthed little brats who are the despair of the English teacher and the bearers of diseased language to other children?

It is only fair to note however that sometimes loudness and coarseness of parents' speech result in a completely reversed reaction. A teacher will find in her class a singularly silent, reticent child. He can hardly be made to raise his voice to answer questions to which he clearly knows the answers. Perhaps a phone call or a visit to the child's home resolves the puzzle. It may be that the father's roaring speech rattles the windows, or the mother, once she has turned on the tap of her conversation, flows on and on and on until the room is flooded with her talk and the listener is washed out on the tides of her purposeless, repetitious, tiresome speech.

Children sometimes meet parental loudness by unconsciously cultivating almost mousy voices; or they counteract the flow of endless chatter with a painful silence.

PROFANE, EVIL SPEECH

Correct speech is a fine art. It is an art that descends normally from parents to children. That is true both of the form of speech and its content. Bad grammar is an ugly heritage. But so is bald profanity. Sloppy sentences are caught up from parental lips and repeated, as is an interest in the common and trivial and unimportant that marks so much of the chatter about the house.

One horrible travesty on training is the encouraging of children in bad habits of speech. Some people think it funny to hear a child break into bad grammar or vulgarity. They even teach them profanity, slightly off-color songs, stories, and poems that are mildly (or not so mildly) shocking, on the supposition that the babies do not understand. They understand enough, believe me, to become copies of the "Dead End Kids."

Protestant writers who in the early days of the Protestant revolt loved to scoff at Catholic saints used to sneer at St. Stanislaus Kostka. According to the record, on a certain occasion when he was still a very little boy, one of the guests at his father's table told a filthy story. The visitor took it for granted that the youngster in his mother's arms was too young to understand. But the child fainted and became so deathly ill that he had to be carried from the table.

"How ridiculous!" commented the scoffer, referring to the event. "Here is a boy who is going to be held up as a model of purity. Yet almost in infancy his mind is dirty. If he was so innocent, how do you explain that before consciousness he recognized dirt?"

The answer is quite simple. Aside from the special protection which God may have thrown around this future pattern of youthful innocence, Stanislaus was merely in amplified fashion manifesting the reaction of normal children to evil. They sense it long before they understand it. They pick up a dirty word and know it is dirty before they have any idea what it may happen to mean—as for that matter they will often spot and shy away from an impure man or a soiled woman whom their elders have not as yet classified. That same strange protective sense will sometimes exist in young women. They will know that a joke is dirty though happily the point of the joke escapes them. They will suspect a man of evil long before he has stopped playing the pseudo gentleman.

So children who hear from their parents and their parents' associates indecent words, smutty songs, purple jokes, and profanity are likely, at a time when their parents regard them as unintelligent and unobservant innocents, either to be shocked by it or to garner it for future use.

The "Dead End Kids" are simply the product of "Dead End Parents." They get their name from the type of street on which their home is located.

Cultivated Vulgarity

When parents deliberately inculcate in their children bad manners, disgusting speech, brashness, and vulgarity . . .

Some years ago I was asked to attend an exhibition of dancing put on by a teacher in a city other than my own. I dropped in to see the youngsters, all of them of grammar- and high-school age, and quite enjoyed the performance—that is, I did until one little brat appeared.

I dislike the word brat, but there is no other name for this poor little obnoxious girl. She could not have been more than five years old. Yet she danced with the knowing leer of a hardened chorus girl. Her voice was brassy. Her manners were brassier. The dance she did was not in itself either vulgar or indecent; but she had somewhere picked up little tricks that made it seem almost shameful.

I hoped to high heaven that when she left the stage she would be met by an angry father and an indignant mother who would turn her over their respective knees, tan her well, and then tell the dancing instructor what they thought of him.

Alas, it was not the dancing instructor, poor man, who was to blame. After the performance I walked down the alley to our residence and thereby passed the stage door. It opened, and out catapulted the five-year-old dancer. She threw herself into the arms of a man who was waiting outside and greeted him with a loud "Hiya, daddy!" It was her father, right enough, and I took him in with one swift survey: hat cocked on the back of his head, loud suit, cigaret defying gravity as it clung limply to his lip even while he talked, and a tilt to his shoulders that suggested the Bowery of the nineties crossed with a flea-circus barker on 42nd Street near Broadway.

He grabbed the baby and threw her into the air. Then in a voice that was intended to embrace all of us and compel our attention, a voice that seemed to come out of the side of his mouth with the impact of a circus trumpeter, he cried: "Baby, you were a wow! Baby, you're a regular Broadway chorine!"

To which the baby, in perfect echo of his voice, replied: "I'll say I wowed 'em, pop. I'll say I laid 'em in the aisles."

Poor kid! I wonder what she is like today, twenty years later. And I wonder if that father ever even guessed what he was doing to his little girl.

INITIATION INTO CULTURE

If parents are the fundamental and only really successful teachers of English, they are also, consciously or unconsciously, the ones who initiate their children into the whole field of culture.

I am thinking of the pictures that hang on the walls of the nursery and the pictures which later the children see on the walls of the rest of the house. I am thinking too of the type of music loved by the parents, whether they themselves are singers and performers or just people with an appreciation of good music. Children are going to be affected for life by the programs which the parents select on the radio and by the records which they play on their recording machines. A child is never going to outgrow altogether the early contact with lovely pictures, nor are the melodies and harmonies that he heard in his earliest days ever going to leave his memory entirely.

Fortunate the child whose parents love the beautiful and early surrounded him, according to their means and opportunities, with things that woke his infant mind to charm of color and grace of line. Fortunate too the child who heard good music before he had a chance to be spoiled by the percussion of cheap, transient stuff. Here again the parents make or mar. They are the only lasting guides to culture.

TALK AND BOOKS

The same influence is exercised by the type of conversation at table and in the living room. What are the parents interested in? What do they talk about? The children will in later years find themselves recalling those subjects and gravitating toward them unconsciously but by remote control.

It is impossible to overestimate the impact of books upon the child early in his life. Suppose the parents read to the child, and read to him from his early years the things that he will find of lasting value. His good luck is something for which he can thank God gratefully.

Some weeks ago I had a letter from a young woman whom I had known when she was in college. She had since then married happily, and she was expecting her first baby in about six months.

"I should like," she wrote, "to be a really successful mother. If there is anything to prenatal influence, can you tell me what I should be reading in preparation for the coming of my child? It would be wonderful if I really could give my baby a beautiful start in life."

I answered somewhat to this effect:

"Actually what effect it would have upon the baby to have you read poetry or other beautiful things right now isn't too clear. If you are happy and your mind is full of wholesome things, if you are spending the days close to God and feeling around you the guardian angel of your little child, you are doing what you can be sure will make happy his arrival.

"But let's look a little beyond his arrival. Your mind will be the cultural matrix into which his mind will first be poured. So how about reshaping that mind of yours with all the beautiful things you'll want to give your child?

"Read the life of Christ carefully and pick out the episodes you'll want to tell your baby when you begin to tell him stories. Read the lovely legends of the saints and tuck them away as the great adventures that will make your child open-eyed with wonder.

"How about refreshing yourself with the nursery rhymes so that as you chant them to your baby you'll give him a sense of poetic rhythm that he will never outgrow?

"There are the great classical fairy tales that should be part of his equipment—the international stories like "Cinderella" and "Bluebeard" and "Rumpelstiltskin." You won't want him to miss the great Greek myths, which though they are fairy tales are yet so eminently true. You'll probably want to tell him the fairy tales of Ireland and let him meet the heroes and heroines of Hans Christian Andersen and the brothers Grimm even before he has learned to read.

"And how about looking over the lovely children's poetry and renewing acquaintance with the children of Shakespeare's plays and with the plots that he uses so excitingly? Dickens has in his books a lot of charming youngsters that your baby ought to meet as he is growing up.

"If you want to be a mother who will leave her cultural impress on her baby, get ready to tell him the stories early, for he will love anything that comes to him by way of your voice. Then when he is a little older, read the stories to him. Finally he will be ready to have the books themselves placed in his hands when he is able to pore over them for himself.

"But yours is the taste that will determine his. I should say that you had plenty to do before your baby is born in order to make yourself the one who will form his tastes and introduce him to the culture that should be his heritage."

The Little Child's Books

No one can possibly overestimate the impact of books early in childhood. They hit the mind in unforgettable fashion. If they are great books, part of the tradition of all mankind, the child's mind is enriched before ever he enters a classroom. If he has not had all this by the time he gets to school, he has probably had his mind corrupted and vitiated by the flood of "comics" and "funnies" and newspaper strips and movie magazines which unfit many children for the eternal and glorious books and stories that should be the foundations upon which a genuine culture is built.

Anyone who has ever taught knows that it is practically impossible to make a child love great literature unless he has met it before the age of five. When however he comes from parents who themselves love literature and have made it easily and happily accessible to the child, he is a sheer delight to teach and an easy disciple to help climb higher and higher on the cultural mountain.

Children Collect

During those earlier years then parents turn their children toward those cultural habits which may last for life.

The tiny youngster is encouraged to start his own library and care for his own books. Too he is inspired to start other collections: pictures that he cuts and mounts; musical records that he himself plays as part of the family program; anything of cultural value that turns his mind toward beauty and sets his feet on the upward path to Parnassus.

Hobbies should be started, not during high-school days, when it is too late, but during these preschool days. Any sort of collecting, whatever it is, is prelude to a lifetime of collecting, which is one of the natural and joyous human experiences.

Train at Once

There is no really effectual disciplining later on if the child has not been well trained before the age of reason. Yet during that period parents who can afford it will carelessly turn their children over to the care of nurses, casual governesses, even the little girl who earns a bit of money for the motion-picture shows by wheeling babies in the afternoon after school.

Said a great baby doctor to me once: "If the rich people of our city put in one tenth the time training their children from babyhood that they spend on their young jumping horses and their hunting dogs, the headlines of our papers would not cry aloud the scandals and divorces and social and spiritual failures of their sons and daughters."

Law and the Child

Children in infancy are not conscious of law or the meaning of law. They cannot be argued into noble courses or talked into goodness. But they can be made very conscious of the operations of law. They learn that rapidly.

When they are good, they experience reward.

When they are bad, there is a swift and inexorable punishment.

Even the youngest child seems capable of making those simple connections. A burst of anger (and how little babies can put it on!), and he gets a sharp, immediate punishment. A smile and a control of his temper, and there is a bit of sweetness in his mouth.

Unfortunately—or fortunately, depending upon your point of view—God and nature have seen to it that the only early approach to the disciplining of children is the very approach used with animals. You cannot argue with a litter of pups—or with a baby in his cradle. A talk on the nobility of goodness and the punishment of vice is wasted on a kitten or on an infant; but rewards and punishments speak eloquently with either.

Spanking?

And that brings me to the subject of spanking—a subject from which I promptly shy away. Who am I to tell parents whether to spank or not to spank? I merely call their attention to the fact that God and nature have centered a great many nerve ends in a spot where they can be reached effectively and utterly without harm. When they are so reached, the child knows he has been punished, and he doesn't enjoy it one bit. He is likely to avoid the things which in the past have led to that irritation of those nerve centers. Thus has been developed a wholesome fear that is first-rate prelude to nobility of conduct and the avoidance of vice.

Bluffed by a Baby

On the other hand the infant soon learns that he can wheedle, and he proceeds to wheedle most efficiently. He knows how soon the parents, exasperated by his yowling, will give in and let him have what he wants. He whined and howled last night, wanting to be carried; mother finally broke down and carried him. He'll keep it up tonight until he gets the same result—to the destruction of discipline.

Infants learn too when threats mean nothing. Parents who talk big and do nothing get no results whatsoever, except the early development of the children's shrewd manipulation of mother and dad.

Children well below the age of reason come to know when parental whim is what determines the punishment for bad conduct and when justice is the dominant factor.

The truism can simply be stated thus: Well-trained adults are developed children who were well-trained from birth. Man has a soul that makes him radically different from animals; yet in those early days of infancy the soul is restricted in its operations. That is why the child must be trained in somewhat the same way that well-trained animals are trained. Whether or not we like it, children in those early days respond to the same sensory impacts that dominate an animal's reactions.

Again I say lucky the child whose parents have loved him enough to be firm with him when firmness was called for, to discipline him when he needed discipline, to reward him for things well done and punish him for a display of temper or selfishness or a nasty disposition. He is the one who is really loved, not the child whose parents are so doting that they cannot punish him, that at his slightest whimper they smother him with affection and love, and that they bring him up to be a selfish, egotistic little bundle of emotions and unrestrained impulses.

EARLY RELIGION

I shall talk much more at length on the subject of parents and their children's religion. Right here and now though I again stress the obvious: Long before the priest, the religious teacher, or the catechist enters the life of the child, the parents have been turning him toward God or away from God. They have been making religion attractive, unimportant, or positively distasteful to him.

All this is of course largely a matter of example. In religion, as in all else, what the child sees in his adored parents he copies in his own life.

We have all come to feel a sentimental love for that picture of the young mother sitting in a chair while her little child kneels at her knee. The mother's-knee theme is however more sentimental and pretty than actually effective. If the parents wish to leave in the child's mind an example the child will never forget, let them kneel along with the child. Then they are not teachers instructing a child in the course of conduct they recommend; they are companions doing the thing which the child loves to do right along with them.

I shall later spend more time on the religious atmosphere of the home. In passing, we might glance at the religious pictures which are on the walls of the child's room or are seen later all around the house. We could ask whether the celebrations of Christmas and Easter are merely gay and pagan or deeply Catholic and in the spirit of the feasts. Is there a shrine in the baby's room? Does he early come to know the picture or statue of his Mother Mary? Does he become acquainted with the charm of his little brother Jesus?

The recurrence of the names of Jesus and Mary on the lips of the parents early in the life of the child is a wonderful start for his whole life. Grace said at table, the sight of dad and mother kneeling together to make their morning offering or to say their night prayers, the stories of Jesus and Mary and the saints that are early made a part of his mental equipment, the religious books that are placed within reach of his hands—all these things are starts, but most important starts along the road to religious maturity.

THE GREAT NATURAL VOCATION

Is it possible to overstress the importance of parents to their children? It seems to me that quite obviously the answer is a loud and unquestioned no.

Should any woman regard the job of motherhood as of entirely minor importance, or any man be willing to play father only after he has cared for "the really important things"?

Those questions need no answers but the echo of the first answer. You can echo it as loudly and as emphatically as you wish. You cannot make the echo speak too strongly.

I once made the rash statement (I have been held accountable to it by my friends) that granted the absurd supposition that I should ever be placed in charge of a crowd of young religious or future priests I should engage at once the services of a first-class psychologist.

"What about parents?" demanded one of these friends. "Don't they need that guidance quite as much as does a religious superior?"

To that my answer would be a prompt yes.

I should think it most wise for a young Catholic couple to come as early in their married life as possible in contact with a good Catholic child psychologist, either by listening to his lectures or reading his books. I can see a tremendous lift that would be given to their future burdens if they knew in advance just what such an expert could teach them.

More than that: I can vision a wise young couple's taking their children—and quite early—to such a good

Catholic child-psychologist. Certainly many of the quirks and twists that appear in later life might have been eliminated in children had the advice of a good psychologist been obtained. The fears and inhibitions could have been caught in time and done away with.

In time to come, won't smart parents who see to it that their children's teeth are regularly cared for by a dentist and their eyes by an oculist and their stomachs by a dietician see to it that their habits, nerves, and brain will be studied by a good psychologist? And won't we as a result produce a race far more balanced and sane, with less nervous twist and emotional upset?

III

THE PARENTS TAKE OVER

It's high time that parents reclaimed their right to their children.

I suggest that instead of some of the silly picket lines that indicate merely the struggle between labor unions to see which union can collect the union dues we see some picket lines made up of parents marching up and down in front of many a modern school.

The pickets could carry banners like these:

"Down with the monopoly of children by schools."

"We parents demand our rights."

"All parents are not morons, whatever some teachers think."

"We can take care of our children's teeth . . . and food . . . and play . . . and nerves . . . and health."

"We're tired of being treated like perils to our children."

"Give us back our children."

"You can have them five hours a day. We want them the rest of the time."

A lot of us who are not parents but who sympathize with the cashiered mothers and fathers of the present would gladly join the picket lines.

Homes and Schools

We have nothing whatever against the school that knows its place—an auxiliary to the home and not a substitute for the home. We have the firmest admiration for teachers; after all we were once a teacher ourself. But even the best of teachers is only the assistant to the parents, taking over those assignments which the father and the mother are too busy or too lacking in specialized knowledge to handle.

In an ideal society home and school both work in close collaboration, the home always in first place. Parents and teachers are partners. But the parents are always the senior partners, the ones with the real voice in the training of the children.

The finest school in the world labors ineffectively and alone unless it is backed with the fullest possible child training already given the child and then continuously supplemented in the home. The most expert teachers can, we repeat, work only with the material sent them by the parents who have placed the lasting impress on the children and determined the fabric on which the teacher will further elaborate.

PROTESTED INVASION

Some years back there was a fairly widespread uproar over the fact that the schools not only wanted to do everything but were actually trying to do it. Henry L. Mencken, who speaks loudly and with deliberate exaggeration, maintained that only about one in three of the people connected with the public-school system was actually a teacher. The others were dieticians, psychologists, dentists, health experts, vocational guides, dancing instructors, music appreciators, and an enormous army of secretaries and file clerks who classified and put on record the state of the children's eyes and teeth and dispositions and grace in doing the conga and liking for classical as against swing music and ability to be a trap drummer or a traveling salesman.

Maybe the howl was an exaggerated one. Maybe it was meant merely to reawaken parents to the fact that it is their privilege and responsibility, not the teachers', to care for their children's bodies and minds.

PARENTS' FUNCTION

Let's start with the simple fact that the care of the child's body and his health is properly the function of the parents. Even when they summon the services of a physician, they do so in order that he may advise them on how better to guarantee this mental and physical health for the child. They do not expect him or permit him to take over and push them aside. He gives his expert advice; that advice the parents then carry into execution.

CARE OF THE BODY

Parents' care of the child's body begins with their inculcating in the child right attitudes toward that body and toward health.

REVERENCE FOR THE BODY

The first of these correct attitudes is a simple matter of respect for the body that God in so wonderful a fashion fitted to that soul.

I don't know where in the world the modern pagan gets the idea that Christians hate and despise their bodies. Rising as it did in the very heat and fury of paganism, Christianity was bound to experience some swing away from the body worship which the Christians saw all about them. Worshiping the pure spirit, who is their immaculate God, they were likely to be revolted by the worship of Venus and Bacchus and Hercules, whose souls were pretty twisted, ugly things, even if their bodies were lovely to look at—and dangerous to have around.

The shameful games in the Colosseum and the disgraceful orgies that racked the bodies of the pagans made the Christians think tenderly of modesty. Christians veiled their bodies because the pagans shamelessly exposed theirs. They fasted for the reason that the pagans feasted in frankly animal fashion. They saw what nakedness had done to the generations around them—corrupting the young, making impurity inevitable, disgracing the human body into a thing of seduction and sin; so inevitably they banned nakedness and covered the sacred thing that is the human body, as we cover anything we regard as precious and holy.

Even our mother's lock of hair we enclose in a gold case. We drape a masterpiece with cloth against the light that would dim and eventually destroy it. The Christians draped their bodies against the aggression of beastly passions and the hot, destructive desires of lustful eyes.

DISCIPLINED BODIES

Quite rightly Christians have had a wholesome distrust of their bodies. For Christians had the common sense to realize that bodily appetites can easily undo a man and ruin a woman. A well-disciplined body they felt to be a glorious auxiliary of their soul. An uncontrolled body driving heedlessly toward too much food or too much drink, a body easily stirred to destructive passion, a body grown lazy and slack and unwilling to work, a body reverting to animal instincts was something of which they must humanly be ashamed.

So they disciplined their bodies. But they never hated their bodies. They never regarded them as ruthless enemies, no matter what the smart-alecky modern pagan, in his desire to restore the dominion of flesh over spirit, of body over soul, may contend. That hatred was felt by the Hindu fakir on his bed of spikes. It was expressed by such heretical groups as the Manichaeans, who were solemnly condemned by the Church—and by the Puritans, who thought that God was best served in ugliness and misery.

The Body Must Serve

The Christian has always taken the noble middle course of a divine dualism. He admitted the God-creation of his body. He acknowledged the eternal importance of his soul. To him the body was the gracious companion of his spirit, moving with him through earth until it was briefly laid aside in the grave. Even the grave was only a checkroom. When the resurrection morning dawned, his spirit would return and reclaim that body, and body and soul together, a complete human being, he would spend his eternity with God.

He knew that a well-disciplined body was invaluable in his progress through the world. Strong legs made him a better missionary. A fine throat and vigorous lungs made possible the clearer speaking of the good news Christ called His Gospel. If he was to be an athlete of God, good health might be a valuable asset. A vigorous body could help a vigorous soul to do more and better work. A sick body might hold back and handicap a soul fettered and braked by the inadequacy of its body companion.

The Christian believed and still believes that the human body is the special creation of God. For all its likeness to the higher animals it is amazingly different. No one in his right mind ever mistook, no matter how dark the night, a chimpanzee for a human being. The young lady who opens her door to an expected caller does not fancy that the gorilla in tux who is carrying a corsage is the young man she thought to welcome. No man, however remote from human society, has thought it as pleasant to walk the woods with a female orangutan as with a debutante.

It is a tenet of Christian belief that the human body is basically the creation of God, but certain evolutions regarding size, shape, and characteristics are not absolutely excluded by Christian belief.

God's Creation

The Christian believes that at the very moment of conception there are for the formation of the human being, not two, but three who participate: the father, the mother, and God, the father and the mother as God's agents, God as the creator.

Hence it has been the Christian who has always struck the nice balance between pagan worship of the body and Hindu neglect of the body. That balance does not follow Bernarr McFadden in his cult of muscles and the flowing lines of a beautiful figure; it does not follow the Christian Scientist, who tries to abolish the human body by pretending it is only a gigantic mistake of the misguided spirit.

The Christian believes that a body must be trained and disciplined, brought into subjection when it rebels, and never allowed to become the master of the superior soul. He does not believe that it should be killed or made weak and sick or treated as a drag or a nuisance or a mistake that God has hung around the neck of the soul.

Body Worship

There is evident today a return of pagan body worship. We have grown so accustomed to it that we hardly notice it any more. Beauty contests are merely an external and silly manifestation of that pagan deification of the body. Not long ago the newspapers reported in a "sob sister" feature story the triumph of a young college woman who won a prize for a short story she submitted in a nationwide short-story contest. Said the gushy reporter: "And she could not have been happier had she won a beauty contest." That's the modern ratio as the pagan sees it; the girl surprisingly thought it as important to have a lovely mind capable of creating a great work of fiction as to have the most beautiful body to walk the Atlantic City pier.

So Catholic parents from the beginning instill in their child that noble middle course followed by Christians who know their faith.

HEALTH

They teach the child to respect his body. They teach him to care for it, to keep it immaculately clean, to work for its development, to avail himself of the bodily strength and skill innate in the human nerves and muscles. Yet they refuse to let him worship his body or regard it as the supreme concern of his life.

Health, the child should learn from the beginning, is valuable. Like anything else that is valuable, it must be safeguarded with normal rational care. It is however by no means invaluable. Men have risen above ill-health to become what Francis Thompson has called "the world's great dyspeptics." Women have triumphed over ill-health by sheer courage of soul and the greatness of mind. Bedridden invalids have influenced the course of history. Cripples have, with a pad of paper resting on their chests, written great books. Milton in his blindness saw paradise lost and regained. Steinmetz developed despite a twisted body his incredible power over electricity. Sick mothers have given the world healthy children and lovely, orderly homes.

NOT NECESSARILY BIG MUSCLES

Important though health is, the importance of big muscles and tremendous strength is decidedly doubtful. Professional athletes do not always find it easy to adapt themselves to anything else but the gridiron, the basketball court, the squared circle.

In seminaries and novitiates of religious communities strenuous athletes often break under the strain of adjusting themselves to a hard routine life, while boys and girls of good, normal development fit themselves without problem into the difficult vocation they have undertaken.

Many a great athlete has made a great priest or religious. To our Jesuit novitiate however came some years ago a great football player. He had been a star backfield man and a long-distance runner in the spring track events. In the novitiate he nearly went crazy because of the demands of his big, bulging muscles. Late in the evenings when the other young men were sitting peacefully doing their spiritual reading, he had to put on track pants and two sweaters and with a pair of heavy dumbbells in his hands run for half an hour around the garden cinder paths. In the end he was beaten by the cry of his muscles for physical labor. He had to give up his attempt to be a Jesuit.

I have seen quite too many star athletes and professional muscle men crack up under tough jobs and the normal routine of an exacting life to be convinced of the personal value of bulging biceps or a chest covered with athletic medals.

No Cranks or Fads

By their whole attitude parents must impress their children with the value of health as something extremely useful but by no means indispensable. Heaven help the poor youngster who is born into a family where the father or the mother is a health crank of any sort. I have seen children subjected to a series of food crazes—to the children's alarm, resentment, and disorganization. One family I knew ran the youngsters through a diet of peanuts; a diet of prunes; a period when the father spoke so disgustingly of any form of meat that was brought to the table that, far from making his children vegetarians, he made them loathe food in all its manifestations; a period of raw carrots and lettuce; a period of nothing but soup.

If parents insist on following the fads in foods as they do the fads in hats and automobiles, they will probably bring up a family of health cranks and food faddists. Most of these fads are dangerous nonsense, repudiated by sound physicians yet capable of making health a monomania and food a hysterical preoccupation.

DOCTORS AND DENTISTS

As part of the rational attitude toward health a friendly attitude toward physicians and dentists should be inculcated by the parents.

The normal place that the doctor and dentist have in the life of the civilized man should simply be taken for granted. The family doctor is a wise institution. He becomes more than merely a physician; he is the family friend, the family trouble shooter, and his pleasant recurrence in the family makes the children accept him as a normal visitor whose visits are not to be dreaded or regarded as extraordinary portents of danger but to be regarded as the kindly arrival of someone who is connected with their speedy recovery from illness and their fuller health.

For physicians and dentists there must be no wild praise and no exaggerated credulity. That sometimes happens. Parents talk of the doctor and the dentist as if they were miracle men, and often the children are disillusioned at the quite reasonable limitations in the doctors they themselves seek out later in life.

On the other hand parents may inbreed in their children a lifelong contempt for or fear of physicians and dentists. The father at the table some night, irritated at the physician who on that day won five dollars from him on the golf course, pontificates: "These doctors are all a lot of quacks. I wouldn't trust a guinea pig to the whole college of physicians and surgeons. Look what they did to Smith. They cut him open, and he died ten years later. They don't know anything about what's going on inside a man. A bunch of fakes, I call 'em. Don't let one near me if I ever get sick."

Needless to say, all he is doing is letting off a broadside of blank shells. If he had a pain in his stomach that same evening, he'd have his wife on the phone pulling the doctor out of bed. Since however infallibility seems to speak in the person of the father, the children put doctors down as frauds whom they will avoid with all the concentrated craft of their youthful natures. In years to come, at another dinner table that same speech is likely to be repeated by a grown man who doesn't even recall that he is echoing the voice of his father.

Doctors have a normal place in the life of the child. They should not be built up to be made to seem magicians. They should not be pulled down to be made to seem ignorant frauds.

HOSPITALS

The same attitude in measure must be developed about hospitals. Time was when the children of the poor all knew that anyone who went to the hospital had a first-rate chance of being given a drink out of "the black bottle." They were told of the hearses which were lined up at the back doors of hospitals to carry the patients from the ambulances and through the front door. To this day many an otherwise intelligent person looks on a hospital as a place where men and women are taken to die.

NO SILLY FEARS

Careless talk about operations—the horror, the pain, the peril—makes children develop a lifelong fear of even the most kindly and harmless gesture of a surgeon's scalpel. Every man and woman (not to mention youngsters) has enough normal fear of the operating table and the downdrop into unconsciousness as the anesthetic captures his brain; he does not have to be taught by his parents to regard a surgeon as a hooded, sinister figure out of the pulp-paper pages of "Tales of Horror and Purple Crime."

In the same way the attitude which children take toward dentists is one they get from the parents. If parents take the child to the dentist as casually as they take him to the barber, he will soon come to regard the dentist as one of his normal friends. The care of the milk teeth is now strongly advocated. But whether or not this care highly affects the character of the permanent teeth would be unimportant if the mild treatment of these early teeth succeeded in killing forever the child's sense of strangeness or fear toward the dentist's office.

On the other hand it is hard to overestimate the amount of fear engendered in youngsters by the gory tales parents love to tell about their terrible experiences at the hands of the dentist. There are women who love to tell about the horrifying sound of the drill and just how they felt when the brute of a dentist hit that exposed nerve. Fathers come back to give grisly and probably entirely fictional details of the agony they went through when the dentist practically dynamited that impacted wisdom tooth. The children listen with all that morbid curiosity they reserve for any tale of horror, pain, or sudden death. Then when later the parents announce calmly, "Now, dear, we must make a visit to the dentist," the parents themselves are amazed at the fright and terrified rebellion of their offspring.

Many an adult who normally becomes quite sleepy in a dentist's chair and has never had any experience more harrowing than the scraping of tartar off his bicuspids will still shudder at the thought of his visiting the dentist. He is not suffering from any pain he ever personally experienced. He is suffering from the fictionalized agonies related with all the ghastly details by his parents.

Food

It's a lucky man who moves through life with a normal appetite for food. If he can eat everything, he's twice blessed. If he has a pleasant curiosity about new and different food, he is likely to know quite thrilling adventures. If his digestion is one of the things he can dismiss as never requiring his attention, he probably also radiates a good disposition and a vibrant energy.

Now the normal, healthy appetite that is given to almost every child will remain normal and healthy if the parents cultivate, train, develop, where necessary curb, and always rightly direct it.

The child's chief lessons in correct eating are given to him by the examples of the parents themselves. For the love they bear their children parents must eat reasonably, with a real degree of relish, without gorging and yet with a frank appreciation of food. If parents say, "Eat your carrots," and then push their own carrots aside, the child will push his aside in exact imitation of his parents. If dad says, "But Popeye eats spinach," the child is unconvinced unless dad eats his spinach too.

Eating Everything

The rightly trained child who eats everything has parents who eat everything.

I have been among families where the parents like so restricted a menu of foods that their sons and daughters regard with distaste every type of food but the few kinds that have recurred and recurred on the family table. Poor kids!

One case I ran into was that of a young man who couldn't eat anything but beef. (He was in his way almost as pathetic as the deaf-mute girl I once met who for fourteen years had eaten nothing but soda crackers.) Even on Thanksgiving Day, though the rest of the family and the guests had turkey, he had his slice of beef.

A child brought up to disdain all foods but those few items to which he is accustomed is going to be regarded as a bore when he dines out. When traveling, he is going to be a nuisance. In new surroundings he will be utterly without imagination. And whether his family is wealthy enough to disdain any food less rare and rich than caviar and mockingbirds' tongues, or hillbillies who starve to death if they can't get corn bread, molasses, and hog meat, the youngster has been deprived of the wide gamut of foods which God has prepared for the health and enjoyment of his children. For that crime against his health his parents are very largely responsible.

To the mother falls of course the tremendous assignment of dietician in chief to the family. It is her role to plan the varied menus which according to her means and the needs of the family will bring to the table the widest variety of foods. Hers is the responsibility to see that the children learn to eat everything.

Indeed the simple rule of the family should be that anything which is fit to place on the family table is fit for anyone in the family to eat.

FANCY FOODS

Fancy food, desserts, sweets, and other delicacies have their place. The sugar they contain is, as we all know, a power producer for the youthful body. These can come as a reward for the eating of the substantial food. "When you have eaten your vegetables, you may have your chocolate eclair . . . . No spinach, no strawberry ice cream."

But the parents, concretely the mother, early see to it that the candy bar between meals or the dessert piled up at the end of the meal does not become the substitute for the food the children need for their proper growth.

One morning in the course of my duties I dropped in at a most casual household shortly after breakfast time. Yes, they assured me, they had finished breakfast—all, that was, except the youngest daughter, and she had "gone out to get her breakfast." That sounded a little weird for a twelve-year-old. When the twelve-year-old returned, the sequel turned out to be weirder still. For her breakfast she had bought a bag of peanuts, three greasy doughnuts, an ice-cream cone, and a chocolate nut bar. Distributed over four days, these articles of food might have been reward for the eating of good breakfasts of fruit, cereal, milk, and eggs. As substitutes for real food they were simply destructive.

FOOD HABITS

Food habits are formed in infancy and last through life. A terrible sin is committed against the health of the children if they are not trained to eat everything that is wholesome, to have an open mind for food that is new to them, and to put aside forever the contempt for and shuddering revulsion against any food that may not up to this time have been included in their pitifully limited diet. Limited diets can nicely (or pitifully) be left to the rice-eating nations of the Orient.

CLEANLINESS

Though in recent years neglect on the part of parents has given the schools an excuse to take over the care of the body as well as the instruction of the mind, the care of the child's body is most emphatically the duty of the father and the mother.

Parents should rightly regard this as part of their routine duty. The unlimited supplies of water in modern America make almost daily baths—and there is no real reason for the adverb almost—a practice to be initiated early and kept up throughout life. The child who dislikes baths is a creation of the "funnypapers," along with the bathless hobo. The truth is that children who are accustomed to regular bathing regard it either as a joy or as a standard routine.

Physical odors and their origins should be carefully explained to children as soon as they start to care for themselves. Amazingly enough children, both boys and girls, come into adulthood apparently unaware of this if parents fail to take care of what "even their best friends won't tell them." The effect of perspiration either on the body or on the clothes, the need for constant cleaning of the clothes, the use of gargles and, if necessary, of deodorants are subjects about which the child should learn early.

From the beginning the care of the teeth is also part of standard routine. The individual toothbrush and gargle cup, the personal supply of tooth powder or paste are given to the child emerging from infancy and treated as part of his essential belongings.

PLAY

God and nature put into youngsters the love for play. That love exists, as we clearly understand, not merely for the sake of the fun they can get out of it but because exercise and games are the most effective ways to develop muscles and coordination and the skilled use of hands and feet.

Nature sees to it that the child does not walk if he can possibly run; nature is driving him to the building up of sinew. No child can resist the lure of a ball or a hoop or a chance to yell at the top of his lungs—with important results to arms and legs and lungs.

Even the natural instinct to play can be wisely guided and directed by the parents. Suppose they provide a sandbox for the little youngsters; this serves not only to keep the children quiet and content but actually to stimulate the creative, constructive impulse instinctive in all of us. As for gifts they can present the youngsters with sets that they use for building, from building blocks all the way up to the complicated steel construction sets. Thus the youngsters gain a real increase in skill with their hands and brains.

Dancing and Games

I shall refer to this later on, but the first natural dancing partners of the children are the parents. It's delightful to see a father dancing with his little girl or a mother encouraging her shy young son to take his first dancing steps.

While games among the children themselves are natural enough, children's games in which the parents take part will stimulate even further the wholesome desire for play. No other game is so thrilling to children as one in which adults have a place. If dad takes his turn at bat, the sand-lot game takes on new zest. If mother comes out and cries, "Give me one of those rackets," all the children on the tennis court are instantly keyed to a new pitch of interest and to a new intensity of determination.

Body for the Soul

In all this talk of the development of the body—whether through food, cleanliness, exercise, or play—we are thinking of the body and the soul, those partners which together make the complete and adequate human being. The horrible degradation of human beings who see in themselves only an animal body has led to a cult of bodies, an ostentation about big muscles or the smooth lines of a beautiful figure, an appreciation like that accorded the strutting of a lion or the parading of a peacock. Children should early be taught that the body is secondary in importance to the soul and that the health of the body is important in order that the soul may function unimpeded. A strong, vigorous, well-trained body can be a powerful asset. It may mean more calm of mind, more opportunity for the enjoyment of life's richness. It can never be man's prime concern.

So the game is for the fun one gets out of it, for the delight of companionship, and for the development of bodily muscles and skill and the display of camaraderie, charity, good sportsmanship. The matter of winning is entirely of secondary importance. Conceit about one's muscles or beauty or ability to bat a ball is petty and small and a little below the dignity of a human being.

The Child's Mind

When we come to the parents' care of the child's mind, we are of course thinking of the days that precede formal education. For the mind, like the body, begins to develop at birth. And in the case of the mind, as of the body, the first few years are of really disproportional importance.

Don't's for the Mind

First we can start with the things that parents should not put into their children's minds. Actually in many cases parents pour—quite unconsciously but with painfully lasting results—into the minds and souls of their children weaknesses and limitations of which they themselves should be ashamed.

No Fears

Rule one is quite simple: Never give a child a fear.

I suppose every man or woman in the world has some sort of personal fear—whether of heights or the dark or cats or ghosts or the policeman or crowds or fire or the dead. Parents transfer these fears of theirs, sometimes deliberately and sometimes without thinking, to their children. It's too bad that a child should have to start off in life with an equipment of dreads and fears and instinctive terrors.

How parents themselves act toward their fears, quite as much as what they say about them, leaves a lasting impression on youngsters. If a mother shudders every time a cat comes near her, she is likely to find her little daughter shuddering at the sight of a kitten. If a father talks in all solemnity of the ghosts that lurk in dark corridors, even if he may think this only a particularly fruity joke, his boy may dread dark corridors for many a long year.

So out of love of their children as well as out of a desire for their personal happiness parents should try to get rid of their own fears. Where the children are concerned, they should with the most conscious effort try to hide the things of which they are afraid.

I have known boys, well developed and otherwise normal, to scream in terror when a dog brushed against them. Their parents were afraid of dogs. I've heard from girls the ancient legend of the woman who wakes and finds a cat resting on her chest; and as she cries out in fright, the cat buries its claws in the woman's throat. The story is one of the oldest of old wives' tales. It has served nonetheless to place those girls eternally in terror of cats.

BOGEYMEN

Parents will deliberately go about frightening children in order to make them behave. They may get a temporary result, a sort of cowed silence; but the lasting effects are pretty bad.

"If you don't stop crying, the bogeyman will get you," mothers have said, probably from the dawn of history. Inevitably with every age that bogeyman has undergone transmutations. Over a century ago mothers frightened their children with the threat of Napoleon's getting them, as they probably frighten children today with the bogey Hitler. Anything will serve: ghosts, devils, "a horrible man who jumps out on bad little children," even God as a terrible threat.

Yes; the father himself becomes a bogeyman. "You just wait until your father comes home and I tell him how you've been behaving. He'll fix you." So when dad arrives and cheerily calls to his children, he sees them scurry away to hide in a closet. He, poor chap, wonders why his children act afraid of him, especially since it is all he can do to force himself to speak sternly to them.

DEVELOPED FEARS

Parents develop in their children lifelong dreads. "Stop crying, or I'll go off and turn out the light and leave you in the dark." The mother will hit that word dark as if it were an awful, palpable, living monster waiting to leap out of the corridor and suffocate the child. "There are terrible giants who eat up little children who are bad like you," the child is solemnly warned, and he has something else to be afraid of.

Or in their casual conversation parents admit that they are terribly afraid of being burned alive, of being buried alive, of being drowned, of falling off high buildings—and the children grow up afraid of fire, of even a closed door, of any approach to a body of water, of any height above five feet.

FLIGHT FROM FEAR

Sometimes it will happen that one brave parent and one naturally timid one will result in the death of a great many fears. There is my own case. I had a father who was afraid of nothing and a mother who was timid about almost everything. My father bolstered up my courage in a dozen ways. He loved dogs and encouraged me to pat any strange dog I met—while my mother stood by, momentarily expecting me to lose a hand or an ear. He always pretended it was fun to hunt burglars, and he made a great show of keeping his revolver under a carelessly tossed sock beside his bed—while any slightest night noise about the house roused my mother to a sleepless vigil.

As a result of this joint training I was afraid of almost nothing. When mother and I returned in the late afternoon, she inserted the key in the lock, opened the door cautiously, and then sent me on ahead. After I had joyfully explored the house, looking with genuine hope for a burglar or a ghost, I called downstairs that all was clear; then and only then did she enter the house.

There are enough real things in the world to be afraid of without parents' bequeathing to a child a heritage of their fears. A wise respect for buzz saws, the devil, speed in any form, the law, and God is all part of the beginning of wisdom. None of these has anything to do with the unreasonable terrors that can twist and distort the soul of a child.

SUPERSTITIONS

Most superstitions, I honestly believe, were invented by women to keep men from doing things that upset the household. "It's bad luck to spill salt on the tablecloth," women say. But then they prefer to have their dinner tables neat and clean. "Don't sit on a bed; it's awful luck," said the housewife, for the reason that to sit on a bed badly musses it. "It's bad luck to break a mirror," she continued. And who around a house chiefly uses mirrors? "Don't drop a knife or a fork. . . . Don't knock over chairs. . . . Don't rock a rocker unless someone is sitting it it, or a death will follow. . . . Don't let a bird fly into a room; that's a sure sign some-one will die."

All these things upset the routine of a well-ordered house. A nice convenient "curse" attached to them kept men on the alert to prevent their occurrence.

Parents have a way of teaching children superstitions that often affect their lives. Most superstitions are just silly, like thinking that horseshoes bring luck. Some of them are just matters of caution, like not walking under a ladder—from which a bucket of paint or a carpenter might drop onto one's head.

The chief fault of these superstitions lies in a destruction of the logical sense. They establish an entirely false connection of cause and effect.

So we youngsters used to search the highways for horse-shoes. When we found one, that was wonderful luck. The more nails in the horseshoe, the more luck we were going to have. But in the hanging of the horseshoe an exact ritual had to be observed: The shoe must be hung with the points up, otherwise the good luck would pour out and be lost.

There is no possible connection, as anyone can see, between horseshoes and nails, the way of hanging them up, and good or bad luck. An utterly false connection is established. Logic is booted out the window.

So men who as children collected four-leaf clovers carry in later life rabbits' feet. Or if they are actors, they must buy an apple from Apple Mary before they go on for their act. Or they wouldn't think of performing unless they wear the shoes they wore in their first hit, or touch a hunchback on their way to the stage, or shake hands with an electrician.

PRENATAL NONSENSE

Children are presented by their parents with the most amazing lot of nonsense. There are the stories of prenatal influence for example. If a mother is frightened by a fire, the child is born with a birthmark like a flame on his face; if the mother is alarmed by a wild animal, she is likely to give birth to a monster.

I once asked a great baby specialist about these stories which I, like most other people, had learned and implicitly believed.

"I made a very careful study of it," he replied, in a heavy German accent that gave emphasis to his disdain. "I have delivered thousands of babies. Never once have I seen a case where the mother's fright affected the baby. Such nonsense! such nonsense! The most you can say is that if the mother is frightened at the zoo by a bear, that baby will be born with bare feet."

FALSE CONNECTIONS

If the beefsteak meant for dinner disappears, more than likely it is being used by young son to cure the wart which he got because he handled a toad. If he rubs the steak on the wart and buries the meat in the ground, then when the meat rots, the wart will disappear. My dear old grandmother believed that as implicitly as did Tom Sawyer. And

I patiently treated all juvenile warts by filching from the icebox the family supper.

In the same way we all believed black cats were bad luck. "Stringtown on the Pike" did a lot to disillusion me of my acquired superstitions. As I read of those Kentucky hillsmen who were dominated by the most ridiculous beliefs that obviously had no connection with the facts, I began to be ashamed of my own credulity.

Unkind Superstitions

Some superstitions that are passed on to children are utterly unkind. Children are taught to regard as bad luck the sight of a hunchback or a person with crossed eyes. They go along the street looking for red-headed girls in conjunction with white horses—a combination difficult indeed to find these days. They get good luck by counting beards.

As a priest I recurrently find myself in districts where the boys keep spells off themselves by looking at my Roman collar and then rapidly making the youthful mystic sign which consists of wetting the right thumb with spittle, placing the spittle on the palm of the left hand and then hitting it hard with the clenched right fist. Frankly I hate to be regarded as an evil influence to be warded off with protective gestures.

Bad Luck

Children are impressed with the horribleness of the fact of thirteen people at table. When I was a youngster, I attended a party with twelve of my peers. About a year and a half later one of the little girls of that group died. Someone happened to remember that the thirteen of us had sat down to table together. Instantly throughout the entire neighborhood ran the horrified whisper that the child had died because of the fatal thirteen.

The idea of thirteen at table being bad luck originated of course through reference to Judas and the Last Supper. Undoubtedly the events of the Last Supper were fatal for the one traitor. But how marvelously wonderful was the good luck that flowed to the rest of the Apostles, and how glorious has been the luck that has flowed to all the Christian world from that dinner of thirteen.

Friday became an unlucky day because on that day the Lord died. Yet we call that special Friday on which He died Good Friday; and though it was a day of horror for Him, all the good fortune of mankind began with that day of the week that the superstitious term unlucky.

"Cross hands as you are shaking hands," we youngsters were told, "and one of the four will marry." To this day I get a lot of fun out of one of these cross-hand shakes when all the people involved are priests or nuns. I don't feel for a second that I am endangering their vocations. Once on a time, in my prepriestly days, I should have regarded this as prelude to marriage.

FORTUNETELLING

Children get from their parents an implicit trust in fortunetelling. They hear their families discuss how "that gypsy said I was going on a long journey, and three years later, you remember, I made that trip to Burlington." Grandmother, if she came from Ireland and grew up before the superstition was given a setback by the development of tea bags, told the whole family their fortunes by a look into the teacup.

Within families good-luck pieces and charms and taboos will pass on from generation to generation, often, as my good Irish grandmother used to say, "in half joke and whole earnest," always leaving a slightly subhuman impress on the youngsters.

CRITICAL HABITS

In the main superstitions can be viewed with a bit of condescending smile, though fears should always be regarded as real perils and dangers. Toward the critical habits passed on by parents to their children however there can be no attitude other than that of real repugnance.

Yet the critical talk of parents creates in the children like attitudes that often last for life.

There are parents who in the presence of the children criticize the whole of life. "I didn't ask to be born," growls the father, after a bad day in the office, "so why should I be thankful to God for life?" In later years the child grown to manhood will repeat this taunt word for word, in perfect echo of his father.

"Oh life is all such a mess! I'm sick of it," the mother cries, when things become too heavy for her. The children listen, their sober, intent little faces lifted to drink in her pessimism. And their souls are soured even before they are quite sure what she means or why she distorts her face in so frightening a fashion.

Perpetual grouches pass their grouches on to their children. Constant criticism breeds criticism. I have seen too many children whose bitterness toward life was merely a rebottling of the poison distilled by their parents, who as a matter of fact may really not have meant what they were saying.

SUSPICIONS

So the careless talk of parents about government will in the children's mind breed a suspicion of and contempt for government.

"That man in the White House!" howls the father of the family. And the children who are listening make no distinction between the particular individual who is the President and the high office which he holds.

"Did I ever put it over on that traffic officer!" mother boasts, after she has told how she wept and cajoled her way out of a parking ticket. She has incidentally made the children contemptuous, not of an individual policeman, but of that mysterious thing called law.

"Oh the Church is always talking about money . . . . The Church is so doggone old-fashioned. Why doesn't it become up to date? . . . Believe me, I'm not going to help that bishop with his charity drive. He has a lot more money than I have; let him take care of the poor himself . . . . Why do we have to have expensive churches like that? Seems to me the money could be used for lots of better purposes than to build a monument to that pastor of ours."

Then the unblushing criticism of the priests and the sisters: "What an awful sermon! That man talks like an illiterate. I could give a better sermon with one hand tied behind my back. Anyhow all he can talk about is money." The youngsters, intent and alertly listening, know only that their parents are taking the hide off someone they had thought pretty important. Religion to them is symbolized in the person of the priest. When parents are bitter about him, the children's whole attitude toward religion takes a terrific fall. A critical mood is born in their souls.

DISTRUST

It is quite possible that the critical attitude of parents can breed in children an almost total distrust of humanity. It can knock over their belief in the value of institutions. I know young people whose distaste for entire races is a reflection of their parents' sweeping condemnation of the Jews, the Polacks, the niggers, the dagos, the "shanty" Irish. I know young men and women who sneer at democracy or at all politicians, who deny the sincerity of charity workers or the disinterestedness of religious people simply because they have received as one of their heritages the eternal carping of their parents.

Whatever a mother's and a father's disparaging opinion of people or institutions, they are wise to reserve those opinions for each other's ears alone. It is too bad that children should be poisoned early in life by cynicism, criticism, bitterness poured out at a time when the youngster can make few distinctions and will fail to differentiate between a grouch and a reasonable comment, the dislike for some individual and the condemnation of an entire race or class of society or institution.

ALERTNESS

Of the many things that parents can directly place in the minds of their children, let's take a few now—and more later.

I should like to place high on the list Alertness, and with deliberate purpose I use the capital A.

For as one who has had to deal much with young people and who has faced a good many audiences and more than a few classes, let me say that there is hardly another natural quality that seems more important.

The alert child is the alive child. The alert child is the one who learns, who wants to advance, who has a real hunger for truth and beauty and whatever falls within the range of his observation and mental grasp.

Now the child's own alertness is in direct relation to the alertness the child has observed in his mother and his father. If they are enthusiastic for a wide variety of things, he is likely to be so enthusiastic. Indeed their interests are likely to be his. Their lack of interests will result in blind spots in his own mind which probably will never be cured.

Maternal Heritage

Let's take the negative for a moment. I happened to have had a mother who was totally disinterested in the country, in animals, or in anything that grew in the soil. To the end she thought that all flowers were bought directly from florists. Occasionally she attempted to raise one of the hardier plants, a palm or a rubber plant; but it died promptly and with suspicious dispatch. She regarded the country as a horrible place where women were worked to death, where there were none of the joys of life, and where the night was filled with hideous noises—all frightening, all sinister.

The result on me is a complete lack of interest in anything outside the city's high walls. With the years I have come to appreciate a beautiful scene. I love—because I have personally cultivated the love—a summer sky, the charm of flowing water, a rolling hill. But anything that grows in soil is an utter mystery to me and, what's worse, a mystery that has never seemed worth the solving.

So as a Jesuit novice I lived in the beautiful and fertile Florissant valley and didn't learn the name of a single growing thing around me. I worked in the garden for six consecutive weeks under the guidance of a dear old brother who simply loved every blade of grass and bush and growing flower. I think that at the end of the six weeks I knew the difference between a rose and a peony; I had discovered that flowers had pistils and stamens. That was all. I still hardly know an oak from a maple. I walk through a garden and don't recognize by name anything more complicated than a petunia or a geranium; and I've never had the slightest urge to plant a seed and watch it grow.

But my mother had the keenest interest in people. She found them absorbingly interesting. And so do I. She loved books, and her life was surrounded by them. There too I am in measure like her. She adored music. That love too she graciously woke in my soul.

It is possible for a genius in the family to develop specialized interests that his parents have never known. But his general alertness, his wide-awake mind and trained senses are almost inevitably the gift of his parents.

So children can be deeply grateful if their parents are alert. If they walk through the world seeing the things around them and talking with interest about what has happened, about the people they have met, the conversations that have taken place, the new things that impinged upon their senses, the books they have read, and the music and plays they have enjoyed, the children will inevitably find their own minds waking up, their own interests being stimulated to responsive activity.

Encourage Questions

That is why parents are smart if they encourage their children to ask questions. Even, as I indicated before, if the youngsters seem to pay no attention to the answers and ask the same questions over and over again, the mere fact that they ask the questions is a hopeful sign. At least they are alive. At least their eyes are wandering and their ears are open.

STIMULATING INTEREST

Parents can stimulate this alertness by pointing out the things that interest them. I know a charming mother who loves nature deeply. She simply took her youngsters walking with her in the woods. She pointed out the growing flowers. She called them each by name. As she looked for birds and their nests, she encouraged the children to find them before she could discover them. She made her youngsters conscious of the development of the year, the feel of the seasons, the signs that indicated nature's growth and progress. She loved these things herself, and she thought that it was her privilege to induct her children into the happy mysteries. She did not wait until they could join the scouts and under a scout master first be awakened to the miracle that is the world God made. She certainly did not sit back and wait till they were in a high-school botany class.

Games often add to this interest. We youngsters played authors and thus learned the names of great books before we had had the privilege of reading them. A boy who starts collecting stamps—or almost anything else—has his eyes and mind opened to the vast wealth of interesting things that await the vital person.

How smart and foresighted are the mother and the father who wake to alert interest in as wide a variety of things as possible the child committed to them! and how wonderfully lucky the child!

APPRECIATIONS

From the parents comes a fine, instinctive appreciation of what is good and true. Despite all the courses in aesthetics, I often wonder if one can be taught to appreciate the beautiful in any other way than by the seeing of it through the eyes of people who already love it. If a mother loves good poetry and reads it to her children, they'll need no rules to make them know a beautiful sonnet from a verse form that clothes sentimental slush. If the parents select good pictures to hang on their walls and walk with the children through an art gallery, pausing reverently or even excitedly before the really lovely paintings and statues, the wise rules of the critical writers will later merely confirm in the children the instincts their parents gave them. If they have with their parents heard good music, whether the better broadcasts, the finer records of instrumental or vocal music, however amateurishly presented, they will in years to come still love good music and willingly sink themselves down into its refreshing charm.

THE MORALLY GOOD

From the conduct and approval of their parents children come to know most effectively what is morally good. From the response and selection of those parents they know what is beautiful and sincere and genuine. They will not easily be taken in later on by the morally evil, the ugly, the fake, the false, the maudlin.

SKILLS

There are great sweeping skills that a person learns only in early years. There is for example the skill in listening. That comes from the child's watching how his parents listen to the questions he asks and how they bend their attention to the comments and queries of each other. There is the skill in conversation itself, which is developed at the dinner table, in the living room, in the car as it rolls along the road, at the picnic when all are relaxed in the soft grass. There are right ways and wrong ways of treating people, doing a favor, accepting a gift, carrying through a job, acting in civilized society. All the memorized rules in the world will later on merely give the adult a stiff formality and self-conscious clumsiness—unless he has early seen these things gracefully done by his parents and has in unconscious imitation learned to do them himself.

EMOTIONAL DEVELOPMENT

The whole emotional development of the child rests primarily with the parents.

I have already referred with emphasis to the effect that the love they see around them has upon children. That is much, much more than merely the atmosphere to warm them and the cushion to protect them from the hard world. It is the stimulus that awakens in them right and wholesome love. The love of the parents is supposed to awaken a complementary love in the children. The interest parents show in their children begets a dear intimacy that must be gained in infancy, or it can scarcely be gained at all.

If they clearly expect a return of love from their children, parents will get it. When however the children spontaneously and in a burst of natural affection show the parents love and the signs of love, the parents must respond at once. Otherwise the emotion dies or is driven back as by a blow, to hide in the frightened soul.

I am amazed when I find how many fathers never kiss their children and how many positively brush the child off when he wants to show affection. It is even more surprising to find mothers who come and go without any sign of love given to or demanded of their children. Quite aside from the happiness the parents are missing, these failures to respond will mean that the souls of the children will grow lonely, timid, chilly; and what is even more perilous, later on the children's affection, which should have poured itself naturally upon the parents, will flow out unrestrainedly upon someone who may be far from worthy of that love.

COOPERATION

The spirit of cooperation is something that the child learns in the days before ever he enters grammar school.

At this point I could begin a dissertation (I shall avoid it) on the loneliness and the cramped character of an only child. The cruelest thing that supposedly good parents can do to their child is deliberately to deny him brothers and sisters or to space the children by such long periods that there are wide stretches of years between them. I am not talking now of sin or of evil practices; I am talking merely of the unfairness of this to the child himself.

Even small families of two or three children may constitute a real handicap to the youngsters.

Man, according to the ancient truism, is a social being. Half the success of life depends on one's ability to get along with one's peers. When Dale Carnegie hit the bull's-eye with "How to Win Friends and Influence People," he was merely offering men and women a guide to something they knew to be essential to their life's success and personal happiness.

Where else in the world could children learn cooperation as they can learn it with their brothers and sisters, in the same family? If there are several children of approximately the same ages, they have to get along together. They learn to share toys and collaborate in games. They engage in a wide variety of collaborative and collective projects. They learn to interchange clothes and luxuries. They even develop consideration in their use of the bathroom—how to get in and out and perform a toilet without holding up the rest of the family. In fact the children in the family will act as little emery wheels, rubbing off the rough edges and polishing down the social conduct of one another.

The Sad Only Child

A solitary child on the other hand lives, not with his peers, but with his elders. In a very small family there is no need for collaboration. The only child does not learn the art of getting along with people. He may turn out in later life to be excellent with his superiors and gracious with those under him; he is always at a loss in his dealings with those of exactly his own age and class.

Over the family the parents should, like presiding geniuses, watch this developing cooperation between the children. They are arbiters of strict justice when the need arises. They reward the democratic spirit as it manifests itself. They punish regretfully but inexorably the violations of rights.

In all this they are giving their children a highly developed social sense and an ability to get along with people, faculties that cannot possibly be developed in small, selfish families.

Comrades

When the child grows a little older, he is not keen to have his parents brooding over his games and parties, especially when he is sharing them with his friends. But during the early days parents are wise to keep without intrusion an eye on the child as he plays with his friends. For here again cooperation and comradeship are being developed. The parents must see that the child does not grab, does not hoard his toys and playthings, learns the all-important game of give and take, and develops an ability to get along with people.

Hence the fallacy of siding with one's own children against their playmates. The commonest course of youngsters when they are in their own homes is to run to their parents with every fancied affront or selfishness their companions manifest. The commonest instinct of the parents is to jump to the conclusion that their own children are good little angels who are beset by the cruelty and rapacity and complete lack of good manners manifested by the neighbors' brats.

And clinging to that adjective for one more statement: The commonest mistake of parents is to side with their own children against their children's playmates and to run to settle the squabble with the might of superior size and authority. Quite aside from the fact that *your* child is quite as likely to be in the wrong as is *their* child, your child is likely to believe that he is always right, that his selfishness is quite forgivable and the other child's defense of his own property merely greedy, and that when he can't handle a situation he has only to call in the divine might that is yours, and the balance of power is swiftly thrown his way.

If the other children are using a mechanical train to beat out the brains of your child, you are quite justified to interfere. Or if you realize that your child is so clearly the underdog that his rights and dignity and sheer thread of life are being cracked completely by a young monster his superior in weight, muscle, and reach, you may take a hand.

Since the scene of action is your own house however, you are wise to use the occasion as a lesson in unselfishness. If you can stay out of the squabble and let the children themselves handle their problems, that is ideal. But consistently to side with your youngster against the children who visit

and who play with him is along the same line as siding with
the children against their teachers—a horrible form of youthful mismanagement to which we shall come again in the course
of our peregrinations.

PATRIOTISM

Tied close together and originating in the home is the
respect for authority and that rational yet deep emotional
love of country we know as patriotism. Parents and patriotism come close together. Here again the virtues they impress
upon their children are much more a matter of what they
do than of what they say. They speak with affection of
America. They do this without breeding little chauvinists;
they do not speak contemptuously of other countries. Early
lessons are given the children by the parents' respectful attitude toward the Flag, which, like the crucifix, has a place
on the walls of the nursery and elsewhere in the house.

Parents show a frank gratitude toward their country in
the hearing of the children. If they must crab about the
taxes, they crab when the children are not around. If they
must damn the state officials and pillory their dishonesty,
stupidity, and general ineptitude, they are wise to do this
after the children are in bed and asleep.

Parallel with the children's introduction to the saints
should come their introduction to the great Americans and
the stories of their deeds. The parents' own love for their
country is soon reproduced in the love the children feel for
a land which, whatever the defects of the governors of the
minute or the peculations of the party in power, deserves a
deep love and a lifelong devotion.

AUTHORITY

This attitude is of course something that leads naturally
into the children's respect for authority. Since this is a
virtue which is essential for effective democracy, I ask the
reader's pardon if I come back to it at intervals throughout
this book. Democracies do not fail because people do not
know how to command; they fail because people are unwilling
to obey or have simply lost the knack of respecting even the

officials they themselves have elected and the laws they themselves have put into effect.

So from the beginning parents can simply insist on the general principle that where there are more than two people together one of them has to be at least to some extent in charge, somewhat responsible. If it is an athletic team, someone must give orders. If it is a circus, there must be a ringmaster. An army, a navy, a city—each needs someone to give the commands.

Hence any symbol of authority is in the hearing of the children treated with respect. The policeman is not held up as a bogeyman but as a friend and a representative and guardian of the law. Anyone with the right to command, even to some extent older brothers and sisters, has his proper place in the world of youth.

When youngsters, however tiny they are, play together, it is wise to let them choose a leader and follow that leader as long as he or she is in charge. For a time we Americans swung away from tin soldiers. From the viewpoint that such toys might make the children militaristic, that departure was good. (The armies of tin soldiers and cannon and other instruments of war that filled my youth did nothing to deter me from a lifelong hatred of war and the strongest possible bent toward pacifism.) But if those soldiers can be used to point out the importance of authority, of officers and their orders, of the fact that at the head of every army and regiment and company and squad there is a man to give commands, they can definitely be used to increase in children a respect for democratic authority.

Charity

In a very young child the abstract principles of charity would be just so many Latin and Greek words, confusing and incoherent. But the practice of charity is easy for him to understand.

That begins with the principle of sharing. He shares with his brothers and sisters. He is generous with visitors and playmates.

That practice of charity advances to small personal gifts, the giving of which can hardly begin too early. Children can be taught to give gifts on birthdays, to do the selecting themselves from the counter of the five-and-ten-cent store, to bring them home, to resist the almost overwhelming temptation to keep them or to spoil them with use, to assist in the wrapping of them, to offer them with their own hands, and then to stand back and not grab when the present is removed from its wrappings.

Parents can give their children small coins as they pass beggars and send them back to drop the money into the poor person's hat or cup. That makes a lasting impression on the child, one that is likely to result in an almost involuntary push toward charity always in the presence of the needy.

Parents are wise to train even the smallest children to drop money into the poor box in church, to contribute to the missions, to put aside some of their food (none that they actually need) to add to the Christmas basket for the poor.

All this is simply a development in kindness, the youthful fulfillment of the command to love one's neighbor as oneself. The animal in every little child makes him tend to grab, to hug to his breast, to refuse to share, to be greedy and selfish and bad-mannered and angry if he has not a complete monopoly of things. Parents sometimes actually encourage children in these attitudes, acting on the mistaken idea that they are amusing, or in their own hearts they are selfish and hence back their children in their lust and greed. The parents who look toward a happy, gracious development of their children's characters put into practice for them the gracious gestures of charity and kindliness.

Later the children will be inclined to continue what in childhood they found so supernaturally soul-warming and so naturally calculated to win the affection and gratitude of their fellows.

Then since grace builds on nature, the step to a supernatural love of one's neighbor is not a far or a difficult one.

IV

STEPS TOWARD PURITY

Quite rightly the Church has been extremely reluctant to let children's education about purity and sex pass into the hands of outsiders. This instruction is entirely the function of the parents. Any outsider, however well intentioned, discreet, tactful, and skilled in the theory or practice of purity, touches the soul of the child with alien hands. Parents are the natural guides and teachers to whom God gave the whole responsibility for training in purity.

Indeed in most Catholic countries anything like formal sex instruction is practically unnecessary. Parents and children regard sex as normal, natural, and entirely wholesome. The parents happily discuss the coming of the new baby and in the presence of the children prepare for its arrival.

A pure woman is regarded as an entirely right and normal woman. A good man as part of his chivalry protects a pure woman. He sees in her a future mother of children, and he regards an assault on her chastity as a major offense against the race.

Purity is not a sign of weakness, as it has often been regarded in pagan countries, ancient and modern; it is the strong protection thrown around the unborn child and around the parents' magnificent creative power of sex.

No Pagan Guides

With real justice the Church is afraid of the pagan who sets himself up to teach sex. In my experience I have had to read or to give to others a number of books written by otherwise good men who nonetheless had the pagan attitude toward matters of sex. In every case, though there might be much that was wholesome and good, there was almost as much with which one could not possibly agree. So when I let others read the books, I had to warn them against the false, pagan attitude that ran through and hence vitiated the treatment.

If the pagan regards man as merely an improved animal, his attitude will be animalistic, however delicately he tries to cover this viewpoint. If he is a Protestant, in these days he is likely to be unsure just why purity is important at all; he is likely to be entirely wrong on the subjects of divorce and birth control; he is very probably lacking in that appreciation of the virtue of purity which we Catholics regard as nobly Christlike and Marylike.

When the pagan is frankly bad, he can do vicious harm. We remember with a shudder of sheer horror the terrible days when Béla Kun turned loose in Hungary his hordes of pagans to instruct youngsters on sex. In our own country some years back I ran into an instance where a certain "advanced" principal in a public high school showed a sex film to a crowd of children; over twenty girls fainted during its progress.

No Negatives

There is much too much inclination to teach purity in terms of negatives. "Don't be impure . . . . Don't be dirty-minded . . . . Be careful of social diseases . . . . Impurity is a horrible thing that brings awful consequences to you . . . . It harms your body and soils your soul."

All that is undoubtedly true. As motivation for purity however it is most ineffective. Some years ago a very sincere French dramatist wrote a play based on the horrors of social diseases. He meant it to frighten men and women into a sense of decency. Indeed all it did, all that the play asked people to do was to be careful with whom they sinned.

The stressing of social diseases to the men in the Army and the Navy has meant merely a protection and a prophylactic treatment of the young men, not an incentive to strength and cleanliness and purity in their relationships with girls. Being careful about the consequences of sin has nothing whatsoever to do with being virtuous.

Any indelicate and rough hand or tongue may in the case of a young child do the most frightful harm. The child can be so shocked, his innocence so jolted that for years he will have an entirely distorted outlook on all matters of sex.

No Dramatic Approach

There have been two attitudes in the teaching of sex, both of them wretchedly poor pedagogy. The first is the awesome approach; we may rightly call it dramatic and spectacular. The teacher or guide in a hushed voice approaches the subject. Even if his subject were only "The Care and Treatment of Colds in the Head," the audience would by his preliminary attitude be worked into such a state of expectancy and taut nerves that they would find the subject either ridiculous or vastly titillating.

The blue-light, hushed-voice, sentimental-music approach puts the whole subject of sex in the category of the occult, horrible, mysterious, forbidden, exciting. The subject is delicate enough without the need for our surrounding it with so melodramatic a setting.

No Offhand Humor

On the other hand there is the very casual, offhand attitude. A teacher can approach the subject as if it were something a little funny, just another topic to be tossed off, nothing to be greatly concerned with or taken seriously. He can joke a bit about it, putting into his voice flippancy and disrespect.

This is fatal. For the subject of sex is most important. It is a sacred thing concerned with the whole question of how life shall safely and beautifully and with dignity enter the world. This quasi-humorous attitude levels it to the plane of the off-color story or the slightly smutty song. Disrespect for the tremendous creative power entrusted to men is not the attitude with which to initiate children into one of their most wonderful natural functions.

Parents Teach Purity

So in this whole matter of the instructing of children on purity the Church regards parents as the natural and rightful teachers. Their right to teach their children about this vital concern is clear enough. Their duty would be clearer if they stopped to think how much of happiness and self-control and the future of their children inside and outside of marriage depend upon a clean, clear, rational, yet supernaturalized and spiritual attitude toward sex and personal purity.

If this duty could be easily passed off on others, parents would in many cases pretend they had no obligation at all. Sexual purity is not an easy subject to handle well. The technique of presenting the facts of life to children requires thought and prayer. Hence many parents would be glad enough to let outsiders take care of the whole matter—an attitude which the Church regards as entirely out of line, as a wrong to the child, and as the shirking of a fundamental parental duty.

YET PARENTS DODGE . . .

The fact must be confessed however that in the main modern parents simply dodge the whole problem. A number of informal surveys made by principals in high schools, notably by Father John Francis Quinn, S. J., when he was in charge of St. Ignatius High School in Chicago, indicate that boys are told almost nothing by their parents.

My own experience with young people confirms this conclusion. When you say to a girl who is troubled by sex problems, "Ask your mother about this," her answer is likely to be, "Why my mother would be shocked to death if I suggested such a thing."

For one good Catholic parent who explains this all-important subject to his or her children there seem to be a hundred who let it go entirely or until it is too late.

WHY PARENTS SHIRK

There are many reasons why parents shirk this duty.

Sometimes they simply do not know the necessary words in which to couch their explanation. Or they have waited so long that they are embarrassed about the whole idea. Or they have the shyness which comes from the realization that the child may associate what they tell him with their own experiences. It is not easy to face an adolescent's questioning look that seems to say, "But how do you know all that?"

So while priests and religious should be spared the necessity of their giving youngsters instructions in sex, their duty may well include that of teaching the parents how to teach their own children. If the parents then fail to handle the problem, priests and religious may ultimately find the task forced upon them. Nonetheless the first effort of priests and religious should be, not to reach the children, but to reach the mothers and fathers with the technique necessary to bring the needed information to their boys and girls.

Once more for all that help to parents and future parents I can see priests assembling clubs or discussion groups made up of the young fathers and mothers of the parish. It seems to me that future parents might well be prepared for this essential part of their parental responsibility. Parent-teachers associations would be wise to make this whole problem, the sex instruction of their children, the subject of a series of talks by experts who can guide them in their guidance of their offspring.

"How to Give Sex Instructions"

I might remark that some schools have handled this problem easily. They have simply presented to their parent-teacher associations or to their alumni or alumnae a Catholic book on sex instruction. Such a book is "How to Give Sex Instructions," written by Father Bruckner and published by The Queen's Work Press, St. Louis. One school that I know of made copies of this book the place cards at a breakfast given to the parents of the students. Many of the parents came back to ask for extra copies for their friends.

Another excellent book on this subject, written by Father Gerald Kelly, S. J., in collaboration with Fathers Fulkerson and Whitford, is "Modern Youth and Chastity."

Start Early and Continue

A first warning to parents must necessarily be this: Sex instruction and training rightly begin with infancy. It continues during the days of the child's development. It should be fairly well established by the time of the child's adolescence. Certainly the friendly, natural relationship between parents and children should be established by that time, otherwise there is great danger of that relationship's never being established.

I doubt if once adolescence is reached a father or a mother can start the sex instruction of a child. (Forgive me if I keep repeating all this.) The minute the subject is approached, the adolescent child, now aware of at least the preliminaries of sex, grows acutely self-conscious. If he has had any experiences, even guiltless ones, he suspects that his parents know about them and are talking because they suspect him. He wants to run away. In fact he may dodge with an effectiveness that leaves the parent completely thwarted.

Adolescence Too Late

Even more difficult is the situation of the parents. They are embarrassed at the necessity of their talking to the well-developed boy or girl. How much does the child know? What will he think? How will he react? Will he, all the while that the parent is talking, be thinking: "Did all this happen to you?" Since the relationship between parents and children is intimately bound up with sex, the parents have the choking inhibiting feeling that their children are associating all they are told with their own father and mother.

If the parents are plain-spoken when they talk to adolescents, they are afraid of shocking or disturbing or stimulating the curiosity of the children. If they use veiled terms and soften the expressions and indulge in wide circumlocutions, they leave the children more muddled than they were at the start. All the time the parents keep wondering how much the children themselves have picked up—from the gutter or elsewhere—and how far their minds and emotions are already set in misconceptions and falsehoods.

I repeat: I sincerely doubt that most parents who put off this interview until adolescence or even later will do more than make a horrible job of it; they themselves will blush and will make their children feel like running away and jumping off the nearest bridge.

Some years ago this whole situation of the father's trying to instruct his adolescent son was made the subject of a dramatic scene. The reaction of the adults in the audience was clear proof that they knew the hopelessness of their saying to adolescents: "Let's sit down, and I'll tell you the facts of life."

Hence I repeat again: Sex instruction must be begun when the baby starts to ask questions. If this instruction is delayed, parents will find that it can't be given.

Not Awful

Utterly mistaken is the parent who starts, no matter what the child's age, with an air of, "This is very awful. I'm sorry I have to tell you this. It is too bad to have to destroy your innocence. But there are terrible facts that you must learn somehow, and you had better learn them from me."

I know a case of a splendid nun—splendid, that is, from other viewpoints — who was appointed to teach child psychology. Her class was made up of collegians, all of them girls from a big city. Each time she approached a subject that was really vital or in which the girls might feel an understandable curiosity, she squelched them by saying: "Now, girls, this subject is so unpleasant that I shall skip it. You may read it if you wish. But I have no intention of explaining it myself." Whereupon the girls with highly stimulated curiosity fairly devoured the print off the pages of that outlawed "horrible" chapter.

Natural and Beautiful

Parents dealing with the matters of sex should treat them as a natural and very beautiful process of human development. Virtuous, strong sex life is part of God's plan for the human race. Its operations rank with those connected with the digestion of good food, with the exercise needed for proper growth and development, with the care of the health, with proper hygiene. In this honest fashion the parents should treat the subject when they discuss it.

The Oh - my - dear - child - this - is - so - awful - and - I - hate - to - break - it - to - you attitude will throw any child into panic and make any parent an entirely out-of-focus teacher.

The Child's Development

Before a parent takes up the details of sex instruction, he should realize that every child goes through a series of perfectly normal developments. Little boys and little girls are in the main asexual. Boys are not interested in girls. Girls are disdainful of boys.

Yet even at this early period it is possible for children to be sexually advanced and often extremely curious. Hence a bad little boy or girl in a crowd may easily induct youngsters into sexual knowledge that normally at that age they would not have. The so-called "doctor games," "artist games," or things of that sort may lead a child to curiosity through improper exposure. In these days there has been a terrific drive on little children in the earliest grades by the dealers of pornographic literature, which in the form of comic books and cartoons are geared to the intelligence and emotions of the smallest children. An evil nurse may sometimes stimulate prematurely the sexual life of a child simply to keep the child quiet.

Parents then, though they can regard innocence as the normal lot of little children, are still doing only their simple duty when they watch their children's playmates, are extremely careful in their choice of nurses, and make sure that stimulating information or the filth prepared by devils disguised as men don't fall into the youngsters' hands.

Adolescence Dawns

With the coming of adolescence the entire orientation of the child changes. His sexual organs develop. With that development his curiosity rises very sharply. The girl becomes interested, often quite innocently, in boys. She likes to be liked; she is pleased when boys pay attention to her.

Much more violently is the boy stirred to curiosity. His emotional and passionate nature awakes with a rush.

Both boys and girls suddenly feel the heat of temptation. Imaginings and desires rush through their minds in indecent parade. They begin to feel the start of physical temptations.

Now if parents have prepared the child quietly and beautifully for all this, the child faces his new state of life calmly and with courage. On the other hand if the child is suddenly plunged into the change without warning, a variety of things may happen to stir his mind to turmoil.

Not knowing that his or her experiences are the common lot of mankind and womankind, the child feels himself wretchedly alone. He is alarmed. He soon comes to wonder if he is not abnormal and queer. He thinks that perhaps he is physically defective, on the verge of insanity.

Many a child comes to look with suspicion on his parents. He reasons: "These are horrible temptations. I wonder if I would have them if my father had not been a bad man. Can it be that mother was not a good woman and that I have these temptations because of her sins?"

If he has been properly prepared for the coming of these experiences, he is not alarmed. He realizes that others have had them, are having them, will continue to have them as long as human nature is human nature. He knows he is not abnormal but perfectly sound. Least of all does he blame his physical and mental problems on some secret sins of his parents.

The Little Child's Questions

As the little child grows into curiosity, even when he is very young his first contact with sex may be the perfectly natural question, "Where do babies come from?"

Now there is really nothing else more beautiful in nature than the origin of babies in their mothers' bodies, babies nurtured by their parents' blood and held in the mothers' bodies as in a sanctuary. For years puritan prudery made people ashamed of this shrinelike character of a mother's body. So when children asked that question, they were pushed aside with lies or angry rebuffs.

One good mother that I know of answered her little daughter's query by replying, hotly, "How dare you ask such an indecent question? You talk like a woman of the street."

Naturally the child decided that childbirth must be an utterly horrible and indecent procedure. In addition she became enormously curious about what her mother meant by that fascinating creature a woman of the street.

At any rate because of parents' puritanical distaste for the world as God made it, children were told that babies were brought by storks, carried to the house in the doctor's little black bag, found by their surprised mothers in potted ferns, and dropped down the chimney by the angels.

Later on when the children learned through gutter channels and the halting, half-true, stimulating whispers of their playmates that this was not true, they faced an unfortunate alternative: Either their parents had lied to them, or their parents were woefully ignorant people. Either alternative made them feel that sex and the birth of children must be a pretty shameful affair, and they were alarmed to realize that their parents were liars or stupid people.

One little girl recently replied when her mother told her that storks brought babies, "Oh, mommy! you should know better than that. Babies come from their mommies."

First Opportunity

When the child first asks that question, he is in the most wonderful mental and emotional state to receive the truth. He has no sex stimulation. He is very thoughtless and pays little attention to answers given him. He takes casually any answer that he gets and drops the matter right there without feeling the prod of further curiosity.

Where Babies Come From

So quite calmly the mother may answer his question: "Babies come from their mothers. When you were a little, little baby, you were in my body, right under my heart. I carried you there for a long time. Then when you were a big little baby, you came out of my body and I held you in my arms."

The normal child reacts to that really lovely and factual recital with an inattentive "Oh!" He turns back to his toys without another thought on the matter. The explanation is adequate and beautiful. He likes the idea. He is quite satisfied. Moreover he is likely to forget all but the fact that he was told something important which later on he recalls without embarrassment.

Protect Innocence?

I explained all this in the course of a talk to teachers on a certain occasion. Whereupon I received a violent and of course anonymous attack by a man who claimed I was destroying the innocence of little children.

My answer to that would be first of all that if God decreed that children be brought into the world by this beautiful sharing of the life of the mother and the father, I don't see how innocence could be destroyed by the child's knowing the simple, unamplified fact. On the contrary: When the period of innocence is past and the emotions are aroused and the child is vastly curious, he realizes with a horrible shock that all this time he did not know how he came into the world. He is alarmed to find that his parents lied to him. Were they ashamed of the manner in which children were born? Were they guilty in their whole attitude toward sex?

He is often appalled and in many a case goes around stunned for days at the revelation of sex that has come to him, not from his beloved parents and in the days of his innocence, but from the "guttersnipes" and from the peddlers of pornography and at a time when he has already experienced the temptations of the flesh and regards them with horror or morbid suspicion.

One youngster that was told in the calm, matter-of-fact fashion where babies come from ran to his mother a few days later.

"Mother," he said, "do you know what little Willie wanted to do? He wanted to tell me where babies came from. And I told him, 'Old stuff'!"

The Girl Approaches Adolescence

As a girl approaches her first period, she must be most carefully prepared for the shock by the kindly counsel of her mother.

Once I met a college girl whose bent toward life had already become abnormal. She told me what she evidently had told others, that her first period had occurred when she was a little girl making a trip all alone. Hysterically she locked herself away in a room in the house of strangers and settled herself down to die. Though after a time she knew she was going to live, she made up her mind that she was diseased and that her life was ruined. I doubt if she ever quite recovered from that harrowing experience, which should have been prepared for by the wisdom of a mother.

We shall talk of this and of the preparation of the child for the other manifestations of adolescence a little later.

Who's Going to Teach Them?

What I must insist upon here however is that sex knowledge is going to come. Anyone who first learned about sex from the dirty mouths of evil companions or stumbled upon it in some filthy book or card got a shock that all the years have not quite erased. Sometimes those shocks give a person a wrong mental slant and an emotional kink that perdure all through life.

Parents have to decide for themselves whether they wish their child to learn in this deadly fashion or whether they wish him to learn from clean instruction given by the parents he loves and trusts. It is a clear choice. All the decision needs is a little courage and a little thoughtful, prayerful preparation.

Parents' Own Ideals

Most important in the parents is the dignity and beauty of their own ideals about sex.

For this it is necessary that modern parents, who live in the midst of pagan standards of morality, reconsider and reburnish the standards and attitudes which they should have toward sex.

To state it simply, we Christians know that:

    A. God could have created human beings as He created Adam and Eve, by a direct act of creation.

B. Instead He determined to share here as elsewhere His own powers with His human sons and daughters. He Himself was free, so He gave them free will; He was intelligent, so He gave them intelligence; He was eternal, so He gave them immortality; He had the power to create human beings, so He shared that power with men and women.

C. Hence the thing we call sex is merely that creative power by which men and women help God to people the world with His sons and daughters and to give heaven its immortal citizens.

. D. Mothers and fathers have in consequence a share in God's divine paternity. They are cocreators with God in the making of a man.

E. Because the responsibilities of fatherhood and the pains of motherhood are hard burdens, God repays His sons and daughters for their aid in the creation of His children. He gives to sex physical pleasure. He surrounds sex with the consolations and joys of love. He makes men and women attractive to each other. He asks them to build homes in which they will through peace and security and the union of souls and bodies provide a safe place in which to bear and rear and educate His earthly sons and daughters.

F. To show His sons and daughters the sanctity of all this, He lifts marriage to the dignity of a sacrament. His Church reminds its members that though a marriage is ratified at the altar it is not completed or consummated until the married couple have rightly exercised their great creative act.

G. Inside of marriage men and women may offer to God their sex relations as they offer Him any other noble act of their day.

H. Hence through marriage the life of the human race continues. Men and women should have the highest respect for themselves as the bearers of the germ of life. Men are potential fathers. Women are the shrines and fountains of the future.

I. Impurity is in consequence horrible because it is a violation and a betrayal of this sacred creative power. It

takes the pleasure connected with sex and does not give God
—under safe and sanctified conditions—the children that He
has ordained can be given Him in no other way. It imperils
the whole life of the future. It is less a sin against God than
a sin against the human race, since it corrupts the fathers
of the future and renders debased and unclean the women
who should be the mothers of wholesome, pure, strong
children.

All this, if you care to see it more exhaustively treated,
you will find worked out in detail in a series of ten-cent pam-
phlets which I published through The Queen's Work Press:
"The Pure of Heart," "They're Married," "Why Be
Decent?"

PURE LOVE OF PARENTS

Once more I come back to the importance of the love
which the mother and the father display in the presence of
their children. The children can find this love the reassuring
guarantee; they can never quite forget that love is a pure
and noble thing. They sense, without their knowing how or
why, the respect which their mother and father have for each
other. They later come, when they know more about it, to
be absolutely sure that their parents' use of sex was always
dignified, noble, pure, natural, according to God's plan. They
feel that love is something very splendid. "Look what it
meant to my mother and father," they argue.

So from infancy love takes on beautifully reassuring
associations. The children are bound to think of it as a
beautiful and inspiring thing. For they remember the pure,
strong love in the eyes and lives of their parents.

BOOKS AND MAGAZINES

Parents who are interested in the purity of their children
will be very careful about what books and magazines come
into the house. Children page through them even before they
can read.

"Why," a little girl asked, in my hearing, "are the women
on the covers of those detective-story magazines always
dressed like that?"

In repugnance she pointed to the shocking criminal woman half naked and sprawling luridly and alluringly across the cover of the magazine her father was reading. He was interested merely in the yarns, which were rehashes of stale murders and counterfeitings. She was distressed by the shameless woman flaunted at her from the cover.

Plays and Movies

Plays and motion pictures make a profound impression upon little children, who drink in what they see before they have any idea of its significance.

In the days before the Legion of Decency did its herculean task of cleaning the stables of Hollywood, I was visiting with a friend of my college days. During the course of the afternoon his little daughter, just about six years old, came back from the picture show at which she had been parked for the afternoon. She herself was the picture of innocence, fit subject for a photographer who might want to do in natural colors a study called Guiltlessness.

"How was the picture?" her father asked, in perfunctory query.

Believe me, there was nothing perfunctory about her answer.

"Oh," she answered, suddenly transformed into a little actress, "it was wonderful. It was called 'Dancing Daughters.' I loved it. It was all about two sisters. One of them was such a silly, good girl. And was she ever stupid! She didn't have any boys coming to see her. She just sat home and sewed.

"But her sister—oh she was keen! She was so pretty. All the boys were crazy about her. One night she came home from a party. She ran upstairs to her sister's room. Her sister was in bed. She took off her clothes. And daddy, she had the prettiest underclothes on. She told all about the boys who were crazy for her. Well the other sister got mad. She got out of bed. She put on a dress with oh such a low neck. She was going to be pretty and get the boys to like her too . . . ."

By this time I was fairly choking, and the father was as red as a stop light.

"I think that will do," he said. "You told it very well. Now run and drink your milk."

She ran, once more innocence on the "lam," while her father lighted his cigaret in thoughtful silence.

"Looks as if I'd better do a little supervising of the youngster's afternoons," he said.

There was really no need for me to agree.

THE VISITORS TO THE HOME

If children are influenced by the magazines and films that lie within reach of their curiosity, they can be even more profoundly affected by the type of friends the parents bring home, the conversations at table, the stories that are told in their presence. They instinctively recognize loose conduct. They are shocked, as I indicated before, even by the dirty story or the suggestive song the meaning of which they do not understand.

EVEN BEFORE REASON

Many children are spoiled for purity before ever they reach the age of reason. On the happy contrary many children are established firmly and forever in the way of purity from the days of their infancy.

THE CHURCH'S LAWS

Very closely allied to all this is the attitude the children hear their parents take toward the Church's laws regarding sex problems. All the Church decrees on the subjects of love, marriage, divorce, birth control, and kindred subjects spring directly from the Church's love of life and its determination to protect that life against the beast in man.

Hence when in the presence of the children parents speak contemptuously or rebelliously of these laws, they are really weakening the children's attitude toward purity itself. Children are quite naturally shocked by the successive polygamy which is called divorce. They don't understand and are revolted by that transition of husbands and wives from one bed to another. They are often definitely repelled by the mere idea of birth control. Parents are wise to remember all this when they speak of these subjects in the presence of children.

A young woman once came to see me, a sick, twisted look on her face. She was tense, her nerves on edge, her jaw white with emotion.

"What's wrong?" I asked.

"I shall never respect my parents again," the girl replied, hardly unclenching her teeth. "Last night when I opened the drawer in my mother's dresser, I found a package of contraceptives. I couldn't have believed it of her. Something of my love for her and for my father died at that moment. I can't respect them again."

Apparently it takes a good deal of adult rationalizing to make the unnatural things which are divorce and birth control seem justified. Children see them more clearly and rightly.

Beyond that when the parents practice birth control, their children are likely to feel the aura of selfishness it casts. They come to wonder, as time goes on, why there are not more children in the family. They hear about birth control. They begin to question in their own minds. Often they condemn their own parents. Then if they find proof that their suspicions are justified, their condemnation may be bitter and lasting.

High Standards Perdure

Even if nothing is said on the subject of sex and purity, the whole relationship of parents and children may result in high ideals and right standards. Often you will meet a thoroughly pagan young man who in his dealings with young women will be almost meticulously chivalrous. Likely as not this attitude arises from the high ideals he has of his mother. Quite without planning it, she may have shaped his whole attitude toward womankind. He is gallant and strong toward other women out of the respect which he pays to the mother he loves and honors.

Mothers' Ideals

A mother can however consciously develop in her young son a chivalrous respect for women. If she seems to expect him to be her protective escort, if she sets herself as the high standard for other women, he will respond.

A young man of my friendship brought home a young lady with whom he was infatuated. Thinking his mother was out of the room, he made violent and undignified love to the girl. He did not realize that his mother was seeing in a mirror what he was doing. She said nothing at the time. When the girl left, his mother stood before him very quietly.

"Son," she said, and her voice left no slightest doubt that she meant what she said, "never again in my house will you treat a girl like that. Evidently you forget that when you act cheaply and indecently to a girl you are throwing a direct insult at me. I don't see how you can pretend to love and respect me if you have a contemptuous attitude toward any other woman."

He long remembered that rebuke.

Fathers' Ideals

The conduct of the father toward women also profoundly affects children. It means a lot to the ideals they will hold if they see their father respectful to his wife, his mother, his sisters. They are keen to note the attitude he takes toward the women who visit the house. Quickly they note any amorous or suggestive or familiar gestures. They regard such actions as treason to their mother. They are repelled by the faint suggestion of weakness on his part.

If on the other hand he is chivalrous, friendly, protective and the gentleman, in no slightest way demanding, familiar, inclined to paw or to expect familiarities, the boys take their cue from that conduct. The girls are lifted in their own esteem by the high regard they see him display toward all women.

Protective Attitude

From infancy boys should be expected to manifest a protective attitude toward women. That boy is lucky who has a younger sister toward whom he can display that protective instinct. He is twice lucky if his mother simply takes such an attitude for granted from the start. That same standard he will then much more easily transfer toward other boys' sisters later on.

The good manners demanded by a mother make a fine prelude to the purity of her son. If he rises when a woman enters the room, if he is taught to treat older women with courtesy, if he opens doors for them and carries bundles for them, he is really being trained in that Christian treatment of women which seems germain to purity. Pagans regard women as inferiors to be treated patronizingly or with disdain. They can be the burden bearers for the race.

Pagans are notably contemptuous of purity and bad-mannered toward women. Christian good manners and purity can well go hand in hand.

RESPECT FOR WOMEN

The young girl's self-respect is one of the strong safeguards of her purity. Here again the mother's conduct and the father's attitudes are powerful determinants. Every girl models herself on her mother. She clothes her soul according to the fashions that seem to suit her mother. If the mother has a high self-respect, if she allows no rudeness or vulgarity in her presence, if she accepts from men only fine friendship and admiring regard, the daughter will think that the proper course to follow.

The girl is often puzzled by the male members of her family. She is pleased when her father and her brothers are exacting in her regard. She is flattered when the menfolk expect her escorts to be high type.

"I don't like that young man, daughter; he's not up to your standard" is fatherly advice that may make a grown daughter flare up and strike back in resentment; it is likely to make a younger girl think happily that her father is concerned for her welfare. Girls are instinctively pleased when their brothers warn them away from this young man or that one "because he's not the kind you ought to be traveling around with."

Puzzled by Men

Yet, as I say, young women are puzzled by the strange conflict they discover in male conduct. A young woman once wrote me somewhat to this effect:

"How is a girl ever going to understand men? There's my father for example. He took me out with a party the other evening, a number of his friends and their wives. After the theater we went to a night club to eat and dance. At the next table sat the most shockingly dressed girl I've ever seen off the stage. Anyone could tell by looking at her that she was bad clear through.

"But dad sat where he could keep watching her, and he just never took his eyes off her. I could have hit him, I was so furious.

"Finally he turned to me and said, 'Stunning-looking, isn't she?' But before I could answer, he went on: 'But if you ever look like that or dress like that, I'll choke you to death with these two hands of mine.'

"And he meant it. How do you explain that utter contradiction? It left me simply too puzzled for words."

That is the way a lot of adult conduct leaves young people—especially people in their very youthful days. They find it hard to be impressed with ideals that are held up for them when they see those ideals flouted by the mothers and fathers who present them.

I later found that this particular girl was nevertheless vastly impressed by the fact that her father demanded high levels of conduct and dress from her. She got a new urge to be what he expected her to be, the finest representative of womankind—yes in a sort of way more dear to him even than his wife, her mother.

So these ideals deeply imbedded in parental minds and hearts and conduct are most important. Only on the foundation of these can education to purity become possible.

Prenatal Sins

I might refer, very much in passing, to the fact that there is a prenatal influence where sex is concerned. The sins of the father may definitely be visited upon his children. The silver nitrate used to wash the eyes of all newborn babies is a symbol of that terrifying fact. The modern doctor is so alarmed at the possible effects that an impure father or mother might have on the baby that he guards against the baby's blindness by washing the perhaps present germs of social disease out of the newborn infant's eyes.

Tell Them the Truth

The first time that children ask, "Where do babies come from?" the answer should be given to them honestly, as I have indicated before. In this first answer there is no need for amplification. The child is only mildly curious. He wants only a swift and general reply. Anything further would bore him. Besides with the casual memory he possesses at that time, most of what is told him rolls right off the surface of his mind—or rather rolls down into one of the soft brain ruts, where it remains unnoticed until some circumstance reminds him of the reassuring fact that lies there.

But the fact that he has been told without hesitation and with transparent truth dulls his curiosity. He loses interest in something that has no more mystery about it. When later on he hears incorrect or half-correct or smutty information from an alien source, he knows the truth and has the protection of the truth against the lies and dirt.

Openings

Incidental to all this, once the bond of confidences has been established, it is wise occasionally to give the little child a clear opening or opportunity to ask questions. He may have run into fresh problems, and he may be hesitating to mention them. So the mother or the father opens an opportunity spontaneously.

"You know of course that you can certainly ask me about anything you ever want to know. I like to think that my little son (or daughter) wants to talk things over with me. Sometimes the other children say things you don't understand. They use words you don't know. If you ever want any help, just come to me. I'd love to have you ask me."

More than likely the child will then and there ask a question that he's been meaning to ask and has hesitated about or forgotten at the right time.

But note carefully: A talk like this last one given to a small child or to a child trained from the beginning to confiding in his parents will bring results. Suddenly sprung on an adolescent, used for the first time on a grown child, such a talk will cause only embarrassment and probably precipitous flight.

No Shock; No Surprise

For any question asked, the parent should have a calm, unemotional answer.

"What does such and such a word mean?" the child will ask, practically slapping the parent's face with a simply revolting word made up of small repellent letters.

Mastering any slightest sign of surprise or alarm, the parent explains: "That's an unpleasant word that nice people don't use. Only nasty people with dirty minds ever say it. You see, it means . . ." and the parent in as delicate language as possible goes on to explain. If the word is merely one of the "toilet room," body-function words, the explanation is easy enough. If the word is obscene, a bit of circumlocution may be necessary.

"Dirty little boys and girls, who have no respect for themselves, sometimes do dirty things. They are very immodest. They don't take care of themselves. That word means a very bad and unpleasant action which my fine little son (or daughter) never need come in contact with. You run away from garbage cans or dead dogs. So just run away from nasty words like that."

If when the child grows older the subject comes up again, or if the subject is approached when the child has arrived at adolescence, the explanation can be much more complete.

No Humor or Ridicule

In the whole discussion of sex questions any slightest touch of humor is out. The parent should be entirely cheerful in his or her replies. But the youngster won't see anything remotely funny either in his question or in the answer given. In fact a sense of humor about almost anything develops in the child only after adolescence is far progressed. A sense of humor about sex is denied, thank God, to youngsters until temptations to sin have advanced far.

Anything like ridicule for a question's having been asked or contempt either for the question or the questioner is fatal. The question, be it ever so ridiculous, must be received in all seriousness. The question, be it ever so vulgar or shocking, must bring from the parent not a wince, or a sign of revulsion, or any response other than that of respectful consideration.

SIMPLE OCCASIONS

Often occasions for basic explanations and precautionary advice arise out of the simple processes of cleanliness. Cleanliness of the sex organs may be used as an excuse to explain to the child the need to be very gentle with them as well as carefully protective.

"Because, you see, they are very delicate, and they are so important that they are the things that make you really a man (or a woman) and later on a father (or a mother)." Without sermonizing, the parent can use a bit of frivolity on the part of the child, utterly innocent and without guile, for a brief talk on the sacredness of his organs and the fact that they are the bearers of the germ of human life.

LESSONS FROM THE "HAIL, MARY"

Early in their lives all Catholic children learn the "Hail, Mary."

We who love the prayer are amazed to find out that some puritanical persons regard the prayer as something not to be taught to children. One highly reforming group once rewrote "blessed is the fruit of thy womb" to read "blessed is the fruit of thy love." They were acting on the supposition that the word womb was a highly improper and probably suggestive word.

"I don't know," a good Protestant lady once said to me, "how you can teach that prayer to little children. I should think it would suggest all sorts of unpleasant questions to them."

As a matter of fact I've never known a child who gave it a second thought. Children question it no more than they question the paternity of God expressed in the "Our Father."

Yet as the "Hail, Mary" is taught, it is quite the easiest thing in the world, especially with very small children, to use the prayer as a study in the lovely fact of motherhood.

We tell the story of the sweet, pure Mary, who loved God with all her heart and soul.

"She was becoming old enough now to be a mother. That meant that she was a grown-up young lady and not a little girl any more.

"So one day a beautiful angel came from heaven to see her. Mary was praying. She was telling God how much she loved Him. She hoped that someday He would come to earth and she could see Him.

"Well the angel cried out, 'Hail, Mary.' That was his way of greeting her. It showed he thought she was important. Only important people were addressed with the word 'hail.'

"Then he told her the important news: She was going to have a baby. She was going to be a lovely mother. But her baby was going to be the Son of God. The Holy Spirit was going to be her spouse, which is just another word for husband.

"Now in Mary's body was, as is in the body of all women, a little germ. It was alive. But it wasn't a baby yet. It could be made into a baby though. Usually a man, the father of the baby, makes this germ into a baby. The father has a life germ too, and he gives it to the mother. The two germs make a little baby. That makes the man a father.

"But it wasn't a man who was Mary's Baby's father. It was God. The germ was in Mary's womb, which is the center of a woman's body, not too far from her heart.

"So Mary said she was willing to be the mother of God's Son. She was very happy. Then the Holy Spirit of God worked a miracle. He formed the little germ into a little Baby, and the Baby rested in Mary's womb. It stayed there for nine months. You can remember that easily: The angel came to see Mary on March 25. That was the feast of the Annunciation. And Jesus was born on December 25; that was Christmas. All that time Mary took care of Him. She fed Him with her own blood as He rested near her heart.

"Then Christmas came, and He came into the world out of Mary's body. Then we saw the beautiful Baby that Mary had given us.

"So we say, 'Blessed is the fruit of thy womb,' because the little Baby Jesus came from the womb of Mary, our Blessed Mother.

"And except for the fact that they have fathers who are men, all children come into the world in that same way."

If anyone hesitates about the telling of this story because of the possible shock to the young child, I should say he does not understand children and children's instinctively happy and wholesome reaction to whatever is true and good.

What could possibly be nobler than the way that the Son of God chose to enter the world?

Using the "Our Father"

While we are on the subject . . . The "Our Father" can be used to explain the more difficult problem of fatherhood. For that problem is one that often stumps otherwise frank and honest parents.

It might be handled like this:

" 'Our Father, who art in heaven.'

"Isn't it beautiful to remember that you have two fathers? One of them is in heaven, and one of them lives here with us in this house."

(I find myself always putting these explanations into the mouth of a mother. With simple changes they can be handled quite as well by a father.)

"Both of these are our fathers, because they give us life.

"So let's look at Our Father in heaven.

"Once on a time we did not exist. God wanted us to be His children. He wanted you to be His little son. So He said, 'I think I'll make little James, and then he will be my son.'

"So He made your daddy and me fall in love.

"He said to us, 'Will you help me make a little boy named James?'

"We said we would be glad to. For you see, your father and I loved you even before we saw you. And so did Our Father in heaven.

"One happy day daddy and I were married. Now God gave us both the power to make a new life. Our Father in heaven has that power. He gave it to us. So daddy and I and God made you. We did it in this way:

"Daddy had a little germ of life in his body.

"I had a little germ of life in my body.

"We united those two germs in my body.

"And God helped us. So when the little germs united, God blew a soul into them, and there you were.

"You see, daddy and God and I made you because we loved you.

"And God is your Father; and daddy is your father; and I am your mother.

"And you are our little son, and we all love you very much."

Love Is Productive

As the children grow older, they can be beautifully initiated into the knowledge of the delightful fact that all love is essentially productive. If a man loves music, he produces a tune, even if only a tune that he whistles in the bathroom. If a man loves literature, he is likely to write a book or a poem. If a woman loves housekeeping, she will create a delicious meal, a sunny room, even the wonderfully happy house over which she presides.

God loved us human beings, so He produced us. Furthermore He gave to human love that same power of production.

So a man and a woman fall in love. They love each other so much that they want to be together, and very close together. They want to share their lives. They are eager to live in the same house, share the same room. Thereupon their love, like all other love, becomes productive of something very beautiful.

Each of the parents carries in his or her body a germ of human life. Because they love each other, they embrace and hold each other dearly and protectively close. The man gives to the woman the lovely germ of life that is in his body. This unites with the germ in the body of the woman. Through this union they themselves are united in the closest possible physical way. As a consequence of this union of these two germs, the "fruit of their love" became the precious baby so dear both to the father and the mother.

So a little child, as he grows up and comes to understand things better, can be happy in the knowledge that he is the fruit of his parents' love. They brought him into the world because they loved each other and because even before they saw him they loved him, their little child.

ANIMAL PETS

For very little children and often for growing ones too pets may sometimes serve to help solve life's mysteries.

There is however the danger of allowing children to see only the animal side of this relationship. It would be the gravest mistake if they were not from the start made clearly aware of the chasm-wide difference between love in human beings and animal passion in animals, between the animal born in undignified fashion and the child born as the immortal son of God.

With these modifications children may well be encouraged to have their pets. The birth of kittens can be explained simply and naturally. The youngsters can become aware of the relationship between a dog and the puppies he sired. Lambs have a delicacy of connotation which makes them good illustrative material. The difference between a fertile and an infertile egg can be explained. The spring season will bring to their attention the courtship, homemaking, and egg-laying of the birds around them. The tropical, viviferous fish may prepare them for later knowledge of life's origins.

"BIRDS AND BEES"

It has become fashionable in recent years to laugh with hearty cynicism (if heartiness and cynicism are not contradictory terms) at parental talks that start with references to "the birds and the bees."

God's ways are all essentially wonderful. Perhaps a child who understands the attraction of the bees for the flowers and the bees' consequent part in pollination may find the place of the father in human life rather beautiful and understand more fully the attraction that men feel for a beautiful woman.

The courtship of the birds is not an unpoetic or impractical symbol of the wooing of a woman by a man in the springtime of their lives. The nest-building and cave-seeking instincts of birds and animals might be a sobering lesson to many a thoughtless modern who has no home and is honored by no offspring because of deliberately unproductive love.

Indeed it is a decided question whether any real love can be unproductive. Are the modern childless marriages based on love at all? If so, they are the inhuman and antidivine instances of the only love which is not blessed with sweet and gracious and vital consequences.

THE APPROACH TO ADOLESCENCE

The handling of sex instructions for small children is relatively simple. The real problems arise when the children approach adolescence. The girl looks worried and afraid. The boy often becomes sullen, morose, abstracted, rude. The mother notices possibly with alarm a slight stain on the bed linen. She hates to admit to herself that her children are growing up. Anxiously she faces the task of making them aware of the answers to the questions that may be disturbing if not actually torturing their minds.

I understand that even the dignified "Judge Hardy," though I have not seen the picture, made a fool of himself when he tried to explain "the facts of life" to the adolescent Andy.

I cannot repeat too often though that, if the proper relationship of confidence and open candor has been established between parents and children, the diffidence of the parents and the embarrassment of the adolescent boy and girl can be cut to a minimum.

THE GIRL'S PERIODS

Let's take the easiest of the cases: The mother must of course delicately and carefully prepare the little girl for the coming of her periods. Because mothers do not do this, or because they treat the whole matter in brisk, curt, or even regretful and annoyed fashion, girls grow into young womanhood detesting the experience and giving it any of the dozen unpleasant names by which they stigmatize their "curse." Or the girl has her first painful experience and goes into a complete panic. Like my poor little youngster on her journey, she is thrown into confusion and terror, which may leave a brutal wound on her psychological life for many a long year.

The first approach is the purely hygienic one, the simple matter of how the period is to be cared for.

The girl will be puzzled however by her experience. This reaction affords an excellent opportunity for the mother to explain to the child exactly what the period means and that it is really a beautiful and entirely dignified and reassuring experience.

"My daughter, you are almost a young woman now. When you become a grown woman, a very important thing is going to happen to you. You remember how in the 'Hail, Mary' we say, 'Blessed is the fruit of thy womb'? Well every woman has in her body a little sack that is called a womb. Connected with it are two little chambers called ovaries. These are so called from the Latin word *ovum*, which means a tiny egg.

"As soon as a little girl has grown up, there is developed every twenty-eight days in her egg-bearers or ovaries a precious little germ of life. When you have grown older and are married, that little germ can become a dear little baby. But that won't happen for a good many years, not until you are married and have a home of your own.

"The little germ passes down into the girl's womb. The womb is covered with important little blood vessels and nerves. Those blood vessels will later on feed blood to the little baby that you as a mother may carry in your womb. But when there is no little baby in your womb but only the life germ, those blood vessels open and the blood washes the little germ out of your body. That causes you pain and some inconvenience.

"But you mustn't mind that. It only proves that you are growing up. It shows that you will be able to be a mother when you really grow up.

"So someday if you are to become a mother, that little germ won't be washed out of your body. Instead the little germ will become a little baby, and the blood will feed and nourish him, as the blood of the Blessed Mother took care of the Infant Jesus, who was the fruit of her womb."

It seems to me that if young children were given even prior to their first period this simple but clear idea of the meaning of these periods, they would regard it—instead of feeling a revulsion toward it and hating it and branding it with offensive and often disgusting names—as a sacred and significant thing. Its first occurrence would make in their minds a real forward step in adult development and growth. They would be happy to know themselves to be developing women. They would hold high the responsibility for their future motherhood.

PHYSICAL CHANGES

In somewhat the same fashion it may be wise to explain to young girls the development of their bosom. If this explanation can be mentally tied in with the care and feeding of children, the girls will at once adopt an attitude of respect and modesty.

"God wants mothers and their children to come very close together. When you were a very little baby," explains the mother, "I gave you food from my body. You rested against my breast, and I fed you. Isn't that lovely?

"Well you are growing up now. Someday if you marry and are a mother, you will give your little child that same nourishing milk. He will grow strong because of the food you give him for his body, just as you grew strong and charming because I nursed you when you were a little baby.

"So you see your breasts are very sacred and important. You have to keep them very pure and sweet. You can't let them be touched by evil thoughts or rough people. That is why you must always be modest and pure. You want to be sure that you'll give your little baby only dear, sweet, pure, wholesome food. That is what I wanted to do for you."

Boys' Adolescence

The boy's adolescence presents even more problems. With the dawn of puberty the most violent physical and psychological changes come over him. He is awakened in the night by physical experiences that he does not understand. His former contempt for girls is succeeded by a vehement curiosity about them and an interest in them which he regards as utterly abnormal, stupidly disconcerting, and probably shameful. Temptations to queer thoughts enter his mind. He looks with suspicion on older people. "Have they had these experiences? Have they led, are they actually leading sinful lives?"

The results of these changes may lead to a temporary change in the boy's disposition. Where once he was cheerful, he may become morose and silent. Perhaps he gets a furtive way of having secrets, of clipping slightly immodest pictures of women and hiding them, of trying to find out from his fellows what it is all about or of bragging to them that he knows "all about it"—whereas he is merely in a cloudy haze.

Boys who struggle along in the dark about all this are often a real problem to teachers and parents. They try to exorcise their temptations by loudness of voice, boisterous "roughhouse," a general tendency toward breaking up the furniture. Their interest in girls leads them to a disguise which makes them insult their sisters, pull the hair of any girl they can reach, and kick out defensively at women in general. They hear other little boys say that "all little girls are bad." They wonder curiously if that is true, and then they deny this with all the vehemence of their indignant souls.

PREPARE FOR THE CHANGE

All this can be forestalled or at least palliated if the parents give the youngster a decent preparatory outlook on life.

"Now you're growing up, son. As you become older, a great many important changes are going to take place in you. Some of these are merely interesting and not in any sense disturbing. Your voice will change and become like your father's. That will be a clear sign that you are no longer a little boy but are becoming a young man. You will notice hair beginning to grow on your body. Only grown men have that. So you can say to yourself, 'I guess I'm really growing up.'

"Don't be surprised if in your sleep or at other times your male organ seems to swell. That is merely because blood has flowed to it.

"Now in all probability you will find queer thoughts running through your mind. You may suffer physical temptations that you won't understand. Let me explain that very simply.

"When you were a little boy and still a child, God wanted you to be happy and have fun and learn a lot of things that are necessary for you to be a success. He wanted you just to eat and sleep and play and go to school and have fun so that you could grow strong and be a fine big fellow.

"But when a boy becomes a little older, about the age you are now, he is really on the way to becoming a man.

"God wants most men to be fathers. So into their bodies He puts a most important germ of life. A man carries that germ around in his male organ. That germ is almost like half a little baby. Because if it is united with the germ a woman carries, it can become a little baby. When that germ is forming in your body, you know that you are growing up.

"So if you start to experience these temptations, if you see in your mind strange and unpleasant pictures, don't let them bother you or make you imagine you are queer. Put them out of your mind and say, 'Well I guess I'm really growing up now. And those thoughts just prove that God is giving me that precious germ. All that those thoughts prove is that someday, I guess, I can be a father.'

"Play harder than ever. Eat well. Try to grow into a strong, wholesome, vigorous man. Keep your mind as free as you can from those thoughts; don't waste time on them. When those thoughts come into your mind, get up and turn on the radio or go out and play ball. But don't let them worry you, and don't let them stay in your mind.

"Then God will make you a fine, strong man fit to be the father of a grand little boy like my son."

Night Releases

Even before the first stain on the bed linen announces the boy's involuntary night release, the parents should adjust themselves to a correct viewpoint on the whole matter.

They must know that this is God's and nature's way of caring for the superfluous seed or germs (or the nutriment of those elements) which have developed in the boy's body. Since man develops a tremendous quantity of spermatozoa, some of them flow back into his body to make him a strong, well-matured, adult male. Some of them flow out during sleep, since nature is extravagant with her life elements.

The mere presence of this factor does indicate the development of adolescence, for which a boy must be prepared. Usually he wakes during the course of this nightly release and experiences the pleasure that accompanies it. That may make him curious. Or if it results in his trying to produce the effect himself, this may be the beginnings of self-abuse.

If the boy has been properly prepared for this experience, he may avoid all mental upsets or the forming of any evil habits.

To him then the parents explain a little more fully the fact that he is the bearer of this male germ of life.

"That germ, my son, is very precious and very important. So you must never waste it or use it in any careless, evil way.

"You see, God gives you a great many of those germs. Most of them go back into your own body. They help make you a man. They are what cause your voice to change, your muscles to grow, your body to become more and more manly. So you mustn't waste these germs or they might not get a chance to make you a strong, vigorously developed man.

"If during sleep however nature releases some of these germs, that may mean that there are so many in your body that you will be more comfortable if they are thrown off. Don't let that worry you at all. The experience won't hurt you. It won't, if you yourself don't abuse it, be in the slightest way wrong.

"You may feel pleasure connected with this if you should happen to be awake at the time. Don't think about that too much. God knows that it is hard to be a father and to work for one's children and to give them all the things they need. So he says to men, 'If you will, when you get married, be a good father, I will bless you with happiness and pleasure while you are giving that seed of life to your wife, who will be a mother.' God rewards us for everything we do. He certainly rewards a father who gives Him fine, strong little sons and daughters.

"But you mustn't waste that little germ yourself. That is very wicked. You must say, 'I shall be very pure and modest and take care of myself until I am ready to be a father.' Then God will make you a very happy man, strong, and pure, and fit to be the father of His children."

No Physical Evils

Parents should understand that the loss of seed, either through night release or through the practice of self-abuse, is not, except in the rarest of cases, attended by physical evils. At times parents give their children an entirely wrong idea about this. To frighten them out of the practice of self-abuse, parents pretend that this practice destroys manhood, brings about invalidism, causes terrible sickness. Children will as a consequence grow to manhood thinking that they are physically unfit for life. Unscrupulous doctors who get their hands on boys will persuade them that night releases and self-abuse have caused them to become sick and unable to assume the duties of fatherhood.

Physical consequences of all this are very rare. They need not be taken into consideration by parents, much less be worried about.

PSYCHOLOGICAL EFFECTS

The psychological effects however can be heavy and harsh. If a child worries about night releases, he is likely to brood, think himself defective, and hate the whole process of life. He may be twisted into a sullen introvert, become really maladjusted for any normal life.

If the child begins to practice self-abuse, he may grow utterly despairful. Not understanding the significance of what he does, he may come to think of himself as growing steadily weaker and weaker, as losing his right to decent adult life, as being a pervert, abnormal.

Now pessimism, which may result from the sin, is the worst possible state of mind for a boy who is trying to handle or cure this evil. If he thinks he's licked, he actually may be licked. If he thinks himself defective, that is disastrous.

While the matter should never be dismissed lightly, the real remedies must be kept clearly before the boy. He should be kept busy and happy. His free time should be filled with games and music and pleasant companionship. He should be so tired out at night that he will go promptly to bed. He may be allowed the habit of reading in the bathroom, even if this somewhat inconveniences the rest of the family, who may be delayed by his leisurely attitude.

The prevention and cure of self-abuse in a boy is simply an optimistic attitude toward the whole problem; high ideals of manliness; an exhaustion of the animal nature by lots of exercise, competitive sports, and pleasant recreation; the filling of his mind with music and hobbies and interests of every kind. Prayer and the sacraments complete the cure.

DIFFERENCES IN BOYS AND GIRLS

Between the ages of twelve and sixteen most normal boys go through a period of violent temptation. Tactfully —

without much actual discussion of the problem beyond the initial handling and the advice to choose a confessor who will give them time and gentle, patient, wise advice—the parents can guide them through their trials.

Girls are tempted too. But always it must be understood by parents that especially during these years their boy and girl are very different little humans. The girl sails through her adolescence sometimes with resentment, seldom with violent temptations. The boy is likely to have a period of stormy siege that beats against his body and makes of his soul a fiery tempest. Never is the difference between the male and the female clearer than during these years of physical change. That is why girls of that age will often be a joy and boys a trial, a nuisance, and a mystery.

If parents do understand this difference, their whole attitude toward their son will be marked with gentle understanding, high ideals, and a deal of patience and personal interest. They will encourage his love of sports, his desire to cultivate hobbies and to blow off steam. They will not even mind his loud voice and clumping feet. Wisely they will even be glad of these things, which exhaust the animal nature that might in a brooding, silent, too well-mannered boy result in fierce temptations and perhaps sins.

TEMPTATIONS NATURAL AND INDUCED

But both boys and girls should be made aware of the double aspect of temptation. For their own peace of mind they must be reassured that temptations of this sort, mental and physical, come to all men and women, even to saints. At the same time they must be clearly taught, and by example shown, that to arouse temptation deliberately is a very different matter.

Hence they must be shown that books that are evil will simply make life more difficult for them, will arouse and put on the savage warpath temptations which are already severe enough. The same is true of pictures that normally would excite any boy or girl.

Boys and girls must, as they grow older, be shown the clear difference yet close connection between temptation and sin. There are certain actions which nature designed to excite a man and a woman. Passionate kisses, close and fervid embraces, indecent exposure, immodesty in all its forms —these are in the plan of nature intended to arouse passion and throw the participants into a state of violent excitement.

SUBNORMALS OR LIARS

When young fellows or girls come to me and say, "Oh that sort of thing doesn't bother me, you know; I can kiss and pet and go to immodest shows and look at what you call dangerous pictures without being affected at all," I have one standard answer:

"Then I'm sorry to say that either you are a liar or you are subnormal. I sincerely hope for the sake of your future that you are a liar. For if these things do not excite you, if they leave you cold, if they do not do to you what God and nature meant them to do—excite you, stimulate you to desire, awake your passions—there must be something very wrong with your glandular development. Too I pity the person you marry. You will always be a cold, unresponsive fish and very dull, dreary and unresponsive to the normal love that should cement or rather fuse a man and a woman in marriage.

"If what you say of yourself is really true, you are a person for whom we can feel truly sad. Love will never really touch you. You will know only selfishness. You are a fore-doomed bachelor (or spinster); and I hope you will stay that way, without any approach to the normal marriage of normal people."

SEEKING TEMPTATION

Every young person—and that means youngsters too—approaching adolescence must be made aware that relatively few people really do go questing for sin. They do not say, "Today I shall be evil. Today I shall do something very wicked and obscene."

What happens is something very different. People go playing around the fringes of temptations. They run pleasant, quite fascinating, almost hypnotically delightful risks.

They say, "This is an amusing book; and while reading it, I'll not give consent to sin." Or "This is a delightful person —dangerous of course and likely to lead me into sin, but let's not worry about it. I'll handle all that part of it with perfect ease." Or "This is a show full of temptations for other people, but not for the exceptional person like me." Or "I'll look at this evil picture, always with the understanding that I shan't commit sin." Or "I'll do this and that and the other that should excite and arouse me. I'll enjoy the excitement and warm myself at the pale flames of passion, which I do not mean to fan to dangerous heat."

Occasions of Sin

Hence it is that parents must watch less for sin itself in their children than for the occasions of sin, the people and companions who might teach them sin or make sin easy for them, those objects of whatever nature which are calculated to stimulate the human passions to successful rebellion.

All this in the concrete is clear enough to understand.

Children must have companionship. Parents can do far more to select these companions than they themselves realize:

A. If their friends are the right sort, the children of those friends will be the right companions for their children.

B. If they pick the right kind of schools, they can cut down amazingly the whole problem of temptation. For a Catholic child there is only one kind of school, whatever the apparent advantages of other schools—a school with a Catholic faculty, atmosphere, and student body, from kindergarten to postgraduate work.

C. If parents afford their children the right kind of recreation in their own home and under their friendly and sympathetic eyes, the dangers of wrong entertainment and sinful pleasure are considerably lessened. The children should dance at home or in places that the parents suggest; they will not need to frequent the dance halls and dine-and-dance taverns. They should be encouraged to bring their friends home for a good time, with cold drinks and inexpensive food made available to them; thus they will find less excuse to run out for a coke-and-hamburger topped off by petting in a parked car.

D. Parents can early teach their children by sheer force of their own custom the safety and value of the foursome. A boy and a girl together may each be a danger to the other; that danger is cut to a good half if there are two boys and two girls together.

E. Parents can accustom their children to thinking of them, not as watchdogs or chaperons, but as friendly and animated participants in their good times. Parents as "cops" are unwelcome. Parents as gay and happy fellow "partiers" are quite a different matter.

F. It is a mistake for parents to go off and leave a crowd of young people in the house alone. Some adult should be there, just as a restraining reminder if for no other reason. When parents go off to the movies or to their own parties and leave the house and the children alone, some bright soul will think of kissing games, move on to post office—with a dark room for the post office—and then turn out the lights, to the bewilderment of the innocent and the delight of the initiated.

PARTIES

In that whole matter of games substitutions are essential. If for the children's parties the parents have provided no exciting, laugh-provoking, group-stimulating games, kissing games will inevitably be suggested to relieve the boredom or to bridge the gaps. Then if the parent frowns or forbids, he is merely roughhandling a delicate situation. His preventive games would have made all disagreeableness unnecessary.

CARS

The use of the family car is one of the things over which parents should exercise a wise vigilance. The boy who can have the car in unlimited fashion, going as he wishes, where he wishes, and with no report on his activities, is given the most powerful and efficient adjunct to temptation. Fathers would be smart to check the mileage before the boy goes out and after he returns. Too much mileage is bad; too little may point to an extensive period of parking.

IDEALS FIRST

Yet in all this we are faced with sheer futility unless the parents have built up in their children a strong love of and reverence for purity. Love must be shown to them as beautiful and sacred, and the love of the mother and the father is the strongest proof of this. Affection must be kept for the chosen few, not lavished on every chance partner of an evening or on anyone who happens to have a sudden impulse that says, "Isn't she attractive?" or "Doesn't he look strong and handsome?"

The creative act must early be recognized as the only source of human life, the instrument for the entrance of little children into the world. As such it is a noble and beautiful power. As anything else it is cheap, funny, humiliatingly animal, tantalizingly base. Purity must be seen, not as a weakness, but as the safeguard of that power for the strong future fathers and the pure future mothers of the race.

Around purity must be thrown all the charm of a happy home, of tender congenial parents, of love manifested toward the children by the mother and the father and among the children in the decent courtesy of the brothers and the sweetness of the sisters.

If all this is watched early, later temptations can be handled as they arise. The loud, seductive girl will be seen in her right light as a betrayer of motherhood and a traitor to human life. The vulgar, pursuing boy will be regarded, not as strong or clever or smart, but as an untrustworthy wastrel who is not fit to be directed toward the glorious power of fatherhood.

Loose conduct will seem a betrayal. Immodesty will be the sacrilege by which something essentially sacred is exposed to greedy, lustful eyes.

The children will be pure, not because they are afraid of the sad consequences of sin, but because they want to be worthy to cooperate with the Trinity of heaven in the completion of the trinity on earth, to give God His beloved sons and daughters and the human race strong men and innocent mothers of the future.

V

TOWARD CHRISTIAN (AND CIVILIZED) LIVING

Most adult human beings divide their lives into two sections: their professional sectors and their nonprofessional sectors.

During their professional lives they follow some line of activity in which they earn their bread by working in some way for those who come to them from outside their families. So a man may be a physician, a lawyer, a professional athlete, a merchant, a mechanic, a man of literature, a sailor, a soldier. A woman may be a teacher, a nurse, a social worker, a businesswoman, a doctor, an opera singer, an entertainer, a saleswoman, a factory operator.

In their nonprofessional lives however they are simply human beings, who live in homes, eat more or less pleasurable meals, take their ease or recreation, meet their families, read, relax, sleep, enjoy their hobbies, and try to forget the work by which they earn their living.

Anyone reading the above carefully will immediately demand: "Where do wives and mothers, who are also the family housekeepers, fit into those divisions?" They might with equal justice ask: "What about priests and nuns, who are engaged in their professions twenty-four hours a day?

PROFESSIONALS TWENTY-FOUR HOURS A DAY

Indeed if the question is asked, it becomes a welcome cue for the point I wish to make: Parents are of that peculiar group of people—like housekeepers, priests, and religious—who lead their professional life twenty-four hours a day in a three-hundred-and-sixty-five- (and sometimes six-) day year.

Even the teacher makes a clean division in his life; there are the hours when he stands before a class—guide, director, pedagogue—reaching out for the reluctant hands of youth. But parents are parents all the time, as priests are eternally priests.

Parents can never really slip away for a time and be completely at ease. They stand before their children during all the waking hours. For children never forget that these adults are fathers and mothers, and they never cease to scrutinize them as teachers, examples, guides, and the models of their developing lives.

That makes things very hard for mothers and fathers. It would be such a relief to feel that "today the children won't be watching me." It would be delightful to give an order and then go off, to return only when the injunction has been fulfilled by the obedient flock.

But such escape on the part of a father and a mother is not possible. Even when they slip away for a holiday, if they can manage it, either they have the children with them, or the imaginations of the children follow them with persistent interest: "I wonder why mother and dad went there? Do you suppose they drink more when they're away? Can you imagine dad's being sporty and trying to act young? I'll bet mother is acting kittenish, and she's so silly when she's that way."

CONSTANTLY OBSERVED

However much they may try to dodge it, parents know they are the observed of all the observers in their family circle. And great heavens, how children can observe! One little girl I know is afflicted with parents who give her prolonged doses of absent treatment. They go away for months at a time, leaving her in the care of hirelings. The child spends hours of her waking days following them about with her mind and imagining the worst about them. Their selfishness toward her is justification for everything that she is convinced they do when they are out of her sight.

The result of this being constantly observed however is not without its element of satisfaction. The parent is the one type of teacher who need say relatively little to the pupils. In fact speechmaking on the part of parents is always a little wasteful and more often than not a bit absurd and pompous. They teach without the formality of teaching. In a word they are most effective when their actions speak

louder than could any words and their conduct makes moral
maxims and windy exhortations absolutely unimportant.

By Deed, Not Word

The most effective parents are those whose teaching is,
not formal, but factual. They don't tell children what to
do; they show them by doing it themselves. They go slow
on precept and long on practice. They never say, "Do this,"
or "Be like me." They themselves do this and are such
charming and attractive and splendid people that their children would feel they were missing incalculably much if they
did not make every effort actually to become like them.

The Teaching of One Father

I was well on in years before I realized my father's influence on my life.

When after my mother's death, which followed my
father's by several years, I sat myself down to write her
biography, I found I could remember her vividly. But my
father was almost misty in my memory. He was a delightful
person, full of laughter and good humor, an utterly devoted
husband, and the kind of father whose pockets were always
bulging with gifts for us kids and who had all the time in
the world (despite a working day that took him away at
seven o'clock in the morning and returned him never before
eight at night) for his two boys.

Yet it was my mother's story that I wanted to tell and
tried to tell. All the while I did not notice the way that my
father kept creeping into the story, smiling, shy, never inten-
tionally intruding, but constantly there.

When the book was finished and being read, I became
amazed at the number of people who said, "Ah but I liked
your father. He was a charming man. Why don't you write
his story?"

At first I was completely puzzled. How had dad managed
to work his way into the story at all? Then when I sat down
again to see whether I could write his biography, I realized
that I knew too little about him to fill even a booklet. Finally
I looked back over what I had written—quite without know-

ing I had written it—about him. Only then at long length did it dawn upon me that the man whom I had seen only briefly in the evenings, who had spent his Sundays with us when we kids deigned to stay home, whom I had never regarded as a marked influence in my life, who in everything where the children were concerned yielded to his wife, my mother—that man had been a most powerful force in the shaping of my character.

I was far more like him (I sincerely hoped) than I had dreamed. Though I fell far short of his charm and goodness and gentleness and high regard for women and devotion to a job, still all those qualities had without any effort on his part graved themselves on my own soul.

He was the perfect instance of the silent force, example speaking without need of words.

No Spoken Advice, Yet . . .

For in all his life I can remember his giving me advice or even attempting to give me advice just twice. Once was after I was an ordained Jesuit priest. On this particular evening he walked to the Chicago elevated station with me; and in the most hesitant manner and broken sentences one could imagine, he talked of my mother. Coherently put, his little talk ran like this:

"She is very sensitive," he said. "We, her boys, you and James and I, are all she has. Nobody else really means much to her, you know, and that is why I think we have to remember how much of her happiness depends upon us. Your mother has given her life for us. No other woman in the world has been so good and so unselfish. Remember that. And remember that you can make her blissfully happy or utterly wretched.

"Oh I take it for granted that you'll never do anything criminal. You won't disgrace her. That's not what I'm thinking of. It's the little affectionate word that matters to a woman like your mother. It's the way you look at her and the things you say to her. It's kissing her affectionately just because you seem to want to. It's praising her a little. It's remembering to write her and to thank her and to be grateful for the dinner on which she spends so much time and thought.

"That's all, son. You understand. But do try to make her happy, won't you? You have been given a better training than either James or I. You know more about what should be done and what shouldn't be done. So you can do more for her, you know, a lot more. You will, won't you?"

Gallant Attitude

That was all. But in the fifteen minutes it took him to say it, he had gone through agonies of embarrassment and humility.

With the years I have contrasted my own attitude toward my mother with his attitude toward her, and I hang my head. Even that speech of his, broken and faltering and clumsy, wasn't really needed. Out of his life and conduct I could have written that summary as adequately as I now write it out of his half-formed sentences and hesitating, unfinished phrases. He did during all his life exactly what at that late date he was asking of me. I knew it. How could his little talk do otherwise than affect most profoundly my whole attitude not only toward my mother but toward all womankind, of which she was the example nearest and dearest to us?

A Talk That Never "Came Off"

The only other occasion on which he tried to talk to me I have often used in perhaps callous fashion as an instance of how not to approach an adolescent. A few things my mother had noticed in me—less respectful attitudes toward girls, the type of pictures I hung on the walls of my room, my sudden interest in a young woman whom she regarded, and rightly, as too swift and promiscuous for any boy's good—must have made her reproach my father for his neglect of his duty.

"You ought to talk to your son," she probably said. Of course he always tried to do whatever she asked.

She managed this morning to hurry home after Mass and leave us to walk home together. He had at that time been a Catholic for only a short time; I was just entering college, a self-conscious adolescent, very sure of myself, and very resentful of anything I thought gauche, badly done, clumsy, or intrusive.

In my salad-green conceit I considered that this interview rated all those painful adjectives.

During the long, harrowing walk home he tried to talk. I couldn't figure out what he had on his mind. He was usually bright, witty, and carefree, talking easily to us youngsters, and finding fun in everything. Now he was self-conscious, nervous, twitchy, walking faster than usual, and shifting from fast chatter to tense silences. I guessed there was something up and that I was involved in it somehow, but I couldn't get at what it might be.

It was not until we had reached the front porch that he assembled enough courage and words to make his speech. Then and there in one swift sentence he poured out his sense of futility. "Mother told me that I'd better talk to you about . . . well about anything you might like to know; so if ever there is anything that you'd like to ask me about, well just ask me about it."

He was purple with embarrassment by the time he had finished. I know that my face was burning with shame, indignation, and pity for the fumbling attempt he had made. Yet even before the final period had been slapped on the sentence, he was gone, the door yawning behind him for my reluctant entrance.

That was the first and only time that he ever even so much as tried to talk to me about the facts of life or any other moral or social issue.

WORDS NOT NECESSARY

As I say, I have often thought of this as a horrible example of how not to approach young people. Sometimes I have even quoted it as such. Actually and in all truth as a presentation of principles and as a method of winning the confidence of a youngster or of making him want either to talk or to listen, it was hopeless.

Now though I know something more important. I know that all his life my father had been preaching to me in eloquent example. He never talked about honesty; he didn't need to, for he himself was a transparently honest man. He never gave me panegyrics on the dignity of labor; he gave me the example of his infinitely laborious life. He did not sit down to go over with me the laws and customs that make for good manners or to explain various definitions of a gentleman; he was a gentleman, and I never saw him fail in any of the things that make for essentially good manners. He did not have to talk to me about purity; his pure love of my mother, his devotion to her, complete and unashamed, his own scrupulously guiltless conduct were far more impressive than all the eloquence in the world could have been.

Today I know that, silent as he was on all the issues that come under the heading of child training, convinced as he was that these things belong to the office of a mother, he was still a most powerful teacher and a most persuasive argument for right living and decent conduct.

He was a father who was a father all the time. He had no need to put into words what was already so clear and compelling and charmingly suasive in his own conduct.

PARENTS THEIR CHILDREN'S CHIEF TEXT

Parents must keep reminding themselves that their own personal characteristics are their children's chief textbook. Their own habits are the laboratory practice which the children constantly observe. The way they themselves speak and act make up the essential curriculum that far outweighs any lectures they might deliver or any heart-to-heart talks which, though they are precious and valuable, in the end merely reenforce the convincing argument of parental example.

THE CIVILIZED VIRTUES

There are certain virtues which tend toward the making of an orderly civilization and a pleasant national culture. They are virtues distinctly humane and hence necessary for proper human conduct. We cannot touch them all. So let's consider just some of the high virtues that are Christian and civilized and charming.

HUMAN AND HUMANE

Unfortunately children do not need to live long in this world of ours before they learn the immense amount of unhappiness which is brought about by the underhand conduct of their elders. They soon come in contact with dishonesty in any of its thousand forms. They see their parents take unfair advantage of their peers or their inferiors and hear them brazenly brag of this as of a major accomplishment.

Indeed we can wonder if the word honorable as an adjective is not an old-fashioned and somewhat ridiculous term. "Has the young man honorable intentions?" the father in the melodrama asks. And the audience is expected to think that rather funny. "He is an honorable man" is a phrase we rarely hear these days. Smart men, yes; successful or clever men, certainly; men who get ahead in life and make their way by kicking weaker men out of their path, assuredly: honorable men . . . what precisely are they?

HONOR AND HONESTY

Now it does seem important that parents should give a little thought to the ideas that underlie honor and honesty. Once in a course of lectures I·based much of my discussion of these words on the old English word decent. That word is simply the Latin participle *decens*. It means, "the thing to do," "the proper thing," "the thing that fits in with human nature."

Really back of that word decent could easily be packed the entire series of the theses in Scholastic philosophy that maintain that morality consists in our correct relationship to our human nature. Murder is indecent; charity is decent. Impurity is indecent; purity is noble and decent. Good manners are the decent mode of conduct; bad manners are inhuman and brutal.

So quite independently of whether or not one is going to be caught, one should be honest and honorable. That is the decent, the fitting, the human thing to do.

By way of clarification we could take the relationship of a man toward animals. Scholastic philosophers do not consider that animals, properly speaking, have any rights. For the moment we may skip their cogent reasons. But the fact that animals have no rights does not give a man the right to abuse animals. For a man to beat a horse unmercifully or to mistreat a dog may not in any way infringe on any rights, which the animal does not possess; but such conduct is inhuman, inhumane, indecent. It is simply not befitting a human being. It is an insult to his human character.

Now much of the conduct with which youngsters come in contact they instantly, or at least with slowly growing reason, recognize as inhuman and inhumane. They feel that conduct like that does not befit human dignity. They are shocked at the lies they hear their parents blithely spout. They are startled at dishonest conduct hidden under trickery. They are embarrassed to find their father without honor, their mother careless in matters of honesty. With their logical young minds they are quick to see the indecency of such conduct. They are startled and abashed.

Yet it takes only a short time of exposure to inhuman conduct to make the person exposed incline the same way. So if a child finds his parents dishonorable in large things, he easily becomes dishonorable in small things. He matches the family lies with his petty falsehoods. He sees in his parents major dishonesties that he can imitate with small thefts.

How fierce the need today for honor and honesty! We have lived to see dishonesty become the international law— or shall we call it lawlessness? We are so startled by the vastness of world-wide dishonor that we forget that it took its rise in the homes and hearts of individually dishonest, dishonorable men and women.

Let parents do some quiet, soul-searching thinking about their own sense of honor. Then let them see what they are passing on to their children.

HONESTY

Let's take a look at the noble virtue of honesty.

"Willie," cries the teacher, "you will stay after school and write, five hundred times, 'Honesty is the best policy'."

"So what?" thinks Willie, with deep irony.

He stays and writes the old puritan platitude four hundred and twenty times, but with a little readjusting of the numbers he makes teacher think he has written it the full five hundred times.

"Best policy, my eye!" laughs little Willie, and he hurries out to the waiting gang. For little Willie's father had long since taught him, though altogether unconsciously, that honesty is a sucker's game and that only fools pay honest income taxes or hesitate about a shady deal that involves no risks; and he brags about how he puts it over on the customer, the boss, a competitor.

NOT FRANKNESS

Youngsters today have come, as I have noted elsewhere, to confuse honesty with frankness.

"Whatever our other vices may be," the modern young boy or young girl brags, "you have to admit we're honest."

Which is precisely what I don't think they are.

They are perfectly willing to cheat in exams, to borrow the work of a fellow student, to beat the railroad company or the bus operator out of a fare if they can get away with it. They tell their parents shameless yarns about where they've been or what they've been doing. The boys spin for the girls the most unblushing insincere lines for which they hardly hope a credulous attention.

The girls put boys off or put them on with the flimsiest stories or excuses or pleas.

Yet all the time they brag that they are honest.

What they really mean is that about their faults, which they think rather smart, they will be quite candid—to people who haven't the power or authority to do anything about them.

So they brag about the amount of liquor they consumed and how stiff and "boiled" they became. They list the girls they've kissed or the boys they've strung along and incited to "make a pass" at them. They brag about how little work they did in school and how they cheated in examinations. They borrow freely from each other and are amused when they slip one over on a roommate or a pal.

They call this honesty, when all it is is the same sort of frankness one finds in the baldest and most unregenerate criminal. Bluebeard probably spoke quite proudly to his cronies about the women who were hanging headless in his bedroom closet. The gangsters of the prohibition era hired press agents to keep their crimes in the headlines. Immoral women use their loves and their divorces to get them better jobs on stage and screen. But they don't say, "We are honest people."

Now honesty cannot be taught in formal schools any more than it can be taught in reform schools. Honesty is the ingrained practice of a lifetime. It is passed on from father to son, from mother to daughter, or it never does reach the children.

The children should be made to feel that around them is the most scrupulous honesty. For honesty, like charity, starts at home, though emphatically it extends its influence beyond the home.

INDIVIDUAL FAMILY RIGHTS

A scrupulous regard for the rights of the members of the family should simply be routine practice. Homes are not communes. They are benevolent monarchies with a strong slant toward democratic ideals. Hence a sense of the right to private property should prevail. There are of course a great many things shared in common in a home. These belong to all and are used by all—the furniture, the books in the house library, the normal conveniences and necessities that must be shared in equality. Yet each member of the family has his own possessions—his clothes, luxury items, toilet articles, toys, books, sport goods, his room and its accessories.

Toward these things should be developed a real sense of ownership that should result in each one's respect for the rights of the other and no one's using another's possessions without permission being requested politely and granted explicitly.

In all this the father and the mother set the example. They have plenty of things in common. But each has his or her own belongings; and though ever so generous and willing to lend, each expects to be asked and expects to have to ask before there is any interchange. Mother does not take dad's golf balls without asking him or telling him—and she duplicates them later on. Dad does not take mother's Eau de Cologne to use as his after-shaving lotion until he first gets her leave.

Each has a great respect for the closets of the other, for the drawers in the bureau which contain personal possessions, for such minor but significant articles as brushes, handkerchiefs, jewelry.

Important as all this is to insure peace between the parents, it has the still further purpose of increasing in the children a respect for the rights of others, which underlies all true honesty.

If the owner of property that has been taken or borrowed is not at home, then he should in all fairness be told immediately of the presumed use. This is only decent. It is common courtesy carried into the family circle.

What the parents themselves practice, they demand of their children. The children are not allowed to take one another's clothes or toys or personal belongings without their being granted permission. Older sister may not borrow younger sister's gloves, which she has carefully put away; nor can older brother borrow younger brother's necktie. If anyone wants to borrow a badminton racket or a pair of tennis balls, a bicycle or a pair of skates, he does not do so without asking and receiving the leave.

A little honest consideration like this at home will ultimately go far to make the children honest when they are away from home.

Respect for the Rights of Others

When parents take their children out with them, they have a grand chance to inculcate honesty into them. They themselves protect the property of others or of the state with genuine consideration. A certain type of minor criminal common in all layers of society regards honesty as something that does not apply to any property other than that of the individual. So they will cheat a railroad company or steal flowers from the public park or bring home bushes they have furtively lifted from the county's roadside improvement project. They will put their feet all over the chairs in a hotel, to the destruction of the upholstering. They will in Pullmans use face towels to wipe their shoes. They will pilfer from a public restaurant a spoon or a teapot or an ash tray. Some will carry away from hotels towels and bedding and the cloth covers of dressers.

A hotel official told me that one of the hotel's biggest items of loss is brought about through the thefts committed by supposedly reputable guests. A hotel housekeeper in one of our nation's largest hotels said that the maids are instructed to swoop down on a room the minute it is vacated so that if any serious thefts have been committed the departing guest can be halted and his baggage relieved of its accretion before he gets too far away.

If children see this adult attitude toward property, their sense of honesty will soon atrophy and die. Honesty in such matters will prove a most powerful incentive to honesty on a wider scale.

Paying Bills

Children are keen about the stand parents take toward the payment of bills—keener than one might think. Taxes are something that can—with difficulty—be dodged. Time was when dodging the income tax was a great national sport, and fathers in the presence of their children bragged of the thousands they knocked off—as hunters might brag of the lions they bagged or bowlers of the scores they toppled—to the scandal of their children.

Parents who want their children to be honest will pay not only the large firms, which know how to collect, but the small firms, which can collect only with difficulty. A peculiar sense of furtiveness develops in a house when bills are contracted far beyond the family's ability to pay. Children sense their parents' dodging of bill collectors; and if it does not create in them a sort of dishonest shame, they may come to look on it as a game, which they continue to play all their lives.

Care has to be taken of such things as time payments. Children are amazed and shocked if they see furniture brought into the house and then carted away, or if the parents send them to the door to stall off the installment collector.

To live within one's income is a simple form of honesty that makes a lifelong impression upon the children. It is a great foundation for honesty.

Borrowing

My grandmother, who was born in Ireland but was thoroughly Americanized, hated the casual habit of borrowing. She loved to tell of the old Irish lady who continuously borrowed her neighbor's churn. Happily coming into a little money, she managed to get a churn of her own. So no longer did she have to beg the loan of her neighbor's. But it happened that the neighbor herself broke her churn one fine day. And when she called on her old borrowing friend for the brief loan of the new churn, the erstwhile beggar held up her chin in disdain: "Indade not," she replied. "I'll have yez understhand that I nather borrow nor lind."

Borrowing is at times necessary. Strict honesty about borrowed articles, whether from the family, from friends, from the general public, is important for the honesty of the children. If the children are sent next door for a cup of sugar or a double boiler, those same children should later return the cup of sugar or carry back the double boiler. If they borrow one of the neighbor's sleds or bicycles or lawn mowers, they must be watched until they return it—and in good condition.

Books borrowed from friends or from the public library become more than a trust and a charge. A friend of mine, knowing the way that books linger in the hands of borrowers, had a special bookplate made. In the center was his name and address. And around it was this significant motto: "Never think it too late to return this book."

OBLIGATIONS

One hates constantly to be dragging in personal reminiscences, yet one knows best the effect of conduct upon oneself. It so happens that my mother was honest to the point of fanaticism. To her an unpaid bill was worse than an unhealed wound. She refused for years to open charge accounts for fear that by month's end she might have run up more bills than she could afford to pay. Her honesty positively haunted us youngsters.

In our suburb on the outskirts of Chicago we had a pleasant custom of sharing the carriage that took us to our more formal parties. Two young men paid for the one carriage and brought their two young ladies safely and unmuddied to their destination. Later the livery delivered the bill to one of the two young men.

I frequently shared the carriage with Ed Kenny, glad enough to have someone to halve the bill with me. Once after using his carriage, I promptly forgot all about it. A small matter like a debt rests lightly on the soul of a young man of seventeen.

My mother waited two weeks without comment. At the end of that time, when we had returned from Mass one Sunday, she stood in front of me as I was relaxed and half buried in Sunday papers.

"I don't see how you can sit there like that, apparently without a care in the world. For that matter how could you look Ed Kenny in the eye when we passed him this morning on the street? And you owing him money for the past two weeks!"

"Oh," I cried, in complete vindication of myself, "I'd forgotten all about it."

"Catholics and gentlemen don't forget debts," she retorted.

"I'll take care of it next week," I said, turning back to the sports page.

"You'll take care of it right this minute. Put on your hat and walk over and pay him your just debt. I can't believe a son of mine could so utterly disregard simple honesty."

So I walked over and paid my three dollars.

If to this day an unpaid bill haunts me like Banquo's ghost, and if I have an amazed alarm when I see people wading into debt beyond their depths, I know whom I can thank for my purely involuntary reaction.

Honesty in Conduct

There is of course another type of honesty beyond mere honesty about money or property. There is honesty in conduct. Children have a quick perception of any trickery that exists in the family social relations. Yet on the supposition that children do not understand or have no sense of honest standards, parents will make their children fellow conspirators in arrant intramural dishonesty. The mother who uses the household money for unnecessary luxuries or for playing the races does not scruple to let the children see her trickery. The children are allowed to realize that the father is holding out on the mother or using money for his own selfish gratifications and vices.

Conspiracies With the Children

Parents have a way of forming conspiracies that actually involve the children. Says mother: "Now we're going to the theater and to lunch this afternoon, but don't tell your dad." Or dad: "You and I are going to slip off and see a ball game, but for heaven's sake don't let your mother know."

Nothing else delights the children more than this opportunity to play conspirators or smugglers in partnership with their elders. Nothing else could more quickly distort their sense of honor and honesty.

Honest Work in School

When the child enters school, the parents are wise if they insist upon his honest work in class. They are paying tuition, and it is a simple matter of honesty on the child's part to do a decent job. They are however foolish if they so ride the child that in his struggle to get marks beyond what he naturally could earn he is practically forced to cheat in examinations or borrow the work of others. Sheer fear of parental disapproval will sometimes make little cheats and sneaks and incorrigible borrowers of youngsters who would prefer to be honest but are afraid to face their parents' wrath.

Love of Work

Life is pretty terrible for the man or the woman who hates his work.

Yet all of us human animals have an inertia that can be overcome only by training on our part and on the part of those who bring us to maturity.

Happy the children whose parents have toward work a cheerful, Christlike attitude.

This attitude rests of course on high Christian ideals. God, the Christian knows, in that ideal which he contributes to his children, made the world only to turn it over to the management of His sons and daughters. Hence when a man or a woman works, he works with God Himself. He is by his work making the world a happier place to live in. He is assisting God to bring His magnificent plans to fulfillment. He actually—and possibly notably—benefits his fellow men. He makes the world a joyous, comfortable, attractive abode for his brothers and sisters.

Morning Offering

This attitude can be presented to the children as they are taught their morning offering. By this prayer the whole family offers to God the work of the day. Work cannot be offered to God unless it is in itself dignified and noble. Even if some particular job seems trivial, menial, and without apparent significance, it gains importance and dignity and value by the very fact that it is offered to God and because of the morning offering is done in collaboration with Him.

THE FATHER'S WORK

Eloquent beyond the need of words is the interest that boys feel in their father's work. Even a little child soon comes to realize that his father leaves the house every day because he wants to provide comfort and luxury for his family. The old rhyme about Baby Bunting whose father was off shooting rabbits in order to make of the fur a warm cloak for his child is the nursery presentation of this relationship of love to a man's job or profession. Intuitively children recognize that connection.

The boy watches his father's whole attitude toward his job. He likes to feel that his father enjoys his work. He experiences a childish pride if his father seems to regard his job as important, and he brags of this to his little playmates.

He listens to dad's conversation at day's end. If he is full of enthusiasm about his work, talks about progress and successes, has a humorous attitude toward the problems he has encountered, and seems to be on good terms with the people who are his associates, the child comes to think that work itself must be a lot of fun, and he looks forward to the day when he too will leave the house for a good day's labor.

It should not cause anyone surprise that doctors so often have sons who are doctors, and that a lawyer's son should go in for law, and that a father who is in a successful business has little difficulty inducting his child into it, or that a sailor's boys take naturally to the sea. For these men—the good doctor, the successful lawyer, the man who has done well in business, the sailor who loves his ship—pass on to their offspring a real love of the work they do.

If on the other hand the father complains, if he hates his job and shows that he hates it, if when he returns in the evening he is full of complaints about his boss, his customers, his general hard luck, he thereby creates in the consciousness of the children less a distaste for his particular type of work than a reluctance to face any work at all.

The Mother's Work

In exact parallel is the relationship of the mother to the daughters. The happy mother who loves her home and works in it cheerfully, without reluctance, surliness, boredom, or grudging, creates in the minds of her girls the happiest possible pictures of homemaking. The girls note with pride her interest in well-planned meals. They are aware of her concern about their clothes and proud of her skill in sewing. They see her increase the beauty of the house through her labor in the garden and her adding of new adornments proportionate to the family income.

Often they learn from her without formal instruction the art and practice of the budget. Indeed on the general principle that children like to do what their elders are doing, a mother is making a fine start when her little toddler "helps" her as she works in the garden, holds the chair when she hangs a picture, and a little later sits with her while she totals up her accounts and in woman-to-woman fashion talks over with her the finances of the house.

Children's Work in the House

As soon as they are capable of doing anything for themselves, children should be initiated into work around the house. I have known relatively few wealthy people in my life; but one family of my acquaintance, blessed with far more than average means, required every child to have a job in the house and to do it. Though the family income came from the candy business, the parents considered the children adequately rewarded with nickel candy bars.

So the mother—seldom the father in matters of domestic arrangements—assigns the tasks. Each child should be required to do a certain amount of ordering and tidying up of his own room. He or she should be expected, no matter how many servants there are, to pick up personal clothes, to keep apparel and closet in fairly respectable order, to assemble soiled laundry and to put the clean laundry away when it is returned.

Lazy Sons

I once met a wealthy family in which an only son was brought up to complete laziness and a masterly ignorance of his own wardrobe. He went away to school, his trunk filled with clothes, his pockets lined with money. Yet the bills for more clothes and yet more clothes kept coming home.

At Thanksgiving time the mother called to see him and returned to tell with delighted amusement how the "poor lad hadn't the slightest idea of how to take care of himself. He wore a shirt or a suit of underwear until it was soiled, and then he threw it into his trunk and bought another one. So there was his trunk packed to bursting with soiled laundry. The poor lamb had never even heard of a laundry."

I regret, but am not surprised, to report that he turned out to be a completely useless member of society and ultimately drove his father to drink and his mother to a succession of nervous breakdowns.

Jobs as Symbols and Training

The jobs that children are expected to do are certainly not going to be in every case efficiently done. Rather are these jobs symbols of the children's participation in the responsibilities of the house and a training for willing work in later life.

So when the family goes away for the summer and there is wood to be brought for the primitive stove, a son of the family should be assigned the job. And he does not swim or fish until that task has been completed. The girl has the task of making a certain number of beds. No tennis until this is done.

Rewards and Punishments

For the successful fulfillment of these jobs wise parents give small rewards. One excellent plan is to condition the week's spending money on the basis of the fulfillment of designated tasks. In this way the small allowance becomes, not a gift, but a salary paid for work accomplished. Thus the money takes on dignity and the moneywinner a sense of his own importance.

If on the contrary the work is not done, there is meted out a definite punishment.

"You did not bring in the wood this morning. Sorry but no swim for you this afternoon." . . . "I had to make the beds this morning; just so that you'll remember them hereafter, you are not going to the dance at the hotel tonight."

Work can be a horrible burden crushing the human soul. It can be a delightful participation with earth's creator in the management of that earth. Which attitude the adult will ultimately assume depends largely on the attitude instilled into the child during the days when work can be made a happy game, a chance to imitate mother and dad, a constructive habit, which, once acquired, lasts through life.

Respect for Authority

Democracy, as I noted before, is guaranteed only in a land which has a deep respect for authority. There can be no freedom unless people freely bind themselves to obey the laws. Any other way is chaos—or the highway down which the dictator walks to assume command over a disorganized and disillusioned mob.

So wise and truly democratic parents will maintain not only their own God-given authority but the authority of those who in some way have the right to command their children. Putting it flatly, let's say that the parents who have any real sense and any love for the children and their country will uphold authority even when it is in conflict with their children and perhaps oversteps slightly its just limits or seems to deprive the youngsters of some of their rights.

We'll explain what we mean by that as we go along.

Backing up the Other Parent

Before they come to any matter of outside authority, parents have to agree among themselves to back up each other's authority. A parent sins against authority, obedience, and his own children if he struggles for the right to control the child or tries to bribe him by being more lenient than the other parent.

Obedience is in the hands of both parents. Authority is their joint possession. If he or she wants his or her own authority respected, he or she will demand respect for the authority of both. If they wish anything like obedience, they will back up each other's orders. When each tries to dominate the child or to win him by canceling out the orders given by the other parent, what they are really doing is undermining all authority, their own included. One parent encourages the child to disobey or to trick the other parent, only to find out that the child has learned to despise all parental authority and to pay not the least heed to the orders of either of the parents.

Teachers' Authority

The teacher stands before the child as an important symbol of authority. As a matter of fact the parents themselves gave the teacher that right to command. When they transmitted to the teacher the part-time care of their child, they also transmitted to him or her for those hours their own authority. So the teacher is not just someone who, having no children of his or her own, decided to gather a few children of other people and wield a rod and a brief authority over them. He is a professional person with real authority, which the parents themselves surrendered to him and which the state at their command has sanctioned and approved.

Yet the world is full of parents who side with the child in every argument that involves the teacher. In fact they often prime the child to go back and start an argument with the teacher.

"So that old maid has been picking on you again, has she? Well, my darling, you don't need to pay the slightest attention to her. She has no right to make life miserable for you."

"Believe me, if she treats you like that again, I'll give her a piece of my mind."

"So he called you a liar, did he? Never mind telling me any more. I take it for granted that my son is no liar. Come along with me, and I'll take the hide off his back."

"The idea of a strong man like you browbeating this little kid. You've a grudge against my child, that's what you've got. You never did like him. And ever since he's been in your class, you've made life miserable for him. Well I don't intend to stand it any longer."

"I'm a friend of the mayor; and if you don't lay off my child, believe me I'll get your job."

The variants of that monologue could be continued for pages. Can't you just see the smug, complacent, delighted face of the youngster? He fixed the teacher. He went home and told his ma . . . or his pa . . . and they knew what to do. The next time the teacher wants to keep him in because he threw spitballs or corrects him for coming to school without any homework done, all he'll have to say will be, "Just wait till I tell my mother that you're picking on me . . . . I'll bring dad down to fix you." He'll have the teacher right under his thumb, with which he is even now metaphorically fingering his nose.

Side With the Teacher

Teachers are used to parents like that. They bear them patiently. Yet what a blow such parents strike at all authority, their own included! They are building up a spirit of successful rebellion that will someday explode in their own faces. They are setting a premium upon all disobedience and making insubordination the excuse for their patting the little rebels on the head.

I'd go as far as to say that even if the teacher is flagrantly wrong the parent should side with him or her just to safeguard authority. Most teachers have more than their share of provocation. They do not develop "picks" and grouches unless they have been goaded by the incessant annoyance of human mosquitoes or infuriating little child gnats. The presupposition can safely be that they let a dozen offenses go before they finally aim their corrective punishment.

If by some supposition the teacher is a villain and a conspirator against the peace and balance of the child, even then the worst possible example in its influence on the child would be to let the child be present at the interview. Side with the teacher when he is around. Then if you must, go and have it out with the teacher, far from the hearing and knowledge of the youngster.

Respect for Civil Authority

That same spirit of respect for authority and of obedience to rightly constituted government arises from the parents' attitude toward civil authority. Often at the family dinner table the seeds of real anarchy are sown. The most antidemocratic viewpoints are expressed, and in the consciousness of the children is built up a real contempt for those who by the arrangement of democratic procedure hold the consent of the majority and the power given the civil state by God Himself.

"Indeed I do not intend to support the Government with taxes. What do I get out of it? They can't collect; I'm too smart for them. I'll contribute nothing to the Government."

"You should have seen me put it over on that traffic officer. Did I tell him where he could go! . . . That President of ours is a fool and a scamp. If he says a thing is right, I know doggone well it's absolutely wrong . . . . The governor of this state is a crook and a scoundrel. He ought to be hanged . . . . Well if the party can get away with a little graft, who can blame the cook for licking his own fingers? . . . Oh yes; I believe in the rights of minorities; but I'm all for putting the Negroes . . . the Jews . . . the Catholics . . . anyone I happen not to like . . . in their place."

Children can get from their parents a respectful attitude toward all symbols of authority, from the policeman on the beat to the President on the nation's biggest battle wagon. From parents they can drink in an innate distrust and contempt for authority in all its forms, contempt that eventually blossoms in something like the nihilism of old Russia, the anarchy of Red Spain, the lawlessness of gangsterland.

The Authority of the Church

It is of course important to reverence the Church for supernatural reasons. As the Mystical Body of Christ it has a right to our obedience and loyalty. But here I am thinking only of the effect that a right or a wrong attitude taken within the family toward the authority of the Church has on the mind of the child.

To the child the Church is almost an abstraction. Father Kelly and Sister Mary however are clear and concrete embodiments of the Church the child must obey. So it is almost equally bad for a father or a mother at the dinner table to lash out at the Church's laws on divorce or birth control or a decent contribution to the support of the Church's institutions, or to make fun of Father Kelly, or to speak with contempt of Sister Mary. For children do not distinguish between the institution, its authority, and those of its representatives whom they know.

If dad says, "Don't pay any attention to Father Kelly; he's an old fool that thinks only of his own comfort and the Sunday collection," the children see their reverence for the authority of the Church smashed to bits. If mother says, "Dear me, Sister Mary is an ignorant woman. What bad manners! Really she has no business teaching children," the children decide that neither Sister Mary nor the Church, of which she is their nearest concrete symbol, is going to get obedience from them.

The personal fine qualities of the priest may not be outstanding. Sister Mary may not be the sort of teacher whose work professors come miles to observe. What has that to do with it? To the child's mind they *are* the Church. When parents undermine the authority or prestige of those representatives, they are undermining the authority of the Church itself.

Authority Is Delicate

For in all this training to obedience we must remember how delicate is the linking of all authority into its fragile unity. Man does not like to obey. Young or old he seeks any excuse to break from that particular section of the chain which binds his rebellious will. So when in the presence of children an attack is made upon authority, whether by a parent's undermining another parent, parents' siding with the child against the teacher, father's blasting the Government, or mother's slurring the Church, the fabric of obedience is weakened and the child's sense and value of authority get a blow.

Even in the Army the sternest top sergeant and the most experienced officers cannot do anything with the young anarch who within his home has learned to flout authority and to give his obedience only when it suits his convenience, his likes, or his whims.

Homemaking

After years of neglecting the home, the modern thinkers have come to realize that the home is the seat of the truest form of natural society and the citadel of democracy.

Catholic parents have for generations taught their children the art of homemaking. It has been one of their great contributions to civilization. On the model of that trinity on earth which dwelt in Nazareth they have tried to establish the Catholic home and family.

For the sake of that glorious tradition Catholic parents today must not forget that this age of efficiency apartments and FHA housing projects has not rendered obsolete their high duty and real privilege of teaching their children how to turn a house into a home.

Here as always the real lessons of childhood are learned through actual experience in the parental home. A fine home, be it big or small, elaborate and expensive or plain and "paid for like rent," is the lovely background against which to spend childhood and adolescence. The more real the home, the more surely it becomes quite subconsciously the model set up by the child for the home he means to build when he is adult.

Revolt Against Homelessness

On the other hand the lack of real homes during the last few years has caused a real throwback in the collegians with whom I have been working. In the main they came from families who lived in apartments rather than houses. Many of their parents rented instead of owned. Many of these parents had sacrificed part of the completeness of their houses in order to have an automobile for the family.

From these facts came the throwback: The collegians during their discussion of the question "What kind of home do you want to establish?" agreed that they wanted, when they were ready to found their own family, to live in a house rather than a flat, to own the house almost from the beginning, and — if need be — to think of a house before they thought of an automobile.

That child is very fortunate who is brought up in a house that his parents own. He gets a sense of security that arises from ownership even of a small city house and lot. He feels the charm of privacy that can be found only in a house. There he has elbowroom that is not possible even in the most elaborately expensive apartments.

Homemaking results of course from the kind of place that is the home and from the spirit that pervades that place. Children are quick to observe with approval the interest their parents take in their house. The purchase of a new house is of tremendous interest and concern to the youngsters. They love to listen while father and mother, happily engaged in planning to build, discuss the details of the new dwelling. They are alert while the furnishings are considered and arranged. They get a deeply etched memory of favorite chairs and comfortable lounges, of bookcases and their location, of the tables and what was on them. They are at their parents' elbows as the process of beautification goes on. They are proud of the garden and often interested in claiming some small patch of it as their own.

All this profoundly affects their attitude toward the house they will select for their adult years. They are very likely to plan it against the memory of the house their parents loved. That remains as the ultimate model.

Within the house the home is built around the unifying love that dwells there. So we can simply refer once more to the love of the parents for each other, to the love of the parents for the children and of the children for their parents, and to the love that is expected of the children among themselves.

Unity From Order

Homemaking depends upon more than just unity. There must be order in the unity. We have already discussed the assignments that should be given to each member of the family. When the family takes over a new house and the needs of the house have been duly considered, it is possible to assign jobs that will be more or less permanent. Sometimes the individual children will outgrow these tasks and pass them on to their younger brothers and sisters. Sometimes they are interchanged for the sake of new interest and to eliminate slovenly monotony.

Time Schedule

A wise family has a time schedule which is adhered to with sensible regularity. That word sensible is an important adjective, for it is a wooden household that sticks to its schedule, winter and summer, feasts days and fast days.

There should be a time for rising. For the observance of this the most important factor is the example set by the parents. Dad knows for instance that for a decent departure —preceded by rising, a bath, shaving, prayers, breakfast, and an unhurried farewell to the family—he has to rise at a certain time. Now in the "funnies" the adventures of some comic character's upsetting the peace and calm of his suburb as he dashes for the bus, dripping garments, coffee, and kisses for the family, may be amusing. Actually by his completely disorderly habits of rising he is setting a horrible example for the fictional child.

Rising Time

Rising time should of course be adapted to the age of the children and their hour for retiring. It should however allow time for leisurely washing, prayers, the care of nature's important necessities, breakfast, and a bit of elbowroom before departure for school or the main pursuits of the day. Hence the exact time should be carefully set by the parents.

As for calling the children in the morning, the parents should have a simple technique: The children are called loudly, emphatically, and with the assurance that they have heard. But they are called just once. No more. If they oversleep, it is an offense that is punished by their being deprived of something they wanted to do. Mother however does not allow herself to be constituted a minute gun going off repeatedly until the children have finally been bombarded out of bed.

The hotel phone operators who ring the call bells in the morning are often instructed to ask, "Do you wish one call or two?" One call is for the adults whose parents taught them how to rise without a lazy submerging into a second slumber. The second call is for the people who never pay any attention to the first call and know they will be tormented to rise, until in sheer desperation, sore, irritated, and in a bad mood to start the day, they are finally jimmied out of bed.

The family that is learning order as well as unity then is called just once. That call comes exactly at the right time. The child does not reason from experience: "Oh that call means I still have fifteen minutes; mother calls me early to allow me an extra quarter of an hour's sleep." Seven o'clock means seven o'clock. The whole family knows it and acts accordingly.

All the family is allowed a latitude of course, as on holidays, when sleep is prolonged. But even there order prevails. It is announced to the children that either "You may sleep until you wake in the morning," or "You may sleep until nine o'clock, when I shall call you."

PROMPT RETIRING

I was visiting some time ago a family blessed with five charming little girls. They were exquisitely mannered. They were friendly and sweet, though you had the sense of the order that marked their lives. Each had her job and did it. One of the youngsters set the dinner table. Two of them disappeared after dinner to help with the clearing away. The two eldest did the dishes while their mother sat and talked with her guests.

At eight-thirty we were in the midst of animated discussions, with the five little girls much involved. "It's time for you three youngest to go to bed," said the mother, quietly. Without a single sign of argument or wheedling they rose, kissed the family, shook hands with the guests, and retired to their rooms.

That was a perfect example of the orderly lives that should be arranged for children if they are to be well mannered.

MEALS PROMPTLY

Meals in the well-knit family are set for a definite time, and a time convenient for all. Without fail they take place at that time. The parents themselves take the lead by being on time. The children are expected to be home unless the most valid of excuses can be offered—and then only rarely and most convincingly.

Children will never have any sense of orderly living if they are permitted to straggle in at all hours, holding up the meals, causing the meat to become overdone, the vegetables to become soggy, while with no excuse or the most flimsy ones they have allowed anything that captured their fancy to derail them or hold them at way stations.

FUN TOGETHER

Home is a compound blend of love, affection, unity, order—and enjoyment. Most of youth's normal enjoyment belongs with first right in the family. Much of it can be shared with those guests who come or are invited.

If people really love one another, they sincerely enjoy being together; and if children are early taught to regard their homes not merely as supply depots where they take on food and change hats but as centers of their recreational life, they will not be inclined to escape their homes so soon as their wings are strong enough to bear them.

LAUGHTER AT THE DINNER TABLE

Recreation and enjoyment begin at the dinner table. There the day is threshed over, or—to paraphrase from memory someone's figure of speech—the shining marbles of the day are pulled out to be rolled about by all the family.

Laughter should be easy. Each one should be given a chance to take his part, and the adventures of the child of subkindergarten age should be given their proportional place with the really important business deal about which father wants to brag.

GAMES AT HOME

A well-cemented home has its games, possibly its game room, certainly its intramural tournaments. A ping-pong or table-tennis set will hold a family at home and bring in the neighbors.

Parents owe it to their children to teach them the rudiments of card playing. Once they have mastered the simple games, they will move on to more difficult ones, always with an improvement of that social asset known as card sense. Dart boards are now moving out of the English pubs and into the family living rooms. I know one family that can get all the members together to play domestic bingo at five cents a card.

FAMILY MUSIC

In the living room music will bind the family in a unity that is notably delightful. How wonderful if the children have learned to play musical instruments that make possible their own small orchestra. Families love to rally round the piano and just sing — loudly and with a sublime lack of restraint. The victrola can serve as a binding force if each contributes in turn his records and plays impresario as well as audience.

CHILDREN ARE WELCOMED

The child must have a clear sense of his place in the home. He instinctively recognizes whether or not he is welcome. He likes to be made to feel that he is, not a nuisance, a pest, a disturber of the peace, but a pleasant addition to the family circle, with something to contribute to the family life that is agreeable and happily acceptable.

Children should be encouraged to take part in almost everything. The horrible old principle that children should be seen and not heard has no place in the business of training a child to love his home. What did the author of that proverb want? A house full of deaf-mutes? English children were often trained, I believe, to be inarticulate in the presence of their elders. Perhaps that accounts for the grimly silent men and the terrible teapots of women who fill the pages of English literature. The poor kids were bottled up until they lost the power of speech or until they fairly exploded in an "Old Faithful" of words.

NOT THE SOCIAL CENTER?

It is however treason to the family peace and false to the child's own development if he is elevated to the center of the family life. Adults have a right to protest when babies are made the hub of the evening, with the adults like helpless spokes swinging about them. While children should be made welcome and fitted into the pattern of a complete family, they are not the dominant factors in a family evening. For they have little to say, and don't know how to say it, and can actually contribute to the entertainment only one or two simple gestures which, once seen, need not be repeated.

While the upper-class English system of walking the children through the living room, muzzled against speech and handcuffed to a governess, may produce a race of stone images or babblers, the American system of throwing the adults to the children produces a lot of tiresome little egoists. The children get an entirely false sense of their own importance. Certainly the peace of the family and the cementing of family unity won't be improved by the outcries and athletic exhibitions of infants on parade.

GUESTS

The art of homemaking includes of course the correct treatment of guests. I'm going to ask for more time on this somewhat later. Just now let's merely touch a few points important to homemaking.

First of all all guests should be met by all the family. There is no need for the children's lingering after the introductions, when they would much rather be playing Indians than listening to Miss Longwind describing her operation. But merely as a matter of the participation of all in the life of all, the children should be brought in to meet adult visitors, as the adults should come in to meet the guests of the children. No one member of the family likes to be kept in exile while the rest of the family is entertaining friends.

Guests should be casual rather than formal. By that I mean that frequent callers, old and young, who just drop in and out, play a game or two, take part in a bit of conversation, touch the family circle on the rim and are gone again are more to be encouraged than are guests for whom there must be long preparation, elaborate plans, and a studied party. A real home is a place to which friends come easily. They do not need an invitation for precisely this day or evening between the strict limits of this hour and that one. They come; they are welcomed; they play a brief part in the life of the family; and they are gone till the next time.

FOOD AND DRINK FOR THE GUEST

For their entertainment and to train the children to hospitality, almost any family of even moderate means can have soft drinks in the refrigerator and cookies on the pantry-shelf. Food and drink are great strengtheners of friendship. Easy access to them is one of the signs of a home ruled by liberal-minded parents with the joy of their children in mind.

When the guests have gone, they are spoken of and remembered with kindliness. If parents see flagrant failures in guests, conduct that should serve as a warning to the children, they are wise to point them out, but always gently and with what excuses they can find.

After the guests are gone, the children should not be initiated into a massacre of the now-absent. Parents are wise if they supplement their face-to-face welcome of guests with absentee charity. The receiving of guests is a great lesson to the children. Charity to all is an important element in homemaking.

VI

PARENTS AND THEIR AUTHORITY

Perhaps the reason that so much of the world has swung almost without a protest into the grip of the tyrants is that the vast majority of us humans would rather be ordered than give orders.

Of course there are those humans—a great number of them—who just delight to boss other people around. They like responsibility. They enjoy snapping their fingers and watching the other chap jump. They are either small *Fuehrers* in their own right or just good and wholesome people who are sincerely convinced that the world would be a better place if they themselves and people like themselves took care of the majority of mankind, told them what to do and when to do it, fed them their medicine, supervised their recreation, handed them their thoughts all carefully predigested, and picked out exactly the right persons for them to marry.

If however all the American citizenry were to be assembled in one spot, it would be seen that the group that does not want to give orders or be responsible for the other fellow outnumbers about ten to one the group that likes to do the bossing. Even those who have imagined it would be fun to pull the strings and watch 'em jump soon become bored with it—the opportunity having presented itself. In our heart of hearts we have a deep-seated conviction that the business of taking care of ourselves is a man-sized job. Anyhow not much liking the way we have ordered our own lives, we have a genuine humility about our ability to order the lives of the rest of mankind.

Reluctant Authority

That characteristic American reluctance to assume authority, that preference we have to vote for officeholders rather than be officeholders, that historic inclination to hand over to someone else the job of governing the country while we do the really important things like making money or listening to the radio or going for a ride in the country or playing golf or sitting down with a detective novel in our hands has made even the American parent reluctant to admit that he has authority over his child. He would much rather say, "Please" than "Do this." When the school offers to take his children off his hands and do the ordering for him, he is frankly overjoyed. He wishes his parenthood could be confined to his loving his children and making life easy for them. He hates to give orders at all.

To cover up his hatred of that occasional necessity, he is prone at rare intervals to play the stern parent, blustering to hide his embarrassment, shouting to cover his reluctance, and hoping that the children will want to do his bidding anyhow so that his obviously ineffective authority will be spared the humiliation of being wasted on the desert air.

No Escape From Authority

Yet parents cannot escape that exercising of authority. Indeed a well-ordered home is impossible without that authority. Children are deprived of enormous character training if their parents are either unwilling to give orders, shaky in their whole grip on authority, changeable and "jittery" about what they want from the children, and in the end given to shrugging their shoulders with a helpless, "Oh I can't do a thing with these children of mine!"

Children themselves miss the firm hand and the reasonable control. In that they are once more like any high-spirited animal. Get on a horse and let him know you're the master, and he enjoys taking you for a canter. But if you aren't his master . . .

The last time I mounted a horse was when I was on our Jesuit-directed Indian reservation in Wyoming. The Indian boys saddled one of the mounts in the big corral, held the horse's head carefully while I got aboard, and then with a sharp slap administered to the horse's flank gave him his head and me the helm. The mixed figures match my mixed emotions. Following the fashion I had noted among the better western-film stars, I headed the horse toward the gate of the corral. But it hadn't taken more than a dozen yards for the horse to discover that for once he was being ridden by an equestrian who didn't know what it was all about. So he laid back his ears and in his equine brain concluded swiftly, "Watch me put this chump in his place."

He did. We got to the gate of the corral, but he backed away from it and began to run around the fence. I got him to the gate again; once more he flatly refused to go out. Time and again I maneuvered him to the opening; but he knew who was boss, and he had no intention of taking a jaunt with a man of my weight atop him out over the lone prairies.

To make the long story of my humiliation brief, I never did get him out of the corral. After forty-five minutes of futile coaxing, persuading, and a bit of restrained beating, I knew who was master—a thing he had known fifteen seconds after I'd mounted him. So I reluctantly dismounted and turned the horse back to his Indian caretakers. If ever in history a horse looked down a contemptuous nose at his rider, it was the horse who had beaten me utterly and who now strolled away with an air of, "Did I put one over on that tenderfoot!" He'd done it, all right.

Slipshod Parents

Many a time that I've seen parents struggling with their children, I've thought of myself and that horse. Maybe it's just as well that my parenthood is confined to theory and the spiritual fathering of the children of other parents. Maybe I'd handle them no more successfully than I handled that smart little Indian pony.

Yet I repeat: Children do not like a slipshod parent who guides them with a loose rein and a hesitant lack of control.

"Please Give Me Orders"

Some years ago into the orbit of my concern swept a young college woman. She was the daughter of extremely well-to-do parents, whose idea of child culture was very simple: "Give the girl a good home, but send her away from it to an expensive Catholic school that will take care of her. Give her plenty of spending money; that will prove that you love her. For the rest commend her to God in your night prayers, and trust to luck and divine providence that she will turn out to be what you want her to be."

When I first met the youngster, she had—beyond her tuition and school bills—about two hundred and fifty dollars a month spending money. She possessed in addition an immediate desire to become engaged to a young West Point cadet with whom she had danced on three occasions and all the knowledge of life that you'd find in one of the Dionne Quints. She'd been everywhere, but she'd got little out of it. She treated classes like relaxation periods during which to catch up between week ends. She was as untrimmed as the hedge that grows around a haunted house.

Some queer quirk of youthful interest made her fairly throw herself into my obedience. She demanded that I order her about. She insisted that she was going to report to me on everything she did, everywhere she went. I was living in the midwest; she was in a school a thousand miles away. I should not be able to see her more than twice a year, but she insisted that even at that I could give her orders and she would follow them obediently.

For a time I turned into a tough parent. I made her give up the ridiculous idea of becoming engaged at the age of seventeen. I insisted that she do well in class; I had the principal send me a duplicate report card, which I solemnly signed, reported on to the school, and, when it was not properly satisfactory, used as excuse for my laying the delinquent scholar low. I "hopped" her by mail when she did silly things, and I insisted that her week ends be sane and reasonable and not a mad succession of sleepless evenings and crazy orgies of shopping.

THEY LIKE TO BE BOSSED

At the end of about three months of this, I received from her a letter which I offer to parents for their thoughtful consideration. The girl wrote:

"I'm out on the week end I wrote you about. It's been fun, but no smokee, no drinkee, no neckee. Though we were out late, everything was on the up-and-up. Now I'm home with Margaret, reporting in to you.

"I wonder if you know how much a girl loves having someone to report in to, and how much it matters to a kid to feel that she can expect to be 'hopped on' if she doesn't behave. If my parents had only waited up for me . . . 'hopped' me when I didn't do what they thought I should . . . been interested enough to care that I was out late . . . loved me enough to bawl me out . . .

"Please keep it up. Make me come in early. Make me report what I am doing. 'Jump on' me when I don't report. It means just everything in the world to know that there is someone willing to be that much interested."

I was giving her by long distance testers the precise control which she deep down in her heart would have loved from her parents and which subconsciously she had always known she missed.

American parents must remember that they have that God-given authority, which, as I have insisted before, they cannot shirk or pass on to someone else. All the love they show their children is so much sand piled around a building if there is not first the strong steelwork of authority demanding obedience to reasonable love-inspired commands.

AUTHORITY BELONGS TO BOTH

We must remember that both the father and the mother share the job of parenthood. Authority is vested in both, though primarily it rests with the father as the head of the family. If the two labor together in the forming of their children and share their authority in the single purpose of bringing up strong, well-trained, self-controlled, and splendidly disciplined children, then there is family unity resulting in youthful strength.

If the father gives the example of the masculine virtues and the mother that of the feminine virtues, and if both unite in the commands that make the house a civilized place to live in, the parents have gone a long way toward making their children complete and in measure perfect human beings.

ORDERS SHOULD BE CLEAR

There is an art in the giving of orders, and parents should learn that art. Before doing anything else, they might try to recall the kind of orders they liked—and still like—versus the kind that left them irritated, foggy, completely at sea. If over them even now there is someone who is in a position to give them orders, his well-given orders might be a standard, his badly given orders a warning.

It sounds almost silly to insist that in the giving of orders parents should be clear. An order that people do not understand is no order at all. So when parents mumble their orders under their breath or express them in words the child doesn't understand, what right have they to be irritated if the order is not obeyed? All of us at some exasperating time or other have received orders from someone who shot them out of the corner of his mouth or left before the commands were half finished.

A secretary once told me about a boss of hers who would come in from luncheon, rush through her office, and over his shoulder cry, "Get me a ticket on the afternoon train."

There were — conservatively speaking — fifty afternoon trains in that particular city. So at once she got him on the interoffice phone.

"Afternoon train to where?" she asked, mildly.

"New York of course," he roared, as if New York were the only city on the map and a fact any moron should know. He rang off immediately. That information did not help much, since there were not less than ten afternoon New York trains on three different railroads.

"What line?" she began. To which he shouted the name of the line and again rang off before she could ask about the time.

So with all the patience she could muster, she got him again and only after a series of cross-questions obtained the information which he should have given her when he tossed the initial order.

Have you met people of that type? Who hasn't?

Are parents sometimes like that? Ask the poor child who after having received a slovenly issued order stands utterly bewildered about what to do or how to do it.

POORLY WORDED ORDERS

My own most vivid recollection of an order of this sort must be laid, not to parents, but to a priest. That mother and father of mine always gave me orders in words of one syllable and with a clarity and comprehensiveness that left me no easy "out."

This particular young curate was different.

I was in third grade, but I was large for my age. I had just been transferred to the parochial school from a public school. As I walked down the corridor one day, this young priest stopped me.

"Go up to the sacristy," he said, "and get me . . ."

He uttered a word that might as well have been Hindustani, for all I made of it. I had however a perfect excuse for not doing anything about it.

"Father," I explained, "I'm not an altar boy."

"What difference does that make?" he demanded, a little impatiently. "Trot up and get me that . . ."

Once again he hit me over the head with the unrecognizable word.

Well I'd been trained to regard a priest's word as law. So taking it for granted that the mere command would give me a sort of infused knowledge or some great good luck, I made my way to the sacristy. I'd never been in a sacristy before; and as far as I could see, it was as full of strange, unknown objects as a drugstore shelf. Somewhere in the midst of all those objects was the one unknown thing for which I had been sent. Which was it?

My eye suddenly lit on what seemed the door of a safe; it was slightly ajar. Some childish impulse made me decide that beyond that door was precisely what I'd been sent for. I opened the door, reached in, found something in a cloth bag; I took it out carefully and with thumping heart carried it back to the young priest. I didn't know what I was supposed to get. I didn't know what I actually had got; but at least it was a token of my good will and obedience, and perhaps God would turn it into the object of my quest.

When I found the priest, I held out the cloth-covered object hopefully. He looked at it in horror and fairly snatched it from my hand.

"You're a stupid, bad boy," he cried, in real dismay. And he dashed back to the sacristy with what I now know was a ciborium in a chamois bag. At that minute though all I knew was that I didn't know what I'd done, as from the beginning I hadn't known what I was supposed to do. I was hurt and indignant; I felt completely abused; and I was disgusted with the world of adults who sent children on wild-goose chases without even explaining to them what a wild goose looked like.

Careful Directions

The wise adult, especially the wise parent, makes sure that when he gives an order the child knows the words he uses and is clear about what is wanted, when it is wanted, and —if that is important—how the order is to be carried out.

"Get me a loaf of bread," says the mother, "when you get around to it." Well children never get around to anything. And if two hours later she asks, indignantly, "And where is that loaf of bread?" the child really has the just though quite unacceptable excuse that the order didn't mean a thing.

"Run to the drugstore and get me some potassium cyanide," says the father. The last two words completely escape the youngster. Even if he knew what they meant, he still wouldn't know how to get poison from a druggist. His father has sunk back into his paper, his work done now he has issued the order; the youngster drags himself to the druggist, wondering if he can ask the druggist to name over all the things on his shelf until he happens to hit on the article wanted.

Not Minor Servants

No child should be turned into a sort of minor servant. Yet parents do that too readily. It is quite too simple for adults to sit back and dispatch the children hither and yon on necessary and unnecessary errands. The children quite rightly resent it.

Children, with their young legs and tremendous vitality, should naturally be trained to do small errands for their elders. But it is one thing on occasion to ask a child to do an errand and another to keep him shuttling back and forth as an unpaid messenger.

"Darling, run up to my room and get me the scissors . . . . Will you trot down to the tennis court and see if I left my sweater there? . . . Run out to the kitchen and fetch mother a drink, will you? . . . Is that my pipe over there on the table? Just get it and hand it to me . . . . How about chasing up to my room and bringing down my slippers? . . . I forgot the paper tonight. Here's some money; run out to the store and buy one—and bring back the exact change."

Any one of these orders is in itself fully justified. Children should be trained to a politeness and unselfishness that consider the comforts and needs of their parents. But an incessant barrage of orders that ship them about like page boys in the Senate is clear indication of parental laziness and lack of organization.

ORDERS THAT INTERRUPT

Especially are children justified in resenting these constant orders if in addition to their being frequent they interrupt the activities to which children have a right. In the life of every child should be periods of play which he can regard as his own. Nothing else is more likely to inspire him with resentment of orders or with a real dislike for authority than recurrent interruptions of his legitimate play.

The bases are full; little Willie has just stepped up to bat, his whole determination bent on knocking the ball over the fence. The fate of the "Little Catamounts" rests with his bat. Then from the family back door comes a peremptory, demanding voice:

"Wil-lee! Come here right away. I want you to go to the store and get me a cake of yeast."

No wonder Willie shudders at the sound of his mother's voice. No wonder he is fuming when he comes to her. He is convinced that a little more system around the house would prevent her running out of yeast in the ninth inning with the bases full and the score four to two against his team. And in that he may be right.

Orders That Tax Memory

Orders have a certain element of annoyance about them when they demand a strain on the memory. My own dear mother had the habit of giving me an errand to run "on the way home from school." The events of the school day were always engrossing to me. They drove everything else out of my mind. I had the gift of concentration, and I worked hard at whatever I was doing. So by the end of the day any order that had been given me in the early morning—"Buy me a spool of thread that matches this one" or "Be sure to pick up a loaf of bread on your way home"—had been completely knocked from my memory. Oh I was perfectly willing to trot back and complete the unfinished business. But it really is asking too much of youthful concentration for a child to remember a trifling order for some seven busy, exciting hours.

No Humiliating Orders

Parents can well consider the advisability of asking children to do things which children find humiliating. Of course it will be to the good of their character development to overcome this reluctance. But does an order that shames a child improve obedience?

My mother must again provide the example. I had the usual youthful fear of seeming to impose on people. And for some reason I regarded it an imposition to present a large bill when I was paying a small debt. In that day storekeepers did not keep a lot of money on hand. So often they didn't have change for a ten-dollar bill—especially didn't they have it if the one who presented it happened to be a youngster they could wave away.

Yet in order to break a bill, my mother would send me to the grocery store with a ten-dollar bill and tell me to buy some five-cent article.

It took all the courage of my youthful soul to go through the ritual of saying, "Please give me a package of crackers," and then proffering that "big bill." I expected to be told to make my purchase elsewhere. I even should not have been surprised if the storekeeper had tossed me and my impertinent intrusion on his cash drawer out into the street.

There are orders that boys just cannot abide—anything for example that they regard as sissy. Many boys—though not all—hate to be sent to the store to buy anything feminine, even a spool of thread, a package of safety pins, or a filler for mother's compact. They hate to be told to do things they regard as the office of a girl. Willingly will they mow a lawn if they are at all well brought up; but they blush at and hate the idea of running a carpet sweeper or dusting a room. This is an extreme case: The boy would regard as normal an order to beat the rug hanging on the line and as altogether out of dignity a command connected in any way with dressmaking.

Say "Please"

Parents do not lose caste or weaken their authority when they precede a command with, "Please," and follow its execution with, "Thank you." Many a child has a queer but altogether understandable human instinct that makes him utter, far back in his throat, "I don't mind doing it; not a bit. But why can't they say please when they ask me?" Any adult who has had to take orders without the soothing lubricant of good manners knows exactly how the child feels—and girls are as quick to resent the "un-pleased" command as are boys.

. . . and "Thank You"

As for "thank you"—that is a wonderful way to make authority not only respected but loved. "That was a good job you did; thank you very much . . . . I'm grateful that you took care of that so promptly." The child smiles. The parents smile. The order has been forgotten in the child's pleasure of having done something for an appreciative elder.

Punishment When Deserved

The obverse of this spirit of gratitude is of course the clear and proportionate punishment meted out for authority flouted and orders disobeyed. Children are only a little less thoughtless than their elders. How we oldsters need constantly to be reminded—by the law, the prick of our conscience, the supervision of those who employ our services—of the things we have neglected or completely forgotten to do!

So the connection of an order obeyed with a proportionate reward or the failure of execution with a proportionate punishment will be a strong nudge to the memory as well as an effective threat to the recalcitrant.

"You've done your work well this week; I'm delighted. We're all going to the movies tonight."

"You simply disregarded my plain wishes in this matter. Sorry but you are not going to the show this evening."

The Punishment of Loss

Whatever may be said for spankings as punishment for very young children, it is my conviction, based on what little experience I have been able to gather, that the far more effective punishment is the depriving them of things they want or want to do.

"You were downright disobedient in this particular case. You can't go out with the rest of the children this evening. I dislike to do this; but since you seem not to want to do what I ask, I just can't let you do what you yourself want to do."

Depriving youngsters of the things they love to do (never of essential food or other necessaries of life) is the best possible sanction for obedience. It does no slightest physical harm, yet it makes perfectly clear the parents' intention to be obeyed. That procedure is as effective with young people in college as it is with the little five-year-old.

No Reasons Given

Orders pertaining to obedience to parents really belong in a realm that is beyond the reach of discussion, wheedling, parental capriciousness, or favoritism.

For the ordinary orders that are given, no reason need be assigned. For extraordinary orders that are unusual and that demand perhaps more than customary obedience, a reason may well be given.

So "Turn off the light and go to sleep" needs no long explanation of the value of sleep nor vivid examples of what happens to children who stay awake nights and don't get their proper rest. This holds for all the normal rules by which a well-trained child lives; it is not necessary to explain why he must eat everything that is placed before him, why he mustn't whine, why he must practice decent good manners, and why he must go to bed at a certain hour.

Unusual Reasons

As the child grows older, he is dignified by his parents' offering some reasons for unusual orders. "You are going to bed earlier tonight because daylight saving starts tomorrow and we lose an hour's sleep . . . . I don't want you to play in that park because you have to cross unguarded railroad tracks in order to get there."

Without Discussion

If a reason is given, there should normally be no discussion.

Now it may be that the reason is not valid; the child knows something that cancels that reason. In a well-ordered house the child may present his counterreason.

"But, mother, I don't cross the tracks to go to that park. There is one place where the street is below the tracks, and I always go that way."

Presenting a counterreason respectfully is one thing; arguing and discussing the value of the parents' reason is quite another. That sort of debate is unpardonable. "Oh, mother, don't be silly; I know how to cross tracks. All the kids cross tracks. Don't be so scardy-cat, mother. Nobody ever gets hurt there."

Anything of this kind is destructive of well-ordered authority.

Real, Not Fake Reasons

Whenever a reason is given however, parents must be sure that it is the real one. Little children may be fooled into eating their carrots by the promise that carrots will give them curly hair; older children will not be taken in by a fake reason.

If parents give fake reasons for their refusals or orders, then they take the chance of the youngsters' removing the reasons. Little daughter wants to go out with some newcomers in the block whom her mother doesn't approve of. Mother doesn't want to give the real reason for her refusal. So she says, "No; you can't go. It's chilly, and I haven't your winter clothes out yet." The child disappears. Minutes later she reappears fully clad in her winter clothes. She had gone up and got the clothes out of the trunk and put them on. "Now can I go, mother?" she demands. The mother is stuck with a false reason on her hands.

This danger holds especially with older children. If no reason is given, they have no barrier to remove, no way of justifying their disobedience or twisting their parents their way. If they are given a false reason, they despise their parents. If they are given a true reason, they may go out and get this removed.

"No, daughter; you can't go out tonight. I don't want you traveling in the streetcars late at night."

Daughter listens to that reason; the real reason is that mother wishes her to stay home and study. Daughter calls up friends. In five minutes she is dressed and ready to go out.

"It's all fixed, mother. I shan't have to travel in the streetcars. Bill is taking me in the family car."

Again mother is stuck.

Wheedling and Whining

Along this same line is the whole matter of wheedling. Even the youngest child learns whether or not he can wheedle his parents out of an order or by whining make them give in.

"Sorry, my child, but you can't go out."

"Ah, mother, why not? . . . Please just this once . . . .
I think you're mean . . . all the other children are going
out . . . . Why are you so cruel to me? . . . Please, can't I?"
—to the accompaniment of tears.

At length in sheer despair the mother lets the insincere
little nuisance have his way.

You may be sure that a child who has once learned the
power of his own wheedling and whining will capitalize on his
nuisance value. He soon wraps his parents round in the
"tyranny of tears." He tries it once, and it works; he tries
it a second time, and it works. From that day on he knows
that all he has to do is make life sufficiently miserable for
his parents and in sheer desperation they'll let him have his
way, just to be free from his pestering and wailing.

On the other hand no child wastes his energy on this sort
of thing once he has learned it doesn't work. In fact he may
be wisely taught that pestering and wailing result in an
increase of his punishment. So he does as he's told or takes
his medicine calmly. He can't crack over his parents' ruffled
heads the whip of his wheedling and whining.

Capricious Parents

The shifting capriciousness of parents works enormous
harm to authority. Children regard such weather-vane
standards first with amazement, then with suspicion, and
finally with a conviction that they're dealing with parents
whose orders depend entirely upon what they had to eat or
how restfully or restlessly they slept last night.

Thoughtless parents will shift in chameleon fashion.
What they sternly forbid today, they permit without a mur-
mur tomorrow. What drives them mad during an afternoon,
they think a big joke in the evening. They announce formally, "Believe me, we'll never have that sort of nonsense
again in this house," and then they promptly forget all about
this anathema. They are smiling approval when their children are fresh little brats in the presence of company, and
they bat them over the ears for precisely the same conduct
when there is no stranger around to see them.

Children soon argue to the conclusion that authority is dependent upon digestion or some other whimsical factor that they, the children, certainly can't control. They do not grow obedient; they become watchfully observant of their parents' moods.

"How's dad feeling today? Fine? Go ahead then; it's O. K."

"Mother has a new hat? Swell. Now's the time to ask her for that permission."

"Duck, kids; dad lost at golf."

"Don't bother mother today; she and dad had a fight."

GOVERNMENT BY WHIM

Like the husband who remarked that his wife was endowed with a strong whim, the children feel that they are governed by the law of unpredictable caprice. There are few more intolerable forms of government.

LAWS, FIXED OR TRANSIENT

Certain regulations for the house should stand permanent and fixed: promptness in rising, good manners at table, the performing of assigned tasks, friendliness and decent courtesy among the children, respectful ways of addressing elders, prompt retiring, and other things of that sort.

Certain regulations should be known to depend upon circumstances: going out, companions, amount of time for fun, running errands, and other things of that nature.

Exceptions should be made—but they should be clearly indicated as exceptions.

"As a rule I don't let you go to the drugstore for sodas unless a grownup goes with you. But because you've a little cousin visiting you and I think it would be pleasant for both of you, you may go by yourselves and order whatever you like."

"Tonight your aunt and uncle are going to visit us. You may stay up past your regular bedtime, but that is just for tonight."

A thing absolutely to be prevented is the child's becoming convinced that he is governed by unpredictable adults who don't know their own minds and yet are trying to form his. That results in chaos.

FAVORITISM

It is hard for a parent not to have favorites. If his extra affection for any one child however makes him treat that child differently from the rest, his whole system of discipline is shot. Or if he does not like one child quite so well and is in consequence harder on him than on the others, the structure of his authority collapses.

If the child is weak and sick, discipline in his case may have to be different—though frankly too many children have been spoiled because they were pampered and allowed to run wild during some period of illness. When the child has been notably good, discipline can be relaxed in his case. The understanding must however be clear that he must keep that high standard if he wishes the favors to be continued.

Any parental favoritism creates the clearest excuse of injustice. The favorite crows over the others and comes to be cordially disliked. The underdog is taunted by the rest of the children and develops into a little enemy of society.

However much parents may be drawn to one child or repelled from another, if they value their own authority and the training their lessons in obedience are meant to give to all the children, they will be just with an even hand and will love all their children deeply enough to give them the unquestionable benefit of discipline and training and the touch of a firm, guiding, and sustaining hand.

VII

THE ROAD TO GOOD MANNERS

Good manners are the easiest things in the world to recognize.

That fact does not however prevent them from being extremely difficult to define. Certainly they do not consist in the use of the approved fork-of-the-moment or in the precise sort of letter paper to differentiate a letter of condolence from an invitation to a cocktail party. We all realize instinctively that good manners are far beyond these transient trifles. But to give a very clear explanation of just what makes manners good—that's a difficult assignment.

With us who live in the Christian dispensation, good manners are the immediate corollary of Christlike charity. They are a beautiful expression of our love for our fellow men and of our desire to make life a little easier and smoother and happier for them. They are the curb we put upon our animal instincts, which would lead us to grab, push, shove, make unpleasant and grating noises, become involved with the sensitive nerves or the reasonable reticences of others.

They are really charity in action.

Pagan Bad Manners

Bad manners on the other hand are oftenest the reflection of pagan standards. Anyone who has ever read one of Aldous Huxley's novels has shuddered almost as much at the ghastly rudeness and deep-seated verbal cruelty of the men and women characters who seem to regard themselves as "ladies and gentlemen" as at their bad morals. They blast one another with a phrase. They reach out and with carefully manicured fingers clutch anything they may want—a love, the center of the stage, the innocence of the unwary, the headlines, the ideas of a friend, the laugh that can be awakened by some ruthless thrust of poisoned tongues. They are of the social uppercrust; but you feel that the crust is made, not with wholesome flour, but with a heavy mixture of arsenic, talcum powder, and rat bane.

So the proud man will usually show a savage contempt for others. He will ride right over their feelings. He will regard their wishes or prejudices as beneath his consideration. He will be arrogant with those he considers his inferiors —that is, the major slice of humanity—and will be insistent about his own "rights," no matter how much this insistence may inconvenience the rest.

Pride and good manners cannot go together, except in brief interludes when the proud man regards good manners as profitable to himself or as a means whereby he can condescendingly prove his nobility of blood or magnificence of manners.

Sin Is Bad-Mannered

Selfishness, whatever its form, is bound to be marked by rough, crude grabbing. And invariably in life it is just that. Sin, whatever figure it may for the moment assume, is sure to betray itself in bad manners. Doubt and blasphemy are bad manners toward God. Lust will not stop at the worst of bad manners to find victims for its crude animal passion. Murderers cannot bring to their profession politeness; in the end their objective must be reached over their victim's rights to life itself. Theft is never regarded by its victims as "the thing to do." An evil tongue is a bad-mannered, heedless, cruel tongue. Indeed this unpleasant litany could go on straight through the catalogue of sins.

Saints Are Well-Mannered

The saint on the other hand, though he may know nothing of the current rules for the eating of asparagus or the leaving of cards on New Year's Day, is invariably blessed with good manners. He is infinitely considerate of the feelings of others. He does not like to hurt anyone. He is quick to put his own wants or desires in a place second to theirs.

Goodness and good manners are first cousins. Stated better, good manners are born of Catholic faith and Christian charity.

Charity at Home

Charity, runs the threadbare proverb, begins at home. And the cynic promptly adds, ". . . and usually stays there." Would that the first part of that ancient truism were really true! For if charity did begin at home, it could not conceivably be content only to stay there. Charity, love, is the most expansive thing in the world. It must seek opportunity for expression. It must affect as many people as possible. So were it true that charity begins within modern homes and that there love is taught expertly and learned naturally, good manners would be the rule of modern living.

Perhaps we have been tricked by the word charity. That beautiful old transliteration from the Latin word *caritas* has come to mean of course the penny dropped into the poor man's hat, while it should mean human love in all its finest expressions. Yet we need to know little indeed of life in order to see the connection between love and good manners.

There is the young man who falls in love with the one-and-only girl. During the period when love is deep and tender, his manners are startlingly fine. He thinks constantly of her likes and shields her against any least blow from rough circumstances. He brings her flowers. He consults her wishes on everything. He steps aside for her, places his hand assistingly under her elbow, phones her on any slightest pretext, writes her constantly. Later on as love cools, he may develop his ursine nature. As long as love is warm, politeness blossoms in its radiance.

Real Love

Hence if the home were a place of real love, we should have to spend but little time worrying about good manners. Perhaps it would be wisest for a time to forget all about manners and to spend our energies to build up love. For with love come politeness and courtesy and consideration, all of which must be present if good manners are not to become as topical as the etiquette put on and off with formal dress.

I have emphasized recurrently the importance of love between the mother and the father. That is the source of the family's love.

But all of us have heard, times beyond recall, the opinion that children are lucky who are brought up in big families. Often the propounders of this sage human experience really mean that big families are likely to keep the parents from spoiling the children. The mother and the father of twelve children are not likely to have time to convert little Millicent into a neurotic or to coddle little Percy when he stubs his toe or to side with Marmaduke against Myrtle when he demands exclusive right to the dumpcart.

But that is merely the negative side. Big families are important because they can be such magnificent schools of human love. The parents find their capacity for love growing with each new child that God sends them. The children themselves, instead of developing into self-centered little egoists, have, because they are surrounded by those near them in blood, the chance to express love naturally, simply, and easily.

Among these "carefully spaced children," so much praised by the modern birth controllers, there is often likely to be a vast difference in years that separates the youngsters from one another. To a child of eight a child of four or three seems absurdly young. A boy entering high school refers to his brother in fifth grade as "that baby." If the children are quite close together in years, they develop toward each other a closeness not only of blood and natural affection but of interest.

Closely Knit

It has been my pleasant experience to see three little girls out of a charming and large family knit together from the days of their babyhood. They are grouped together with a total age span of hardly more than three years. So that their interests through childhood, girlhood, and into their maturity have remained closely interwoven, deeply saturated with understanding and sympathy and love. We have seen instances of men twins who have been almost as close as the Corsican brothers not only because they were twins but

because they had the same age level, with a consequent camaraderie possible only to those who are at close age range.
Later in life five years separating a man of forty from his
friend of thirty-five seem slight indeed. Five years separating
a girl of twelve from her little sister of seven or a high
schooler of seventeen from his kid brother of twelve seem
wide as a chasm.

Lucky then the children who at home and under the eyes
of their parents are taught the basic lessons of human and
humane love.

They are taught to share their belongings out of love
for one another. They are trained to care for the needs of
one another. The girls are expected to care with a love at
once motherly and sisterly for the new babies that come into
the family. The boys are trained by their parents to show
an affectionate concern for their younger sisters. The family
is made into a well-blended unit by parties enjoyed together,
by happiness in birthdays, and by communal feasts. The
parents' quick and transparent love for their children is
reflected in the love of the children for one another.

There will always be in later loves something of selfishness. And selfishness is a handicap to good manners. But
love within the home can be tinged with the unselfishness of
mother love itself. That kind of love will blossom into a
politeness at home which will be carried beautifully and permanently into later life.

Good Manners at Home

So it is impossible to talk of good manners without the
wistful hope that they will spring from the deep and paren-
tally cultivated love which exists in the home. Only there
can the child be equipped with the foundations of good manners. Only there can he be provided with that politeness
which is based on a respect for the rights of others. If the
parents set the children the example, the children will be
attracted by the charm of good manners as they see their
elders walk these gracious ways. If the parents expect good
manners between the brothers and the sisters, those good
manners later on will be part of life's equipment for those

children. If the parents are interested in instilling into their youngsters that gentleness which is the essential element that makes of a mere man a gentle man and of a plain woman a lady, their influence will be plainly marked in the conduct of their children.

If the parents' manners are bad and their training of their children's manners slovenly or nonexistent, their children will, unless by some miracle, turn out to be little barbarians or boors or hoodlums; or they will recurrently break through the thin veneer of overlaid politeness and betray what the English language has come to call, devastatingly, "bad breeding."

Not Sissy

Early in their life children must be impressed with the fact that good manners are not sissy. A certain type of American seems to think it manly to be loud and rough, to use a pointed elbow or an acid remark, to prove his superiority by insulting waiters or bawling out the girl behind the counter. He even thinks he indicates his manliness if he eats noisily and tosses furniture around.

What Are Good Manners?

No definition of good manners will ever be final. But we offer this addition to the long list of definitions: Good manners are the expression of controlled strength. The weakling who does not hurt his fellows is not necessarily well mannered; he may be only afraid. The strong man or woman who is kind to others and respectful of their feelings has learned the magnificent art of directing his or her strength and controlling animal vitality.

Modern business has long been aware of the value of good manners. Big concerns that deal with the public insist on the utmost courtesy in their employees' attitude toward the customers. "The customer is always right" is a platitude of salesmanship. One big chain of retail cigar stores insists that if a buyer mispronounces the name of a cigar the salesman must carefully mispronounce it after him lest the customer be embarrassed when he hears the correct pronunciation.

The filling-station employee has become a legend of polite service. Salesmen learn to smile in almost exaggerated fashion. Railroads win wide patronage by schooling their staffs to courtesy. Good manners pay in all dealings with the public, and the smart modern professional or business man knows that art and practices it.

Real Value

So from the beginning children can be made aware of the enormous value—here and now and just from the standpoint of temporal advantages—they get if they learn and practice good manners. In good manners lies the true art of winning friends and influencing people.

It should not be difficult to show children by example and out of their own growing experience how welcome the well-mannered person is in any circle. They can see that exemplified among their own little friends. Parents can further point this out. People like to have visit them the child who is well behaved, who has a decent regard for their rights, who asks permission before he touches their things, who thanks them after he has played with their things, who willingly shares with them his own things. Children cannot fail to notice how impressed adults are with the youngsters who know how to accept an introduction and to meet strangers.

Road to Popularity

Lifelong good manners mean real popularity, with the later success in life that comes from popularity. Good manners bring their possessor to the attention of the right people and make easier the climb to positions worth striving for. Social success and financial success are enormously facilitated for the person who knows the right thing to do and does it.

One of the funniest of modern comedies was "The Man Who Came to Dinner." It was uproarious fun, and it left the audiences sick with laughter. But when the laughter died and the fun was over, many a member of the audience had the same second thought: "From even chance contact with an ill-mannered smart aleck like that, O Lord, deliver us!"

Seen on the stage and from across the safe barrier of the footlights, the main character, a blustering, brilliant, selfish, egotistical, self-centered boor, was as funny as a goat in a laundry. In one's own parlor that same man would have been too horrible for anything but the swift point of one's well-directed boot.

The main character was, according to the universal and often printed rumor, based on a famous American writer. I happen to know of a young lady reporter who was sent to get a story from that writer when he visited her city. She was trying to make her bread and butter in the way he did, by getting other people to talk for her or give her help toward the writing of a sellable article. He treated her as a nuisance and a pest. He flatly refused to give her any story at all. He was dressed in a disreputable dressing gown when he greeted her. He was the complete oaf and boor. Finally after refusing her a story, he terminated the interview with as vulgar and coarse a comment as a man could throw in the face of a woman.

His replica on the stage may have been as amusing as a monkey in a cage. In reality he was as unattractive as a monkey running loose among one's favorite bric-a-brac and treasured letters.

Bad Manners Not Clever

Bad manners are not a sign of cleverness; they are the clearest indication of selfishness. A bad-mannered person may actually betray a real stupidity which holds that the rest of the world is unworthy of his effort to win and retain anyone's friendship. Bad manners do not even suggest strength. They mark merely uncontrolled greed and selfishness. They are not the mark of sophistication. They often indicate crass ignorance of the most fundamental human likes and dislikes. They are a sign that one has not learned what to do and how to do it. They show clearly that one has not been places or done things.

Egotism

Bad manners are an easily recognized sign of the most ungracious disregard for others. They flow from utter egotism and egoism. Let's remember that from the viewpoint of the parents bad manners indicate in a child his emergence from a home without charm and culture and from parents who either did not know how to train their children or were too hard at work earning the necessities of life or too unaware of the decencies of civilized living to pass on to their offspring a knowledge of the proper things to do and the proper way to deal with people.

Pretense

Because all this is so platitudinously true, bad men and bad women will often try to hide their evil morals under the surface gloss of apparent good manners. The Don Juan of whatever age tracks down his victim with an exquisite courtesy that suddenly melts away as his desires flame up. The café-society maiden will know exactly how to balance a fork and order a dinner or greet the columnist who may give her a good notice; she will curse in truckman fashion her chauffeur if he keeps her waiting briefly at the door of the night club.

For a Gentler Life

The general principle that underlies all good manners is simply this: Good manners are those acts or habits which make living a little smoother and simpler for others. They are the manifestation of consideration for others' shins, nerves, prejudices, likes, wants, tastes, comforts, general happiness and well being. Really that makes them no more than a practical expression of the golden rule.

Customs Versus Good Manners

Good manners are eternal and unchanging. Customs on the contrary and etiquette may change with every season.

When I was a lad, I served my term in learning how to manipulate my fork with the approved grace of the period.

It was held, this important fork, in one's left hand while one cut the meat with the knife, which was held in the right. Then the fork was transferred easily and with as little waste motion as possible to the right hand, which hand alone carried food to the mouth. One did not use the left hand as a food carrier. The honor of conveying all food to the mouth was conferred exclusively on the right hand.

Nowadays a person will convey his food to his mouth with his left hand in order to prove that he has been in Europe. He will hold his fork in his left hand, cut his meat, and then carry the morsel upward with a sweep of that same left hand. That is called the continental use of the fork and has in many parts of the country superseded the American transfer from left to right hand.

That custom, like many another, has changed. So has the mode of eating fried chicken or asparagus.

The dropping of cards at the door to simulate a visit is the proper thing in certain diplomatic circles, yet it would be regarded as the sheerest affectation in most social levels. Customs of one age demanded that men's trousers be without crease to prove that they were tailormade and had not been taken down from the shelf, where they acquired their crease; today uncreased trousers indicate a tramp, a man who last night was locked out and had to sleep in his clothes, or a sophomore in one of the swankier colleges.

UNCHANGING

But good manners do not change. A tendency to gulp one's food is always bad. Failure to thank a hostess for her entertainment can never be other than rude. Deliberately to cultivate sloppy dress on occasions that call for dignity and reverence can never be anything else than boorish.

It is rather significant that good manners proceed from good homes but not necessarily from wealthy ones. Some of the worst-mannered whelps I have ever had the misfortune to hear yelp came from homes that were rotten with money. That seemed to be the point: The homes and the samples sent from those homes really were *rotten* with money. Some of the finest youthful manners I've ever encountered were displayed by children of the poor. Many a newsboy who sells you a paper on the corner could teach the sons and daughters of many of the rich all about the good manners which win friends and attract people instantly. The best manners however are likely to come out of good, normal middle-class homes, where the parents have enough time to pay attention to the training of their children and just enough money to make possible pleasantly comfortable surroundings and not so much that they can spoil their children or give them the arrogance, human indifference, boredom, and callousness that come with too liberal an income.

Home Over School

In the whole question of children and their manners the school cannot possibly counterbalance the influence of the parents. Good parents and the training they give their children will triumph over the apparent bad manners prevalent in some boys' schools. Bad parents and their lack of interest in their children will mean that girls will go through the so-called finishing schools and emerge with a finishing that is not even a real polish but an undeceptive shine.

No Domestic Letdown

Hence within the atmosphere of the home parents can never afford to let down. Good manners in the home are in reality far more important than are good manners outside the home. Without the solid foundation laid there, the on-parade manners are so much cheap shellac.

Good Manners Between Parents

The display of good manners between parents themselves is the first great lesson given to the children.

The parents' way of speaking to each other is most important. If their speech is affectionate, if they address each other gently, no child can escape the influence of that example. Between them are hurled no jibes, no insults. When they want something done, they ask for it politely. Absent are loud commands, orders without the prelude "please," or favors accepted without a thank-you. Never in speaking to each other do they use unpleasant or objection-able—much less insulting—names. And their attitude toward "kidding" is that it has no place between them.

"KIDDING"

May I pause just for a second on that matter of "kidding"?

It can be the curse of families, a source of endless annoy-ance to the sensitive members, and the basis of real friction and misunderstanding.

In the first place I've never yet known a family "kidder" who could himself take "kidding." He offers the perfect instance of the type who is able to "dish it out" but utterly unable or unwilling to "take it." The most incessant "kidder" I have ever known in my life refused to speak to me for almost a month because in mild fashion I dared to "kid" him one evening. He thought "kidding" was amazingly funny only when he was the "kidder." As a "kiddee" he was a dismal failure.

"Kidding" produces in families an atmosphere of the most continuous suspicion and distrust. I am thinking of one family where "kidding" was the universal rule. On a certain occasion the mother of the family was returning from New York and passed through, let's say, Omaha, the family's home town, on her way to meet her husband, who was, she thought, in California. Arrived in Omaha, she called the house and got on the phone one of her elder sons.

"Just thought I'd say hello," she said, "before I hopped the train to join dad."

"It's lucky you called," her son, a notorious "kidder," replied. "Dad's not in California. He came home yesterday, and he's down at his office right here in town."

"Isn't that sweet," the mother replied, ironically. She'd heard that sort of "Wolf! wolf!" story before. "Well thank you, dear, for telling me. Give dad my love. And I'll drop you a line from California and ask dad to sign it too."

"But, mother!" the now alarmed son shouted into the phone, "I mean it this time. Dad's here."

"Yes I know," soothed the mother. "And so is the President and Clark Gable and Mickey Mouse. Well take care of them all for me, but don't tell your poor old mother such yarns, you cute little kidder."

Whereupon she rang off and boarded her train. And it was some hundred miles further west before the distracted and penitent son finally caught up with her and brought her back with him. Even then she was quite sure that it was some new twist to his peculiar brand of "kidding." She'd suffered from it so often that even when he told the plainest truth she declined to believe him.

RULES FOR "KIDDING"

The only sensible rule for "kidding"—and it should be taught early by example—is that one may "kid" another person only about something that the other person is sure is not true. If someone has beautiful eyes and knows it, one may say, "Don't you find people turning to stone when you level those simply horrible eyes upon them?" If they have just given a talk which has plainly left the listeners gasping in amazement, one may comment, "Did you notice how soundly everyone slept through your talk? How can you be such a bore?"

But most "kidders," especially those within the family circle, have the unhappy art of being, as the Irish say, "in half joke and whole earnest." They can always find the one defect about which one is really worrying and drag that out for their impaling. They can hit on a quality that a person is not sure he possesses or on something that he is afraid he has done badly and then stick it full of verbal pins. That type of torture should come under the law that forbids unusual and inhuman forms of punishment.

The good rule for parents to follow is never under any circumstances to "kid" each other. And "kidding" among the children, except when it is obviously untrue, should be instantly squelched. Nothing else is more embarrassing to visitors than their having to listen to the elder children "ride" the younger ones until the poor youngsters are practically in tears. Later more than one quirk of temper, petulance, or shyness will appear as the result of this entirely too frequent form of domestic assault and battery.

POLITE PARENTAL SPEECH

Children learn fundamental good manners from the way that parents speak to each other or about each other. It is bad to let the youngsters hear any of the unpleasant names that are used even jokingly to designate parents. There is nothing really funny about "the old lady, my old man, the ball and chain, the old grouch, the straw boss, the nuisance," or any other names of that kind. It is deplorable manners for the man to introduce his wife with a casual "Folks, meet the wife"—almost as bad as the old custom of signing the hotel register, "Mr. George Jones and wife."

Decent parents will realize the utter bad manners of their talking about one another to strangers—especially if one of the children happens to be listening. Infinitely worse is the habit of parents' talking slightingly to the children themselves.

POLITENESS BETWEEN PARENTS

Politeness toward each other is something that parents actually owe to each other—quite aside from the fact that that politeness will profoundly affect the manners of the children. So a civilized husband gives to his wife exactly the same polite consideration that any gentleman is expected to give to a refined woman.

He helps her with her chair when they sit down to the table alone or with the children. He relinquishes this only when he has taught his eldest son to do it in his place. He stands on those occasions when a gentleman stands to welcome a lady, and he expects the boys of the family to do this too. He helps her on and off with her coat; and if the wrap is heavy, he hangs it up for her. When his wife drops anything, he hastens to pick it up for her—until his sons in their youthful agility have reached the point where they can do it more readily.

He shows real consideration for her in the way he lets her have those parts of the newspaper that she prefers. He does not take her detective story away from her until she has tracked the unknown murderer to his unmasking. He lets her have her turn to select the programs on the radio. If they go to a motion picture, he may suggest his choice, but with due regard for her veto or her countersuggestion.

All this could be summarized thus: that the children find in their parents the manners that mark the courtship and the honeymoon. Their attitude toward their mother and ultimately toward all other women will be largely influenced by their father's blend of love and politeness.

These good manners are displayed in parallel ways of course by the mother. She remembers her husband's tastes and defers to them. She treats him with the same politeness that she shows to other men. She is a lady measuring up to his stature as a gentleman. Through her example the good manners of her children will inevitably be insured.

TABLE MANNERS

The table is one of the first classrooms of good manners.

Fastidiousness and finicky ways are not, needless to say, good manners. They are the sign of poor training or a bad digestion, and neither makes for a pleasant social being. Early, indeed from the very beginning, the youngsters are taught the general rules of good manners.

No noise is permitted in the consumption of food. In the Oriental lands—I have often heard this though I have not always been able to credit it—appreciation of food and gratitude to the cook are expressed by loud noises, smacking of lips, and even—I crave pardon for mentioning it—belching. The Occidental races have learned that any form of noise at table is distressing and often revolting.

Children easily come to think that such noises are funny and, if they are not instantly corrected, make a great joke out of inhaling their soup and chewing their meat in noisy fashion. The mechanical limitation of the sound-recording devices in the films tends to exaggerate the sounds of people's eating and drinking. Apparently a certain class of café society seem to have made a custom of bad manners and are apparently reviving noise in eating. Yet none of these factors must deter the parents from their duty of early teaching their children that Christians do not emphasize with sound effects the necessity of eating; they conceal this animal need for food in the quiet way that they consume their food.

No Grabbing

Among the children there must be no grabbing—either with the hands or with a whine. Like little animals they tend to reach their chubby little hooks for what they want, even on the plate that is next to them or across from them. Or like the reasoning little humans they are, they soon learn that they can trick their elders or even their peers out of choice bits if they put on scenes, whine, or make an intolerable fuss.

So children will grab for candy; or each of six children at a family board will demand a drumstick from the Thanksgiving turkey, which clearly is not a centipede.

Religious communities have the custom of someone's reading out loud during meals. I doubt very much if the wise founders of the orders believed that the monks and nuns would learn much from the books the reading of which furnished the obbligato for dinner and supper. They did hope however through this pleasant distraction to deter the members from a purely animal concentration on food. A dog over his bone develops a singleness of purpose that is often amusing. In a pig that same exclusive application to the task in hand is unpleasantly revolting. In a human being, even in a child, such concentration is inhuman and completely bad manners.

Conversation With Meals

Hence the importance of cultivating conversation at the dinner table. Into this conversation children must early be drawn. They must learn to talk in the intervals of eating and not permit either operation to impede the other. A man who has learned simultaneously to handle the main course and a pleasant topic of conversation is likely to be a well-mannered man.

BASIC PRACTICES

Individual customs for eating may change with the times. Once on a time no one dared tip a soup dish. Now, I believe, it may be tipped slightly, away from the eater. Once on a time a diner proved his mastery over his appetite by leaving a small quantity of food on his plate. Now he indicates his regard for economy by eating everything down to the last crumb.

Despite such changes a gentleman needs no rule book to teach him that the consumption of soup should never be a vocal affair and that one should not clean one's plate in the manner of a starving man who is down to his last sea biscuit.

Children can be given quite early the reasons that underlie good manners at table. A man proves he is human by his control of that animal appetite which might make him wolf his food or tear it greedily from the hands of his neighbor. As a Christian he tries to demonstrate his control over his lower, physical nature. His good manners, which are rooted in his social, spiritual nature, triumph over his greediness and hunger, which are instincts that he shares with the animals.

SIMPLE FUNDAMENTALS

Little children are seldom more charming than when they are displaying a mastery over their knives and forks. They know how to hold them, lightly yet firmly, with grace yet without a grip. They learn to guide them to their mouths without spilling the food in a greasy train along the plate and their clothing. They learn not to bite the fork as if they were relishing the tines. They do not scrape their knives or forks against the china. They do not so overload their spoons and forks that the others at table anxiously watch the progress, convinced that the safe arrival of the food into the mouth is impossible.

Any sign of haste or greed is outlawed. In the Army the officers are rather in despair because no matter how attractive the food is made the soldiers persist in bolting it in less than a quarter of an hour. Authorities in boys' boarding schools are constantly struggling against the speed with which youngsters plow their way through a plate of food as if it were a snowdrift between them and the playing fields.

STAYING TILL THE END OF MEALS

If the parents adopt at home a leisurely method of eating, this is bound to affect the children. To make this certain, children should early learn that even if they bolt their food and are finished before the rest they still will have to remain at the table for a reasonable time. If in their mad anxiety to get back to their games they eat their meat in two canine bites and decline to partake of dessert, that is not going to help them one bit. Meals take a full half hour or more, and everyone remains at the table until the entire family is finished.

Under no circumstances should the parents let a child leave the table without his first asking permission and explaining why he has to be an exception to what is really a sort of sacred family ritual.

UNSELFISHNESS

We all of us get a trained eye for the better cuts and the choicer bits of food. In a well-mannered family however mother gets first choice. After that dad sees to it that each on successive days gets what is regarded as the choicer item.

A lot of men and women would be much better-mannered if they went through something like a religious novitiate. For nowhere else do really rough, selfish manners get a swifter and more effective planing than in a novitiate.

TURN AND TURNABOUT

So children must be taught to take their turn at the better cuts and be satisfied if once in several days they get the piece of layer cake that has the heavy outside frosting or are served the crisp, top piece of the beef.

All through the meal the mother, with the same tact and mastery of her dinner table which she would show if at the table were invited guests, leads the conversation. If a child is silent and too concentrated on food, she tosses him a question that demands more than a yes or a no answer. The table is one place where surliness and moodiness cannot be permitted. If such moods are controlled there, they are much easier to control elsewhere.

CLEANLINESS AND PROPER CLOTHES

Prior to all meals the parents set for the children an example of cleanliness and proper attire which all must follow. Hands are washed and, if need be, inspected before meals. If a child comes to table with unwashed hands, he is sent away to wash them before he is served. No soiled clothes are permitted to be worn at table, nor outfits that reek of the ball field or of manual work.

It is decidedly worth considering whether, except in very hot weather, coats or their equivalent should not be worn by the men and the boys. Certainly in the case of the girls boudoir apparel should be outlawed. The rest of the diners should not be required to sit across the table from a female in a wrapper, her hair in curlers, her face covered with cold cream.

In this as in other things the children will follow, not the commands, but the example and lead of their parents.

PARTIES

In civilized, Christian society the social party plays a most important role.

In practice parties may be not only the expressions but actually the schools of Christlike charity and good manners. They manifest friendships and promote them. They develop the natural social instinct. They make us more fully human and more completely humane.

From the years before the dawn of reason children actually experience the most intense interest in the parties given by their parents. So if parents are interested in teaching their children good manners and social usage, they are wise to let them feel they have a part in the shaping of the parties.

They can be allowed to remain to watch and listen while the lists are being made. A mother and a father can for the direct benefit of their children discuss why they are inviting this friend and why they are not inviting that acquaintance.

Listing the Guests

"I think we should invite the Browns; they invited us to dinner two weeks ago . . . . The Smyths are new in the neighborhood; this would be a pleasant opportunity to have them meet our friends . . . . The Greens are always such charming guests; let's have them . . . . Wouldn't it help your business if you were nice to Mr. Blue? Let's invite him and his wife."

Or . . .

"I don't think the Scarlets enjoyed themselves the last time they came. Perhaps we can leave them out this time . . . . The Blanks are so noisy; they wouldn't fit into a party like this . . . . We've had the Exes twice now, and they've not invited us; I think we'd better wait until they ask us before we invite them again."

As children listen with the engrossed alertness of all youngsters following the plans of their parents, they get a realization of the fact that though parties are primarily for fun and good times they should be used to repay debts, establish friendships, make new and worth-while connections, and welcome newcomers. At the same time they can learn that people are not invited again if they are bores or act bored, if they are boisterous or bad mannered, if they selfishly expect to be asked continuously and make no effort to repay the favors they have received.

Subtly children must be made aware however that guests are not restricted to the profitable and personally attractive. That would be the normal tendency of the child: to pick as his guests the children who would be sure to bring a present to the party or those whom he personally likes. The wider range of charity as it is exhibited through parties must be made quite clear to the child.

Pleased Watchers

Even a small gathering will throw the children into a pleasurable flurry. They can be allowed to watch the progress of the preparations. The food is discussed in their presence. They hear mother and dad deciding what to do with the guests when they arrive; what games, if any, they would like to play; how the guests should be seated at the table. The woman, as the dominant social factor in our American social life, is seen always to be exercising her right of management and jurisdiction.

When the actual party convenes, if the children are at all old enough, the wisest policy certainly seems to be to give them a brief taste of such a social event. They can be dressed and allowed to meet the guests. They can even sit around for a brief time before they are exiled to their own quarters and bed.

Even from their exile the children will be following the course of the party. They come to know that mother and dad can put on a party which is wonderfully pleasant and free from any sign of boisterousness. They know that fun can be had through activity unmarked by romping. They come to see the relationship of good food and drink to conversation and social friendships. They can see too the adult practices of self-control in eating and drinking.

Games and Conversation

They come to know with interest the value of civilized games and conversation. They may even watch their mother and father handle expertly but without offense those who tend to slip slightly out of line. They can learn how to draw out the shy and the hesitant and to subordinate their own personal preferences to an attitude of friendliness toward all.

Then when the children come to plan and arrange for their own parties, under the direction of their parents they can develop small replicas of their parents' achievements.

The Children's Parties

As soon as the child is old enough to have friends, he should begin to have small parties of his own. During his very early years these are arranged and prepared for almost entirely by the parents. But as soon as possible the child should be encouraged to take an active part in the preliminaries.

A list of his young friends is drawn up, modeled on his parents' procedure in that matter. He is encouraged to repay obligations, to win friends, to destroy any growing cliquishness. He is reminded that it is important to invite the shy and diffident and to include the less attractive as well as the very self-assured and popular. The fun element in the party will be clear enough in his mind; the charity and social-obligation elements will need parents' emphasizing.

PLANNING ITS COURSE

The child and his mother—and even his father, if the father is smart and willing—plan the course the party is to take. Successful children's parties are not left to chance or the ingenuity and resourcefulness of the youngsters. The parents should talk over with the child the things he'd like to have his guests do. Into the child's mind can deftly be inserted ideas which he will think he originated and which he spontaneously suggests for the program. But the fun must be directed long in advance, the games selected, the course of the party mapped. Otherwise the first half hour to hour of silent, solitary getting acquainted will be followed by chaos and "roughhouse" for the remainder of the afternoon.

RECEIVING

Even the smallest child must be made to feel that he or she is the host or hostess of his or her own party. As such he is dressed and ready to receive the guests when they arrive. Again we can point to the charm of a child who knows how to meet his friends when they arrive, to shake hands with them, and to say however formally and stiltedly the necessary words of welcome.

PRESENTS

If it is a birthday party and there are presents, he accepts them and says the proper words of thanks.

Custom seems to disagree on whether he opens the presents while the guests are with him or whether he puts them aside to be opened after the small guests disappear at the end of the afternoon. My mother was of the put-away-till-later school. She maintained that all children could not afford to bring equally good presents; hence if none of the presents were opened till after the guests' departure, no one was embarrassed by the inferiority of his gift. Besides she thought that if the gifts were taken out of their wrappings while the guests were present, the small guests were likely to wreck them—to the sad loss of the recipient. She felt that the unwrapped gifts would serve to interfere with the planned party.

I merely present her reasons. Whatever the attitude, the child should be taught to be grateful, to say a proper thank-you, and to be really appreciative later on.

Introductions

The youngster can early be taught how to introduce to one another those of his friends who have never met before. Those formulas are simple enough for youthful mastery, and they are part of life's social equipment.

Wide Friendship

Once the party begins, the mother—or the mother and the father, if both are present—should watch whether or not their child is playing with only a few or is universal in his friendship. He must learn that the host or the hostess is obliged to take care of all the guests. Hence he, the host, must concentrate universally, not alone on the pretty little girls whom in unaccountable fashion he finds himself trailing; she, the hostess, must bestow her favor universally, not alone on the boy who for the moment has captured her admiring interest.

If more of this wide friendliness were taught to youngsters from the very start of their social life, we should not be afflicted by selfish adolescents and young people who won't go a step out of their way to dance with anyone but the belle of the ball or the hero of the hour.

SOCIAL LEADERSHIP

The leadership in the fun belongs to the host or the hostess, however young. Hence before the party the parents and the child can go over the games so that he knows just how they are played. He can be consulted beforehand on the seating of the guests at table, so that he will be able to indicate this arrangement when food is about to be served.

Stupid indeed are the parents who let their child sit in the corner while the party is taken over by alien hands. Pretty hopeless are the parents who let their child slip away from his own party to devote himself to just one of the guests or to some minor game or enthusiasm which cannot be shared by all the others. That is the kind of child who will, when he is adolescent, ride away in the family coupe and leave his own party flat while he spends the time with some transient enthusiasm.

DATES TO REMEMBER

Civilized dates are remembered in the well-mannered family.

This happy custom which the child sees around him from his first consciousness becomes part of his social nature. He is taught to remember birthdays. He becomes aware of the existence of anniversaries. In Catholic families his saint's name day is recalled. There are for himself small gifts and a minor celebration. He is part of these family celebrations, and he is trained to give gifts to the other members of the family at these times.

Quite aside from the charming customs, the practice of giving presents and the pleasant knowledge of how gracefully to receive them has been given the child. Both will make him a pleasanter person all through his life.

LETTER WRITING

Letter writing should of course be the routine practice of the parents. Then quite easily and early they can cultivate this manifestation of good manners in their children. Birthdays are remembered with letters; deaths are softened by

letters of condolence. No gift is received without its being
followed by a prompt note of thanks to the sender. After
every visit, however brief, that the child makes, there is a
bread-and-butter letter. Happy events like weddings and
graduations are marked with a letter.

And in these cases, as in a thousand others, like parents,
like children.

Voices

Some people are by nature endowed with charming and
easily modulated voices. Far more people have to cultivate
this through long years of patient training. The civilized
voices of the parents are the living demonstration to the
children. Yet beyond that children can easily be trained to
control their voices and to develop a speaking timbre that is
delightful to hear.

Formulas

Very early they must be taught the formulas necessary
for civilized living and be made to use them.

When a child is introduced to his elders, everyone is
acutely embarrassed if he stands with a finger in his mouth,
pressed against the parental leg, and appearing as if in quest
of a hole to crawl into. On the other hand we all instantly
admire the child who accepts an introduction properly.

"How do you do, Mrs. Jones? . . . Thank you; I am very
well."

Apparently the old formulas, "I'm pleased to meet you"
and "I'm happy to make your acquaintance," have been dis-
carded as notably insincere. Similarly the abbreviation
ma'am has been dropped in favor of the full name of the
person. Indeed the use of names or titles should run through
a child's conversation. Not, "What?" . . . "Wha'ja say?"
. . . "Huh?" . . . "Yes, ma'am," but, "What did you say,
Mrs. Jones?" . . . "Thank you, Mrs. Smith." . . . "Yes, Mr.
Brown." . . . "No, sir."

Handling People

Children can early learn how to deal with strangers, how
to handle bores who obtrude themselves. And if their later

life is not to be complicated by the imposition of strangers, they are happy if they do know how to manage their fellow men.

COMPLIMENTS

The receiving of compliments and the paying of them are arts.

Little girls and boys who are paid compliments can go into a social tail spin, blush scarlet, look helplessly for an avenue of escape, and make the complimenter wish he'd never opened the subject. They can learn to say, simply, "Thank you very much," or "I'm glad you think so," or "You are very kind."

Much selfishness will be killed if they are trained to pay deserved compliments to their peers. "I think that is a pretty dress you have on . . . . Good play! Well done! . . . That's an attractive house you live in . . . . I think your baby brother is very sweet."

All sorts of adults find themselves simply incapable of saying the kind, generous, complimentary things they really would like to say, because in their youth they were never trained to pay such compliments to those who deserved them.

Can it be overemphasized how all these things would improve our social living and make life pleasanter for all of us?

CARD GAMES

The home is the place where, under those natural teachers who are the parents, children can learn pleasant things like card playing and dancing.

All modern children should be taught the simple child card games. If they are taught, they later find the social card games easy to master. I honestly believe that the natural gambling instinct is released and controlled if children have played card games along with their earliest games. And certainly they will have mastered a pleasant and usually harmless form of social entertainment.

Card games in the family are a grand source of fun and union. They help the child to develop concentration combined with a quick sense of partnership. They prepare the child for social life. They are a simple school of applied psychology.

Dancing

In the same way the home is the natural dancing school.

I feel intensely sorry for a boy or a girl who has not been taught how to dance almost from the days he began to walk. At every gathering of young people with which I have been concerned, there has aways been a desolate fringe of many boys and a few girls who hang on the outskirts and make everyone uncomfortable. They are the boys and girls who never learned to dance. They watch the others with genuine envy. They are too old now and too self-conscious to take the leap.

I should be highly in favor of all children, both boys and girls, being sent to dancing school. Even if, like myself, they choose a career or enter a profession in which dancing is superfluous, the mastery they have gained over their feet makes them able to cross a lecture platform or even a sanctuary or a classroom with far less of a sinking feeling than they might otherwise have had. If however they remain "in the world," their mastery makes them better equipped for the normal social life, of which dancing is an integral part.

Dancing at Home

If parents cannot afford dancing school for their children, then the children should, as was mentioned before, learn to dance at home. Parents should start early to dance with their children. Brothers and sisters can dance together. The other children on the block can be encouraged to drop in for an informal family dance. As I see it, the home is the place in which children, while they are avoiding the dangers of public dancing, are trained for their part in the delightful, sinless, and altogether charming social dancing that can well make pleasanter their whole social life.

Brash or Shy

Some children are by nature brash. They want to show off. If there is a party, they are far in the lead. When anything is going on, their voices rise piercingly or compellingly above the rest.

Some children are by nature shy. In company they are alarmed, and their voices shrink to a barely perceptible whisper. They find it a torture to meet people. They cannot take the lead or stand in the center of any space—platform or ballroom or stage or living room—without their wishing to high heaven that they could die.

Somewhere in between these two extremes is the civilized, well-mannered human being. The two extremes are almost equally bad. The brash are a nuisance to the rest of the world. The shy are a torture to themselves.

Parents can in their own homes do much to bring the two extremes somewhere near the ideal center. The shy child can be encouraged to take his part, to perform when his turn comes, to face people or meet them or display what small talents God has given him and his training has developed. The brash child can be made to wait his turn, not to be eternally performing, to stand aside until others have first been introduced, not to thrust his acts in the face of any unprotected audience.

RESPECT FOR PRIVACY

The signs of good manners having been instilled in the child at home are many.

There is that beautiful characteristic which is respect for the privacy of others. Parents show that respect toward each other. They even display it toward their children. They insist that the children practice it among themselves.

Homes are limited monarchies, I insist. They are not little communisms. They are certainly not anarchies.

LETTERS AND PHONE CALLS

Hence in a well-mannered home letters and phone calls belong to the persons who receive them.

"Who called you up? . . . Who's that letter from? . . . What did he say? . . . My you were a long time on the phone! . . . Who's that? Your new girl?"

Almost any of these queries is a small percussion cap that will set off a family explosion. As a plain fact almost no one but the parents has a right to ask these questions.

Parents should of course exercise a reasonable control over the letters and phone calls their children make and receive. This is merely part of the supervision they exercise over their children's friendships.

Yet between themselves husband and wife should set the example of a very dignified restraint. The wife has no right to open her husband's letters or to demand to know to whom he was talking on the phone. Nor has the husband any such privileges with regard to his wife. Hence the training of the children in their respect for domestic privacies begins with the parents' being most careful not to intrude on one another.

Parents should know who writes to their children. They ought to know whom their children are phoning. If the correspondence becomes too frequent and fervent, the parents can discreetly enter in. When the phoning reaches a point where it becomes almost impossible for the other members of the family to use the phone, simple good sense puts a stop to that.

Yet where the letters are obviously harmless, it is better for parents to pay their children the compliment of letting them open their own mail. Should they be rightly curious about the letters received, the parents can ask if they may read them. Only after the request has been refused or given with reluctance or embarrassment need they start to exercise their parental authority.

The children must be taught that among themselves mail is sacred and telephone conversations for the ears of those who take part in them. Mail may be freely shared if the recipient desires it. No one else has any right to intrude or demand. Phone messages may voluntarily be relayed or repeated. They should not be pried out of those who received them. There is much too much of this sort of thing in families:

"Who's that letter from? I recognized the handwriting on the envelope. That's the third you got this week from that person . . . . Who called up? Gosh he talked a long time.

What did he say? . . . Who're you writing to? . . . Are you calling that girl up again?"

This is essentially bad manners, to be suppressed sternly by the parents.

PRIVATE DRAWER AND CLOSET

Both boys and girls like their own closets and bureau or dresser drawers. They enjoy the feeling that these belong to them and that no one without their leave can pry into them. That is a reasonably human attitude and one that any of us should be quick to recognize and understand.

So if the house is large enough, the parents designate a closet as the child's very own. As long as he or she keeps it orderly and clean, it will not be bothered. Occasionally he or she will be asked to open it for parental inspection. For a closet found in good order, there are words of commendation. As a reward the child's privacy is respected more completely. If the closet is in a state of disorder, the child must be warned that this will mean the loss of his exclusive right to use it, since someone will have to take over the task of keeping it neat and clean and in proper array.

If an entire closet cannot be assigned to one child, then certain bureau or dresser drawers should be given him. Here again the child's rights to that drawer should be respected. Only crass disorder in the drawer should bring parental invasion of it.

Among the children in a family these places that belong to brothers or sisters should be in the line with Bluebeard's closet. They should be taught to respect others' privacy as they expect their own privacy to be respected. There can be few finer lessons in cooperation or good manners than this regard for the small private domains.

COLLECTIONS

Most children are born collectors. Boys and girls are alike in this. They are usually alike too in the relative secrecy with which they surround their particular hobbies. It may be that they harbor a suspicion that the elders will regard their collections with contempt. It may be that they are afraid that by parading them too much they will lose them. Whatever their reasons, they like to regard this hobby or collection as their own, something they can show to others only when they wish to do so, something that they can keep for themselves at all other times.

They will get a real lesson in good manners if their collection or hobby is treated with great good manners by the rest of the household. When they present their private museum for admiration, it should be respectfully and attentively admired. No one should scoff. No one should point out its obvious lacunae or inadequacy. When they are not in the mood to exhibit their collection, no one should demand a showing of it or without let or permission go prying around of his own accord.

If in Doubt . . .

It may well be that under certain circumstances parents have reason to suspect the too carefully locked closet, the drawer too watchfully guarded, or the collection not shown to anyone and visited by the collector only in great secrecy. In that case the parents should certainly find out if anything is wrong. Good morals always take precedence over good manners.

Elders and Youngers

Good manners in children are manifested almost equally in the respect they show their elders and the consideration they display toward the younger children in the family. It is lovely if children have been trained to stand when an older person enters the room, if they relinquish the more comfortable chair to their elder, if they say, "Please excuse me," when they pass in front of an elder, if they say, "I beg your pardon," after they have disturbed someone in any way, and if they seem pleased to be of service in small things.

In well-mannered families there is a hierarchy of ages. The children acquire greater privileges with advancing years. Yet the older ones pay the compliment of politeness to the children who are their juniors. They regard even little brother and sister as human beings with rights. They pay attention to little brother when he wants to talk. They let him have a place, even if it is distinctly a minor one, in their games. They take a friendly interest in his concerns, but only so far as he wants that interest.

As always it is the wise disposition of the parents which sweetly and happily regulates all this.

NATURAL ASSET

There is hardly another natural asset that is of higher value than good manners. The person who is punctual and considerate knows the correct thing to say—and he says it; has consideration for the rights and feelings of another; is often enough the adult who as a child under the watchful eyes of his parents practiced these things at home. What finer natural endowment could parents transmit to their children? And what could possibly make them more attractive at home and more welcome beyond the family circle?

VIII

THE HOME - TEACHER OF RELIGION

This is a sector of the relationship of parents and children that seems almost superfluous.

How could anyone fail to see the importance of the parents in the teaching of religion to their children? I feel safe in asserting that of the readers of these pages seventy to eighty per cent were inducted into their religious beliefs by the mothers God gave them. If today they practice their religion with enthusiasm and love, they can trace the origins of that religious practice right back to the practices they learned in their homes.

THE FATHER AS PRIEST

Under the old patriarchal system the father was not only the head of the family; he was the priest of religion. When the Jewish family sat down to the paschal feast, the father, seated at the head of the table, was the one who offered the sacrificial lamb to God and by his prayers and instructions led his family gently to the worship of their God.

It seems simple platitude to state that the home is the cradle of religion and its first school and that the parents are the first and most effective teachers.

HOMES FIRST

We need hardly discuss something we see demonstrated everywhere in our ordinary workaday world. When good Catholic parents who are interested in their religion communicate that interest to their children, it is likely in the overwhelming percentage of cases to perdure through life. Our priests almost to a man come from homes notably Catholic. There are few religious vocations to men's or women's orders that have not in back of them more than ordinarily good Catholic mothers and fathers with at least a goodly measure of religious generosity.

The school on the other hand seems to labor in vain against the destructive influence of an irreligious home or parents who are indifferent to God and the interests of their own souls. We have so-called Catholic nations in which the men of the race seldom trouble the feminine atmosphere of the churches. Invariably the sons, no matter how much the religious teachers have worked on them, give up their religious practices as soon as school is over. They have the theory of religion on one hand and on the other the example of their fathers' lack of practice of that religion. Example and practice always beat principle in any struggle.

From Mixed Marriages

We have too the terrifying statistics on mixed marriage. Men who really know what they are talking about are convinced that the majority of the children of mixed marriages lose their faith. After two generations of mixed marriages almost all the children are lost to the Church. Children know no other authority more persuasive than that of their parents. If only one parent is Catholic, the children are only half persuaded. If the non-Catholic parent is the stronger parent, his practice far outweighs that of the diffident Catholic parent. If the Catholic parent, because of a non-Catholic atmosphere and the indifference he or she experiences around him or her, grows careless, the child follows that downgrade with increasing momentum.

Religious Training a Simple Duty

So all that this brief chapter pretends to do is to remind parents of the plain fact that they cannot pass on the task of the religious training of their children exclusively to the school. It just won't work out that way. Back of the parish must stand the home. Back of the religion teachers must stand intelligent Catholic parents. Five hours a day in school cannot possibly substitute for the youth-long training that children should receive in a Catholic home. The strangers who as professionals talk to them in a classroom of religion cannot expect to have even a fraction of the influence wielded by that father and mother who set for their children all the essential standards of life.

Home and School Together

When the Catholic parents work with the Catholic teachers, and the Catholic home demonstrates in practice the principles of religion laid down in the Catholic classroom, then we have the unbeatable combination. From such a partnership will be developed and brought to strong religious maturity the sons and daughters of God.

Atmosphere

Yet for the reassurance of parents who may be protesting inwardly that they themselves don't know their religion well enough to teach it to their children, I hasten to remind them that they may, if they wish, safely leave the theory of religion to the Catholic school. The teacher and later the professor will intellectually prove the truth of the Church and present to the young people its history and its appealing beauty. To parents is left the far more important task of creating the Catholic atmosphere in which the children live and move and have their youthful being. They illustrate practice. They present viewpoint. Even the least instructed Catholic if he is convinced of his religion and lives according to it can give his children these precious elements.

The Parents' Catholicity

There is no other possible lesson for the children like that of the Catholic virtues of their parents. Unashamed yet not necessarily ostentatiously they lead Catholic lives. They do not hesitate to make the acts of faith which the child can understand—frequent reception of communion, the father's lifting his hat as he passes a church, the carrying of the rosary, the making of a yearly retreat. They are pure and have a Catholic respect for and understanding of purity which they make radiantly clear in their conduct. They are willing to do hard things for God—give Him the children He asks for, fast with joy during Lent, help support the activities of the Church to the extent of their financial ability, give their sons and daughters to the service of God in religious life or the priesthood.

A New Nazareth

A real Catholic child comes to know with the advance of his maturity that around him has been another Nazareth. He recognizes that quite without show or parade his father has been very like the laborious, devoted, self-sacrificing, and pure Joseph the carpenter. He is proud that his mother so unmistakably suggests the Mother of God.

Pictures on the Walls

He notes conscientiously what at first he drank in instinctively and without comment—that there are Catholic pictures on the walls and Catholic statues in accessible places. He realizes that at certain times of the year are set up small altars on which stand an image of Mary, a representation of the Sacred Heart. And the lights that burn before these altars are bright, homely, beckoning.

Religious Days

Feast days are not merely days of food and gifts and pleasure. He realizes that under the Christmas tree, which later on he learns was originally pagan, is the Christmas crib, with the dear, silent, but compelling actors in the drama of the Incarnation. Easter has its rabbits and eggs; but it has its far clearer vision of the risen Savior. The rising sun of Easter is itself not more beautiful than the vision of the Christ of the Resurrection.

Birthdays are important; but so are the feast days of those saints whose names are borne by the members of the family. And Pentecost and Epiphany, even though they have not as yet become commercialized by people who don't even believe in Christianity, are remembered in the household, loved, and honored.

Practices Seen and Imitated

The child will never forget, not even after the long passing of the years, the religious practices he saw performed by his mother and father. He will be vastly affected by the way that they assisted at Mass. His first gestures at Mass will in all probability be a direct imitation of their actions at Mass.

My mother grew very indignant at the children or grownups who knelt and sat at Mass *sans* prayer book or rosary. That was long before the blessed rebirth of the liturgical movement had placed the missal in lay hands. Yet I vividly recall her following the ordinary of the Mass and my paging through my own smaller prayer book till I found the page that paralleled the one she was reading.

Children have the keenest interest in the morning and night prayers of their parents. If by any happy arrangement they all say those prayers in common, the prayers take on a new value for the child. No boy can fail to be impressed for all time by the sight of his fine, respected father kneeling beside the bed in the morning or at night. No child can ever lose the flavor of prayer that has been recited in the company of his mother.

So I repeat: It is much better for parents to recite prayers with a child, kneeling and in the correct attitude for prayer, than for them to make prayers a sort of memory lesson to be recited while the parent in the role of teacher listens, corrects, or prompts.

PRAYER TOGETHER

The modern family seems to be together so little that prayer in common has been lost in the onrush of the modern age. That may be. Yet when first in the rosary drive for October we asked young people to suggest daily family rosary said together, it was the youngsters who took up the idea and pressed it upon their parents. I am inclined to think that the reason that the family rosary failed to make a wider sweep was due much more to the lack of interest on the part of the fathers and mothers than to any unwillingness on the part of the sons and daughters.

Prayer together can be achieved in a family. When my beloved grandmother died, my mother and father decided that we should keep her in regular prayerful remembrance for at least a few months. Mother, always ingenious, found a time. Immediately after the evening meal, before we had dispersed to our several interests, we knelt and said together the "*De Profundis*" and other indulgenced prayers. We ran those months of prayerful remembrance into years.

GRACE AT MEALS

That is perhaps why grace before and after meals is especially important. It is perhaps the one prayer that finds the family together. Anyhow there is something especially liturgical in this turning of the family meal into the *agape* or love feast by the addition of group prayers.

REGULAR CONFESSIONS

In well-regulated Catholic families the elders, quite as much as the children, have regular confession days. It is fine to "send the children off to confession." It is far better to go with the children to receive the sacrament. So if the mother and her youngsters go in the early Saturday afternoon, the mother takes a burden off the confessor, who is rushed in the evening and fairly at leisure in the afternoon; and at the same time she sets a splendid example for her children.

AT COMMUNION

One of the most beautiful sights a priest sees as he walks along the communion rail is a family receiving Holy Communion together — the father, the mother, and then the children, all united in the happy moment of reception. Congregations are quick to notice such lovely groupings.

One big metropolitan cathedral was for a time blessed by the presence of a family in which there were five children ranging in age from seven to fourteen. Busy as the church was and steady as was the flow of the worshipers, the mother and the father accompanied by their five children, all going to Holy Communion together at the eight-o'clock Mass, became a subject for delighted comment. I know of people who went to that particular Mass just to see what they thought so charming a spectacle for God, angels, and men.

Parents who go with their children to confession and communion will need to give them little formal instruction on the use of the sacraments. The way the children see their parents prepare for these sacraments will be the method they will quickly adopt. Children will grasp the value and meaning of the thanksgivings that follow the sacraments largely from their parents' use of these practices. And if the parents, after they have received Holy Communion, remain for a few minutes after the Mass, the children will adopt that lovely practice too and will in the years to come either remain to make their thanksgiving or have a rebukingly guilty feeling about their having rushed out with their thanksgiving unmade or carelessly made.

CATHOLIC VIEWPOINT

Teachers may present to children the theory of religion, the Catholic viewpoint that they should possess. Parents alone can make that theory practical and turn the viewpoint into something that is habitually a reality. Hence within the Catholic home the Catholic viewpoint must quietly but effectively be expressed.

Everything Catholic should be of interest there. The successes of the Church or of Catholics are causes for real joy. The attacks upon the Church or the failures that mar its progress bring forth a sincere expression of sorrow and regret. They are interested, this father and mother, in each new advance that is made by Catholics in education, charity, public service, literature, art. Inevitably their attitude is reflected in the similar interest felt by the children.

DEFENDING THE CHURCH

Instinctively they defend the Church when it is attacked, whether the attack is great or small. Unlike the illiterate Catholics who seem to take it for granted that the Church in any controversy is very likely to be wrong (and they are illiterate, no matter what the extent of their education), they know it is practically certain that the Church is right. They so express themselves.

They know the Church's history well enough to realize that since it has been consistently right in the past—in everything from the definition of the Trinity against the Greeks to the warning of what birth control would, if continued, do to pitiful France—it is very likely that the Church will continue to be right, now and in the future.

So even when they do not know the exact answer to the current heresy that attacks the Church, they quite calmly are sure that the Church is right and that the heretics, like all other heretics of history, will disappear and be forgotten.

When someone in their hearing or in a book presents some argument against the Church, they do not tremble and begin to apologize. They smile with the calm assurance that "this too will pass" while the Rock remains firm against the storms.

An attitude like this on the part of his parents is the child's most conclusive argument for his faith. Supplemented by the training of a fine Catholic school, this home training makes the type of Catholic whose life will be rock-firm, whose opinions will be established in the truth of Christ, and who will meet life's problems and difficulties with calm assurance.

Catholic Literature

In line with this Catholic attitude parents are of course interested in Catholic literature. They themselves read it. They see that it is within easy reach of the children. It has a place on their living-room table, for family and guests. They buy it or subscribe for it, not as a sort of minor penance, but because to them it expresses beauty and truth.

Missions and Charity

They will be contributors to the Catholic missions because this is the simplest way to spread the Catholic cause. They will be deeply and personally interested in Catholic charity, the expression of their living faith. Their children will have a part with them in this too. Mission mite boxes will be as inevitable as the children's toys. They will teach the children to contribute out of their small allowances to Catholic charity. With the coming of Christmas, plans will be laid for the gifts to be given by the whole family to the poor. Children will be taught to adopt a missionary and to regard him as their personal ambassador to the pagan peoples.

Catholic Problems

Children can never quite lose the viewpoints given them by their parents on subjects like mixed marriage, divorce, birth control. Where the parents' attitude on these things is genuinely Catholic, the children will maintain those attitudes as the dominant viewpoints all their lives. On the other hand the most brilliant teacher or the author of the most cogently written book will have to struggle hard to win to the side of Christ those children whose parents thought lightly of divorce, believed that "mixed marriages are about as likely to be happy as are Catholic ones," and regretted that birth control is forbidden to Catholics, because really it is "so civilized and sensible a practice."

Catholic Schooling

The modern attitude of allowing a child to choose his own school is a little along the line of the Protestant attitude of letting a child choose his own religion. Will the day come when children will become Americans only when they are old enough to decide for themselves whether or not they wish to be citizens of the United States? It seems a sort of inevitable last step, though I doubt if the Government is going to approve of that very much.

In the parents' minds there should simply be no question about the choice of schools. Their children's schools will be Catholic, from kindergarten to university. If there is a choice between this Catholic school or that one, the selection may be permitted the youngsters. But their education will be Catholic, and parents can simply take the stand that this choice has been made once and for all. The children will then take that as much for granted as they will take the fact that mother decides the menu for their meals. They won't come with arguments that their best friends go to the country day school, or that they are "tired of being taught by nuns and priests," or that "Catholic schools are too strict," or that they "want a wider experience than the one the Catholic school can give."

When on the other hand the children hear their parents hesitating about the choice of schools, they will hesitate too.

Sometimes parents say, almost with regret in their voices, "Oh yes; we'll send our children to the Catholic school, but still . . ." The children are quick to note all the mental reservations which their parents make in that hesitating—their regret that Catholic schools are not more social, that Catholic graduates are not so likely to get into the "Who's Who," that the parochial schools are old-fashioned and not progressive, that the sons and daughters of the wealthy . . . and the socially prominent . . . and the famous . . . go elsewhere.

The effect of a Catholic education may be largely nullified by any reluctance expressed by either of the parents about their children's attending a Catholic school.

When however parents themselves understand the value of Catholic education—that it is the great guarantee of the only success that matters; that it is the one education that treats the entire human being, body, mind, morals, and trains him for time and eternity; that it is a miracle of heroism and devotion to an ideal; that it stands fearlessly in competition with any other system in the country—when they know this and express it freely, the child follows their lead unhesitatingly, to the assurance of his happy future.

Never a Bore or Punishment

Under no circumstances should religion be made a threat, a bore, or a nuisance. Parents can easily and thoughtlessly do just this.

"So you didn't behave yourself, eh? Very well then. This afternoon instead of letting you go to the movies, I'm taking you to benediction."

"If you don't stop that noise, I'll take those funnies away from you and make you read the lives of the saints."

"Do you know what happens to bad little boys? Father Kelly comes and beats them and tells God about them."

"You behave yourself, or God will lean down from heaven and pick you up and squeeze you to death."

To use religion as a bogeyman is certainly a horrible contradiction of the sweet Christ's intentions.

Not Tiresome

Nor should children be allowed to hear people talk about religion as of something tiresome.

"You bet I'm going to early Mass. Do you think I want to sit for an hour and a half through a tiresome solemn high Mass? . . . Oh Father Smith talked again today. What a windy old fellow he is. I just couldn't listen to him any longer . . . . Friday! How I hate it! I wish I'd been born into a religion that doesn't have abstinence days . . . . I suppose we'll just have to go to the mission this week. But I get so tired of those same old sermons on death and hell."

All this, like all the *ex-cathedra* statements of their parents, children will without shadow of doubt repeat again and again in the course of their lives.

Pleasant and Essential

Religion is as a matter of cold fact simply one of the pleasant and essential parts of a complete human being's existence. It should be so treated. Like all the other pleasant and essential parts of existence it is taken for granted by the parents, made a normal exercise, not discussed in any way other than the way that one discusses the necessity for eating, exercise, cleanliness, or attendance at school. It ranks higher than all these things of course; but no more than these other necessities is it to be made an event, something to be built up, argued about, threshed out.

So of a Sunday the family goes to Mass. No fuss is made about it. No big event is made of the obligation to rise and assist at the Holy Sacrifice of the Mass. Friday is just another day in the week, a day made a little memorable by the fact that on Friday one commemorates the death of our Savior and does something to train body and mind to self-control. The sacraments are normal steps in human growth and development. They are welcomed happily. They are, like other big events, celebrated with real joy. They are not stewed over or fretted about or held impendingly over the child.

The Parish Church

Attendance at parish devotions and participation in parish social life are part of normal family routine. The children go along as a matter of course—and learn to love and thoroughly relish the parish life.

Religion Class the Most Important

From the very beginning the parents take toward their children's religious education the stand that the children's religion classes are the most important classes they attend.

A certain young man I happened to be talking to told me of the lesson his own father had early given him. He did not go to a Catholic school until he was in fifth grade, when the family finally moved into a city that was blessed with a Catholic school. After the first quarter the lad brought his report card home and with complacency showed it to his dad. All his marks were A's and B's, with the exception of catechism. That was a C.

"Very good, my son," the father commented. "But what about this C in catechism?"

"Oh," the youngster replied, flippantly, "nobody worries about that. If you study the other subjects, that's all you need. Catechism is easy. I just didn't bother to study."

To his utter amazement the boy saw his father tear the report card into small pieces and throw it into the wastebasket. Then he towered over the boy, his face set and firm.

"That happens," he said, slowly, "to be the most important subject on your card. You can flunk the other subjects if you're dull and not able to learn. But if you can make A's and B's in the other subjects, you can make an A in catechism. That's the grade I'm always going to look at first. That's the subject you'll study and do well in. That's the one you'll be examined in by God Himself."

"And," said the young man, as he concluded his story, "that was the real beginning of my Catholic education."

The wise parent when he receives the child's report card looks first at two marks—the mark in religion and the mark in deportment or conduct. He can sometimes be a little forgiving about other poor marks. The child himself is amazed and embarrassed if he finds that his parents don't care when his marks in religion and conduct are bad.

Help in Studying Religion

Religion as a subject can be made easy and pleasant if the parents are constructively interested. The child likes to recite his catechism to a willing and appreciative ear. The little one home from school enjoys saying his "new prayers" over for his parents. One little altar boy, greatly encouraged by his parents to serve Mass, greeted me one evening in his home by saying, "Gee, this is great! Look, mom and dad; he's a priest. How about the two of us right here in the parlor putting on a Mass?" We didn't do it. But at least he knew that his parents were interested in this side of his Catholic development.

Early the parents start telling the children the great Catholic stories. Perhaps, remembering the parents of the saints, they try to teach them to say Jesus and Mary even before they teach them to say mamma and papa. They furnish them as spiritual equipment the legends of the saints, the glorious life of Jesus Christ, the beautiful short stories that are the parables, and the most exciting narratives of all time—the great adventures of the Old Testament and the New Testament.

They encourage their children to adopt Catholic hobbies. They are interested if they start to collect copies of famous masterpieces of Catholic art or pictures of the saints. They remark to the children that Vatican City stamps make a fine start for a stamp collection. They suggest their building a shrine and decorating it or making their own little altar and equipping it. When Christmas comes, the crib is each year made more elaborate and beautiful.

Catholic Comradeship

They furnish their children with delightful Catholic companionship in the boys and girls who surround their early years.

Because many parents have regarded all this as difficult and exacting tasks, they have passed too much of it on to the Catholic school. We are justly proud of our Catholic-school system. It is the greatest educational tribute ever paid to an ideal and in some ways the most remarkable offering ever made out of faith and love to the God of heaven and the Savior of the world.

But the great fact remains. Even the greatest school can never replace the home, and the finest teacher can only supplement the work of the parents.

If that is truism for all forms of education, it is more than ever true where religion is concerned.

Holy parents can well hope to have saints for children. Stalwart Catholic fathers and pure Catholic mothers may be sure that their children will be so firmly grounded in their religion that a lifetime of temptation will not eradicate it.

Man thought up the idea of schools. God thought up the idea of homes. Teachers begin where parents leave off. But the plain fact is that parents should never leave off. They may call in the teacher, the priest, and the religious as auxiliaries. Always the forming of the child's character and the building of his strength and purity and faith and the elements of realest success are in the hands of the parents.

PRINTED IN U.S.A.

Lightning Source UK Ltd.
Milton Keynes UK
UKOW04f2111281217
315141UK00001B/4/P